Lorca's Poetic Practice from
Poemas en prosa to *Poeta en Nueva York*

Juan de la Cuesta Hispanic Monographs

Lorca's Poetic Practice from
Poemas en prosa to *Poeta en Nueva York*

Ten Essays

by

ANDREW A. ANDERSON
University of Virginia

Juan de la Cuesta
Newark, Delaware

Juan de la Cuesta Hispanic Monographs
An imprint of Linguatext, LLC.
Newark, Delaware 19711 USA
(302) 453-8695

www.JuandelaCuesta.com

MANUFACTURED IN THE UNITED STATES OF AMERICA

ISBN: 978-1-58871-384-1

Table of Contents

Introduction

THIS VOLUME COLLECTS TEN essays about Lorca's *Poemas en prosa* and/or *Poeta en Nueva York*. They are all concerned, in one way or another, with issues of content, technique, and style, as well as the challenges they present to literary-critical analysis and interpretation. In the pages that follow, I explain the context in which they came to be written, and then how they fit together and the rationale for the order in which they are presented here.

BACKGROUND: THE DEBATE ABOUT THE TEXT OF *POETA EN NUEVA YORK*

My interest in *Poeta en Nueva York* dates all the way back to 1975. In the fall of that year I started graduate studies, and planning for my dissertation topic rapidly coalesced around Lorca's later poetry, that is to say, the verse that he wrote between 1929 and 1936. I had not been working on this for very long when several studies appeared that came to disrupt and eventually refashion my initial project. 1976—the fortieth anniversary of Lorca's assassination—saw the publication of two articles by Eutimio Martín, a critical edition of the *conferencia-recital* of *Poeta en Nueva York* and an essay entitled "*Tierra y luna*: ¿Un libro adscrito abusivamente a *Poeta en Nueva York*," as well as a book by Daniel Eisenberg, "*Poeta en Nueva York*": *historia y problemas de un texto de Lorca*.[1] Martín's two pieces led me back to the opening shot in his persistent questioning of the textual status of the collection, which had come out in *Ínsula* in 1972 and had anticipated in very summary form his "doctorat de troisième cycle" (1974) that I was soon able to consult on microfilm. Disconcertingly, the main theories put forward by Eisenberg's densely footnoted book of 1976 differed greatly from Martín's propositions, but beyond this Eisenberg's work did serve to confirm that *Poeta en Nueva York* had gone through a long and complex process of gestation and evolution, not only

---

1   For full details of all references, see the Bibliography.

from 1929 to 1936, but also from 1936 to 1940, when it first appeared post-humously in its famous two "first" editions in New York and Mexico City. Clearly, there were many questions here that remained to be elucidated, and for a while this became one of the areas on which I focused my own research.

Of course, I was far from alone in this mix of concern, curiosity, and fascination. Martín dismissed the authority of the first editions and argued that there was no alternative but to return to an earlier state of the collection, at which point Lorca was evidently toying with the idea of splitting it into two, as *Poeta en Nueva York* and *Tierra y luna*. Probably the first supporter of Martín in this radical claim was Piero Menarini, who adopted it in his book of 1975 (and followed up with an article in 1978). Miguel García-Posada espoused the same posture in his doctoral dissertation of 1977 and the revised version that appeared in book form in 1981. Eisenberg's position was implicitly and fundamentally at odds with Martín's, though simultaneously he cast severe doubts on several other significant aspects of the textual history of the collection. "Push-back" independent of both the Martín and Eisenberg camps came initially from Mario Hernández and Nigel Dennis. Hernández joined the fray in 1978, with some notes on the subject that attempted to steer a reasonable course based on the facts as we knew them at that time. The following year, Dennis offered a much more extensive treatment, with detailed scrutiny—and often rebuttal—of both Martín's theories and Eisenberg's. A further by-product of this research and the new data that resulted from it was an upsurge of interest in José Bergamín, the publisher of the Mexican first edition. He gave a series of newspaper and magazine interviews over these years, though his understandably imperfect memory of the exact sequence of events four decades earlier did nothing to squelch the controversy.

The publication in 1981 of Martín's edition of *Poeta en Nueva York* (split between the eponymous collection and *Tierra y luna*) galvanized an already nascent polemic. That same year I reproduced an overlooked testimony from Uruguay concerning the state of the collection as of 1934, and in a second article sought to evaluate the competing hypotheses while adding another putative one of my own: Lorca's plan at some stage to compose a book to be entitled *La ciudad*. María Clementa Millán (1982) was largely supportive of Mario Hernández. By 1983 it seemed that enough information was available for me to attempt a comprehensive summary and critical examination of what we knew about *Poeta en Nueva York* over both periods, that is, 1929-36 and 1936-40. The second issue of *El Crotalón* (1985) contained a further two articles on the topic. I developed upon my review-article of the previous year, and argued that greater attention needed to be paid to the first half of 1936 as well as to what went on during the years of the Civil War. Millán explored the problematic relationship between the index of the collection and the poems presented by Lorca in the *conferencia-recital*. By now the two sides in the debate were firmly established, with Martín, Menarini, and García-Posada backing the splitting ("escisión") of the collection, Hernández, Dennis, Millán, and myself advocating for closer study of the prehistory and genesis of the two 1940 editions, and Eisenberg as a kind of outlier, some of whose ideas were taken up by both sides but whose general position was supported by neither.

In 1985 Christopher Maurer showed how the consultation of unpublished correspondence between the various principals involved could help considerably with the investigation of the many still obscure aspects of the textual history, and in 1987 Eisenberg followed along a similar, complementary path. 1987 was also the year of two further editions. One was illustrated by Juan Carlos Eguillor and was printed on eccentrically tall and narrow paper stock. Still, Mario Hernández took the opportunity to incorporate in it an important essay, presenting his own ideas and discoveries that he had been developing and accumulating since the anthology of 1978. Millán was charged with the edition brought out in Cátedra's Letras Hispánicas series, and in a lengthy introduction offered her synthetic overview of the situation as it stood at that date. Maurer completed that hat-trick the following year, with a modern, carefully edited bilingual edition (1988).

Another major step forward was made in 1990 with the publication in facsimile of all the then known first-draft manuscripts of the poems in *Poeta en Nueva York*. Hernández supplied the transcriptions and revised and augmented his 1987 introductory essay.[2] In 1992 I returned to the complex story of what had happened to the final manuscript of the collection, filling in a number of details mainly concerning what must have occurred from the moment it arrived on Bergamín's desk in the summer of 1936 through to when Bergamín had it with him in Paris in the summer of 1938. Then, in the years immediately following 1992, there was little further activity, as we had gone about as far as was possible with all the information currently at our disposal, while of course still lacking the actual manuscript of 1936.

---

2   A few more original autographs have come to light since that date, notably those of "Tu infancia en Menton," recovered by Nigel Dennis in 2005, and that of "New York (Oficina y denuncia)," unearthed by Christopher Maurer in 2011. I present a survey of the poems whose first drafts have yet to be located in Anderson (2011).

As he recounted in his book (2000), for several years during the 1990s Nigel Dennis pursued leads in Mexico, where it seemed most likely that the 1936 manuscript would have remained after 1940, and was able to track much of its rather haphazard itinerary. The Lorca family finally managed to locate it in Cuernavaca, and in 1998 Dennis was able to announce its discovery (Diez). The individual who had possession of it at that time was Manuela (or Manola) Saavedra de Aldama.[3] In December of 1999 she offered it for sale by auction at Christie's of London, but the Fundación Federico García Lorca launched a lawsuit that blocked the sale and led to several years of legal wrangling, complicated not least by the competing jurisdictions of Britain, Spain, and Mexico. A British judge found in favor of Ms. Saavedra in 2002. Consequently, the manuscript came up for auction again at Christie's in 2003, at which time it was bought by the Fundación Federico García Lorca.[4] Early on in this sequence of events, the Fundación had been sent a photocopy of the manuscript, and subsequently photocopies of that photocopy circulated among a few academics who contributed regularly to the Fundación's activities. Maurer's revised bilingual edition (1998) was based on this copy, and consequently, for the next fifteen years, became the most accurate and reliable edition of *Poeta en Nueva York*.

With the complete 1936 manuscript now available for examination and study, many of the hypotheses about the evolution of the collection and what happened to it over the course of the years were either substantiated or disproven.[5] Logically enough, thoughts turned to the preparation of a new critical edition based on the manuscript, which represented Lorca's authorial intent as of June 1936, and Mario Hernández was initially put in charge of this project. In 2007, as was widely reported in the Spanish press at the time, it was hoped that the new Centro García Lorca would open in Granada in 2009, and plans were made for a major exhibition on *Poeta en*

---

3   Briefly, the manuscript had passed from Bergamín to Jesús Ussía Oteyza; later Ussía left it for safe keeping with his uncle, Ernesto de Oteyza; after Ussía's death in 1975, Oteyza passed it on to Ussía's widow, Rafaela Arocena, and she in turn gifted it to Saavedra in 1979. For the next twenty years, it lay tucked away in a sideboard drawer.

4   This sequence of events was covered extensively in the Spanish press. One can also consult Dennis's book (2000) and the articles by Hart (2003) and Barrera-Agarwal (2009). From 1999 to 2003 the manuscript languished in the Christie's vault.

5   Still, in the face of overwhelming evidence, Martín (2001) steadfastly maintained a modified version of his original position.

Nueva York that would inaugurate the new building. Coinciding with this, the new edition would also be published. Unfortunately, neither event took place: the Centro suffered a series of construction and financing delays, and only opened in 2015.[6] The holdings of the Fundación in Madrid were not transferred there till 2018. At the same time, the critical edition was delayed more than once, and eventually I was approached by the Fundación to take on its preparation. For this task, I took into account all the previous contributions that had propelled inquiry forward, and of course I was also able to work with all the new and invaluable data provided by the pages that formed the 1936 manuscript. This edition appeared in 2013 and has been reprinted several times.[7] Finally, in an essay of 2018, concerned primarily with the different English translations of the collection, I was able to treat in some detail Bergamín's contact with W.W. Norton and Rolfe Humphries's overall involvement in the project for the 1940 U.S. edition.

Returning now to the late 1970s, at a certain point I decided to drop *Poeta en Nueva York* from my doctoral dissertation and concentrate on the poetry written between 1931 and 1936, a decision that in retrospect seems to me to have been well-advised. While I channeled my continuing interest in *Poeta* into the aforementioned articles, for my doctoral research I concentrated on *Diván del Tamarit*, *Seis poemas galegos*, *Llanto por Ignacio Sánchez Mejías*, and *Sonetos*. And while I remained primarily committed to the literary-critical examination of the poetry, the example of *Poeta en Nueva York* had alerted me to many issues that could surround the textual history of Lorca's works, particularly those whose first edition occurred posthumously (and which constitute a large portion of his overall output). Consequently, I included in an appendix to my dissertation a critical edition of the four collections that I was studying. With substantial revisions, that appendix formed the basis of my edition of three of those four books in the new series of Clásicos Castellanos (1988), while the main body of the dissertation was the foundation for my first monograph, *Lorca's Late Poetry* (1990).

---

6   There was an important exhibition held in New York in 2013, "Back Tomorrow: Federico García Lorca / Poet in New York," at the New York Public Library, curated by Christopher Maurer and Andrés Soria Olmedo.

7   Since that date, I am not aware of any significant discoveries (for instance, of missing first-draft manuscripts or versions of poems) that would so far necessitate revisions to the edition; see also Anderson (2011).

STRUCTURE OF THIS VOLUME

Running alongside this sustained interest in the textual history of *Poeta en Nueva York*, but rather later in first appearing in print (1991), was a parallel concern with the literary-critical qualities of the poems that it contained and the evolution of Lorca's aesthetic thinking that had led to their composition. The reader who closes *Romancero gitano* and then opens *Poeta en Nueva York* will immediately notice a wide stylistic gulf separating the two, and as a result one early and enduring question that I sought to explore was how and why that radical change had come about. Within the span of Lorca's poetical composition, the one (putative) collection that falls chronologically between those two books is *Poemas en prosa*, which is one of those volumes that Lorca mentioned as planned for publication but in the event never made it into print. The surviving individual prose poems (mainly from 1928) that would have been part of it demonstrate even more extreme stylistic experimentation than what we find in *Poeta*, and so they clearly constitute one telling piece of evidence. As far as more theoretical or discursive writing goes, Lorca's lecture "Imaginación, inspiración, evasión" (1928) is the single most important document that allows us to chart the development of his ideas around this time, and it is supplemented by other prose writings and notably by sets of letters exchanged between Lorca and two Catalan correspondents, Salvador Dalí and Sebastià Gasch.[8]

In 2000 I published a critical edition of the *Poemas en prosa*. Because of its unfinished nature, this cannot hope to be more than a partial reconstruction, but it has more than enough substance to give us a good idea of what the eventual book would have looked like. The works included here are not without their own complexities in regards to their publication history, and these issues were treated in the "Introducción" and "Bibliografía." This edition of *Poemas en prosa*, then, together with the aforementioned edition of *Poeta en Nueva York* (2013), can serve as companion volumes to the ten essays collected here. They may be supplemented on the biographical front by the book, also from 2013, *Federico García Lorca en Nueva York y La Habana. Cartas y recuerdos*, on which I collaborated with Christopher Maurer, which collects all Lorca's correspondence from the period and the *conferencia-recital*, and offers profiles of the people with whom he interacted during that period and a range of reminiscences of him.

---

8   For Lorca's general state of mind at this time, right around the date of publication of *Romancero gitano*, see my essay "Lorca en 1928" (2008).

The articles and book chapters collected here were published between 1991 and 2020, but they are not presented in chronological order. Rather, they are organized thematically. The first four address the theoretical and aesthetic ideas mentioned above, starting with a consideration of the "Imaginación, inspiración, evasión" lecture, and then progressing through Lorca's exchanges with Gasch and Dalí, to arrive, in chapter 4, at an attempt at a full-scale overview of the situation that integrates all of those principal factors and elements. As each of these essays was originally conceived as a freestanding piece, readers will notice some modest overlapping of ideas, but I hope that this continuity will serve to knit the studies together and underpin the development of my arguments.

With chapters 5 and 6 there is a pivot towards matters more of poetic technique—*paysage d'âme*, objective correlative, "hecho poético," image, imagery—considered both in general terms and as illustrated in individual poems from *Poeta en Nueva York*, "La aurora" and "Intermedio (1910)" respectively. Following on from these, the next three chapters are concerned more or less exclusively with literary-critical explications of three more texts from *Poeta*, "Tu infancia en Menton,"[9] "Poema doble del Lago Edén," and "Cielo vivo." Finally, chapter 10 is different again: its comparativist turn aims to illuminate both collections, *Poeta en Nueva York* and Hart Crane's *The Bridge*, by bringing them together in a careful examination of their points of contact, similarities, and differences.

For the sake of consistency, in this volume the punctuation and English/American spelling have been regularized, quotations that were translated into English have been restored to their original Spanish, and when necessary I have converted the footnoting to the format where a list of Works Cited is presented at the end of each chapter. However, I have not sought to update the references and bibliography, even of the older pieces; I decided not to introduce this anachronistic element, as doing so would often have interfered with their internal logic and their engagement with debates current at the time of their composition.

---

9   Nigel Dennis was kind enough to invite me to collaborate with him on the original article about a newly come to light first-draft manuscript of the poem. He was principally responsible for the study of the manuscript and its textual situation, while I was the principal author of the literary-critical commentary that we also presented. Only this latter section is given here.

CHAPTERS 1-10: ORIGINAL PUBLICATION DETAILS

1. "Lorca at the Crossroads: 'Imaginación, inspiración, evasión' and the 'novísimas estéticas,'" *Anales de la Literatura Española Contemporánea*, XVI, nos. 1-2 (1991), 149-173. Reproduced by kind permission of *Anales de la Literatura Española Contemporánea*.

2. "Sebastià Gasch y Federico García Lorca: influencias recíprocas y la construcción de una estética vanguardista," in *Federico García Lorca i Catalunya*, ed. Antonio Monegal & José María Micó (Barcelona: Institut Universitari de Cultura, Universitat Pompeu Fabra / Area de Cultura, Diputació de Barcelona, 2000), pp. 93-110.

3. "'Corazón bleu y coeur azul': Dalí y Lorca en diálogo," *Scriptura*, no. 18 (2005), Monográfico Salvador Dalí, 13-23.

4. "García Lorca's *Poemas en prosa* and *Poeta en Nueva York*: Dalí, Gasch, Surrealism and the Avant-Garde," in *A Companion to Spanish Surrealism*, ed. Robert Havard (London: Tamesis, 2004), pp. 163-182. Reproduced by kind permission of Tamesis Books.

5. "*Paysage d'Âme* and Objective Correlative: Tradition and Innovation in Cernuda, Alberti, and García Lorca," *Modern Language Review*, CX, no. 1 (2015), 166-183. Reproduced by kind permission of the Modern Humanities Research Association and *Modern Language Review*.

6. "Imagery and How It Works in Lorca's *Poeta en Nueva York*: the Case of '1910 (Intermedio),'" *Forum for Modern Language Studies*, LVII, no. 1 (2021), 1-20. Reproduced by kind permission of Oxford University Press and the General Editors of *Forum for Modern Language Studies* (on behalf of the Court of the University of St. Andrews), https://doi.org/10.1093/fmls/cqaa049.

7. "The Manuscript of Lorca's 'Tu infancia en Menton'" [with Nigel Dennis], *Bulletin of Spanish Studies*, LXXXII, no. 2 (2005), 181-204 [excerpt]. Reproduced by kind permission of *Bulletin of Spanish Studies*, ISSN (printed): 1475-3820.

8. "*Et in Arcadia Ego*: Thematic Divergence and Convergence in Lorca's 'Poema doble del Lago Edén,'" *Bulletin of Hispanic Studies* (Glasgow edi-

tion), LXXIV, no. 4 (1997), 409-429. Reproduced by kind permission of *Bulletin of Spanish Studies*, ISSN (printed): 1475-3820.

9. "Lorca's 'Cielo vivo,' the Other Lake Eden Poem," *Symposium*, LXXI, no. 1 (2017), 28-47. Reproduced by kind permission of *Symposium*, https:// doi.org/10.1080/00397709.2017.1277871

10. "Un puente entre dos poetas: García Lorca y Hart Crane," in *América en un poeta. Los viajes de Federico García Lorca al Nuevo Mundo y la repercusión de su obra en la literatura americana*, ed. Andrew A. Anderson (Sevilla: Universidad Internacional de Andalucía / Fundación Focus-Abengoa, 1999), pp. 119-130.

Bibliography

Anderson, Andrew A. "García Lorca en Montevideo: un testimonio desconocido y más evidencia sobre la evolución de *Poeta en Nueva York*," *Bulletin Hispanique*, LXXXIII, nos. 1-2 (1981), 145-161.

———. "Lorca's 'New York Poems': a Contribution to the Debate," *Forum for Modern Language Studies*, XVII, no. 3 (1981), 256-270.

———. "Lorca's Late Verse (1931-1936): A Critical Study. (With, in Appendix, a Critical Edition of the Poems," doctoral dissertation (Oxford: Oxford University, 1982).

———. "The Evolution of García Lorca's Poetic Projects 1929-1936 and the Textual Status of *Poeta en Nueva York*," *Bulletin of Hispanic Studies*, LX, no. 3 (1983), 221-246.

———. "Federico García Lorca, *Poeta en Nueva York. Tierra y luna*, ed. Eutimio Martín; Federico García Lorca, *Obras II. Poesía, 2*, ed. Miguel García-Posada; Miguel García-Posada, *Lorca: interpretación de 'Poeta en Nueva York*,'" *Revista Canadiense de Estudios Hispánicos*, IX, no. 1 (1984), 112-131.

———. "*Poeta en Nueva York* una y otra vez," *El Crotalón. Anuario de Filología Española*, II (1985), 37-51.

———, ed. Federico García Lorca, *Diván del Tamarit. Llanto por Ignacio Sánchez Mejías. Seis poemas galegos. Poemas sueltos* (Madrid: Espasa-Calpe, 1988).

———. *Lorca's Late Poetry: A Critical Study* (Leeds: Francis Cairns, 1990).

————. "Las peripecias de *Poeta en Nueva York*," *Boletín de la Fundación Federico García Lorca*, V, nos. 10-11 (1992), 97-123.

————, ed. Federico García Lorca, *Poemas en prosa* (Granada: Comares, 2000).

————. "Introducción"; "Bibliografía," in Federico García Lorca, *Poemas en prosa* (Granada: Comares, 2000), pp. 9-53, 107-115.

————, with Nigel Dennis. "The Manuscript of Lorca's 'Tu infancia en Menton,'" *Bulletin of Spanish Studies*, LXXXII, no. 2 (2005), 181-204.

————. "Lorca en 1928," in *"gallo." Interior de una revista. 1928*, catálogo de la exposición, ed. Luis Muñoz (Madrid: Sociedad Estatal de Conmemoraciones Culturales / Patronato de la Alhambra y el Generalife, 2008), pp. 102-127.

————. "Los manuscritos todavía por recuperar de *Poeta en Nueva York*," *Granada, Hoy* (Granada), 11 enero 2011, pp. 42-43.

————, ed. Federico García Lorca, *Poeta en Nueva York* (Barcelona: Galaxia Gutenberg, 2013).

————. "Introducción"; "Notas," in Federico García Lorca, *Poeta en Nueva York* (Barcelona: Galaxia Gutenberg, 2013), pp. 7-152, 283-311.

————. "La trayectoria de *Poeta en Nueva York* a través de sus traductores estadounidenses: Humphries, Belitt, Simon/White y después," in *El impacto de la metrópolis. La experiencia americana en Lorca, Dalí y Buñuel*, ed. José M. del Pino (Frankfurt/Madrid: Vervuert/Iberoamericana, 2018), pp. 93-115.

Barrera-Agarwal, María Helena. "Los exilios de *Poeta en Nueva York*, de Federico García Lorca," *Aguilha. Revista de Cultura*, no. 70 (agosto-septiembre-octobre 2009).

Dennis, Nigel. "On the First Edition of Lorca's *Poeta en Nueva York*," *Ottawa Hispanica*, no. 1 (1979), 47-83.

————. *Vida y milagros de un manuscrito de Lorca: en pos de "Poeta en Nueva York"* (Santander: Sociedad Menéndez Pelayo, 2000).

————. "The Manuscript of Lorca's 'Tu infancia en Menton'" [with Andrew A. Anderson], *Bulletin of Spanish Studies*, LXXXII, no. 2 (2005), 181-204.

Diez, Gontzal. "Nigel Dennis anuncia la recuperación del manuscrito de *Poeta en Nueva York*," *La Verdad* (Murcia), 27 marzo 1998, p. 57.

Eisenberg, Daniel. *"Poeta en Nueva York": historia y problemas de un texto de Lorca* (Barcelona: Ariel, 1976).

————. "Nuevos documentos relativos a la edición de *Poeta en Nueva York* y otras obras de García Lorca," *Anales de Literatura Española* (Alicante), no. 5 (1986-1987), 67-107.

García-Posada Huelva, Miguel. "Los poemas neoyorquinos de Federico García Lorca: *Poeta en Nueva York* y *Tierra y luna*," doctoral dissertation (Madrid: Universidad Autónoma de Madrid, 1977).

————. "Nota de lectura. Daniel Eisenberg: '*Poeta en Nueva York*': Historia y problemas de un texto de Lorca," *Ínsula*, XXXII, no. 367 (junio 1977), 10.

————. *Lorca: Interpretación de "Poeta en Nueva York"* (Madrid: Akal, 1981).

Hart, Stephen. "Poetry on Trial: The Strange Case of Lorca's *Poeta en Nueva York*," *Hispanic Research Journal*, IV, no. 3 (2003), 271-284.

Hernández, Mario. "Notas al texto: *Poeta en Nueva York*," in Federico García Lorca, *Antología poética*, 2nd ed. (Madrid: Alce, 1978), pp. 135-150.

————, ed. Federico García Lorca, *Poeta en Nueva York*, ilustraciones de Juan Carlos Eguillor (Madrid: Fundación Banco Exterior, 1987).

————. "Federico García Lorca, 1929-1940: el significado de su muerte"; "Nota a la edición," in Federico García Lorca, *Poeta en Nueva York*, ilustraciones de Juan Carlos Eguillor (Madrid: Fundación Banco Exterior, 1987), pp. 9-22, 133-135.

————, ed. Federico García Lorca, *Manuscritos neoyorquinos. "Poeta en Nueva York" y otras hojas y poemas* (Madrid: Tabapress/Fundación García Lorca, 1990).

————. "Introducción. Federico García Lorca: el significado de su muerte"; "Los manuscritos de *Poeta en Nueva York*"; "Nota a la edición de los poemas," in Federico García Lorca, *Manuscritos neoyorquinos. "Poeta en Nueva York" y otras hojas y poemas* (Madrid: Tabapress/Fundación García Lorca, 1990), pp. 13-29, 31-34, 273-274.

Martín, Eutimio. "¿Existe una versión definitiva de *Poeta en Nueva York*, de Lorca?," *Ínsula*, XXVII, no. 310 (septiembre 1972), 1, 10.

————. "Contribution à l'étude du cycle poétique new-yorkais de Federico García Lorca: *Poeta en Nueva York*, *Tierra y luna* et autres poèmes. (Essai d'édition critique)," doctoral dissertation, 2 vols. (Poitiers: Université de Poitiers, 1974).

————. "La conferencia-recital sobre *Poeta en Nueva York* de Federico García Lorca (edición crítica)," *Les Langues Néo-Latines*, LXX, no. 216 (1976), 52-67.

————. "*Tierra y luna*: ¿Un libro adscrito abusivamente a *Poeta en Nueva York*," *Trece de Nieve*, segunda época, nos. 1-2 (diciembre 1976), 125-131.

————, ed. Federico García Lorca, *Poeta en Nueva York. Tierra y luna* (Barcelona: Ariel, 1981).

————. "El texto de *Poeta en Nueva York*: suma y sigue," in *Surrealismo y literatura en España*, ed. Jaume Pont Ibáñez (Lleida: Universitat de Lleida, Área de Lingüística, 2001), pp. 41-56.

Maurer, Christopher. "En torno a dos ediciones de *Poeta en Nueva York*," *Revista Canadiense de Estudios Hispánicos*, IX, no. 2 (1985), 251-256.

————, ed. Federico García Lorca, *Poet in New York*, translated by Greg Simon and Steven F. White (New York: Farrar Straus Giroux, 1988).

————. "Notes on the Poems," in Federico García Lorca, *Poet in New York*, translated by Greg Simon and Steven F. White (New York: Farrar Straus Giroux, 1988), pp. 257-276.

————, ed. Federico García Lorca, *Poeta en Nueva York*, translated by Greg Simon and Steven F. White, revised ed. (New York: The Noonday Press, 1998).

————. "Notes on the Poems," in Federico García Lorca, *Poet in New York*, translated by Greg Simon and Steven F. White (New York: The Noonday Press, 1998), pp. 287-303.

————. "Lorca: 'Y me ofrezco a ser devorado por los campesinos españoles,'" *El Cultural* [*El Mundo* (Madrid)], 7 enero 2011, 10-13.

————, and Andrew A. Anderson. *Federico García Lorca en Nueva York y La Habana. Cartas y recuerdos* (Barcelona: Galaxia Gutenberg, 2013).

Menarini, Piero. *"Poeta en Nueva York" di Federico García Lorca. Lettura critica* (Florence: La Nuova Italia, 1975).

————. "*Poeta en York York* y *Tierra y luna*: dos libros aún 'inéditos' de García Lorca. Apuntes para una reconstrucción histórica," *Lingua e Stile*, XIII, no. 2 (1978), 283-293.

Millán, María Clementa. "Hacia un esclarecimiento de los poemas americanos de Federico García Lorca (*Poeta en Nueva York* y otros poemas)," *Ínsula*, XXXVII, no. 431 (octubre 1982), 1, 14, 15, 16.

————. "Interpretación de *Poeta en Nueva York* de Federico García Lorca. Contexto y originalidad," doctoral dissertation (Cambridge: Harvard University, 1984).

————. "Sobre la escisión o no de *Poeta en Nueva York* de Federico García Lorca," *El Crotalón. Anuario de Filología Española*, II (1985), 125-145.

————, ed. Federico García Lorca, *Poeta en Nueva York* (Madrid: Cátedra, 1987).

————. "Introducción," in Federico García Lorca, *Poeta en Nueva York* (Madrid: Cátedra, 1987), pp. 19-105.

1

Lorca at the Crossroads: "Imaginación, inspiración, evasión" and the "novísimas estéticas"[1]

IT IS BECOMING INCREASINGLY clear that in many regards 1928 was a crucial year in Lorca's life. In the spring he oversaw the production of the two numbers of *gallo,* in July *Romancero gitano* was published, and in December parts of the "Oda al Santisimo Sacramento del Altar" appeared in the *Revista de Occidente.* In that last month Lorca also joined the distinguished ranks of *conferenciantes* at the Residencia de Estudiantes, speaking on "Las nanas infantiles." Previously he had not ventured to talk formally in public outside Granada:[2] in his home town he had lectured on the *cante jondo* in 1922, on Góngora and Soto de Rojas in 1926, while more recently he had given "Imaginación, inspiración, evasión" and "Sketch de la pintura moderna" at the Ateneo de Granada in October 1928. These last two texts are both significant—but especially the former—for what they can tell us about Lorca's aesthetic orientation at the time.[3]

---

1   Federico García Lorca, *Conferencias*, vol. I, p. 21. All further references to this work will take the form *C* I or II, plus the page number.

2   There seems to be only one—very minor—exception to this general rule, when Lorca gave part of the Soto de Rojas lecture in Zamora in July 1928; see Ian Gibson, *Federico García Lorca*, p. 550.

3   Among other things, the opinions expressed here show how the aesthetic evidenced by "La imagen poética de don Luis de Góngora" (first given on 13 February 1926) had been completely superseded: cf. Maurer's introduction to *C* I, 15-30, and the revisions introduced in the 1930 version of the Góngora lecture (especially I, 91-92 and II, 127-28).

On the personal front, too, things were far from simple. Lorca, who turned thirty in June, was involved in a problematic relationship with the young sculptor Emilio Aladrén, and this seems to have been the immediate cause of an overwrought summer of *crisis sentimental* spent back in Granada.[4] There Lorca wrestled with his own conflictive feelings, and also with the related issues of the place of emotion(s) in poetry and the potential role of poetry in his private life.[5] But this was not his only worry: the overwhelming success of the *Romancero*—from which he was already rapidly moving away aesthetically—seemed curiously unreal and irrelevant beside his personal woes, the book had reinforced the "mito de gitanería" *(E* II, 21) against which he chafed, lubricious readers were endowing "La casada infiel" with an unwarranted and unwanted notoriety, and, worst of all, the book as a whole had been badly received by several friends whose opinions mattered to him deeply, among them Buñuel and Dalí.[6] To an emotionally vulnerable Lorca, their trenchant criticisms—that the *Romancero* was traditional, conventional, commonplace, overly studied and elegant, falsely but not truly modern (to cite only the less scabrous)—must have hit particularly hard.[7]

---

4   Lorca left Madrid at the very beginning of August and did not return until the middle of November. He used that precise phrase—"crisis sentimental"—in a letter of August or September 1928 to Sebastián Gasch: Federico García Lorca, *Epistolario*, vol. II, p. 109. All further references to this work will take the form *E* I or II, plus the page number. Cf. also the letters to Jorge Zalamea of summer and September (?) 1928: *E* II, 107, 108-09.

5   Cf. Lorca's comments: "Ahora estoy lleno de desesperanza, sin ganas de nada, tullido. [...] Veremos a ver si mis versos consiguen lo que deseo, veremos a ver si at fin corto las terribles amarras," in a letter to José Antonio Rubio Sacristán, quoted in "Federico García Lorca escribe a su familia desde Nueva York y La Habana (1929-1930)," ed. Christopher Maurer, p. 11; and "Ahora tengo una poesía [...] con una emoción donde se refleja todo mi amor por las cosas y mi guasa por las cosas" (*E* II, 108).

6   Luis Buñuel, *Obra literaria,* letter to José Bello of 14 September 1928 (quoted on p. 30), and letters to Bello of 5 September 1927 and 1 October 1928 (p. 36); "Salvador Dalí escribe a Federico García Lorca," ed. Rafael Santos Torroella, letter of end-August 1928 (pp. 88-94); letter from Salvador Dalí to Sebastián Gasch of November 1928, quoted in Gibson, p. 571. Cf. also Agustín Sánchez Vidal, *Buñuel, Lorca, Dalí...,* pp. 176-82.

7   The following is representative: "Tú quizá creerás atrevidas ciertas imágenes, o encontrarás una dosis crecida de irracionalidad en tus cosas, pero yo puedo decirte que tu poesía se mueve dentro de la *ilustración* de los lugares comunes más estereotipados y más conformistas" ("Salvador Dalí escribe...," p. 89). After criticiz-

On 8 September 1928 Lorca wrote to Sebastian Gasch that he had been out of Granada for several days and that "he vuelto hoy" *(E* II, 112). Later in the same letter he mentioned that "ayer me escribió una carta muy larga Dalí sobre mi libro (i.e. the *Romancero*) [...] Carta aguda y arbitraria que plantea un pleito poético interesante" *(E* II, 113).[8] Lorca's use of "ayer" must be approximate, as Dalí's letter must have been received before his brief absence from Granada. This would put its receipt at the beginning of September, and Dalí's penning of it in late August (rather than early September, as is usually assumed). These are no mere idle points of detail, however, for the first draft of the *Poema en prosa* which we know as "Nadadora sumergida. Pequeño homenaje a un cronista de salones" is dated 4 September, written apparently under the direct stimulus of (the receipt of) Dalí's letter.[9]

Even before the summer publication of the *Romancero gitano* Lorca had begun to move on to other things; of the book he wrote to Gasch that "se me ha muerto en las manos de la manera más tierna," while "mi poesía tiende ahora otro vuelo más agudo todavía. Me parece que un vuelo personal" *(E* II, 113). What he was referring to were the *Odas*—"al Santísimo Sacramento" and "a Sesostris"[10]—and the *Poemas en prosa,* already initiated in late 1927

---

ing Lorca to Bello, Buñuel listed the poets whom he favored, citing Larrea, Pedro Garfias, Huidobro, and Diego.

    8   A year earlier Dalí had given a mixed review to *Canciones:* "Salvador Dalí escribe...," pp. 58-59.

    9   Gibson, p. 566 and cf. pp. 563-69; Miguel García-Posada, "Lorca y el surrealismo: una relación conflictiva," p. 7.

The first draft of "Nadadora..." was originally entitled "Técnica del abrazo. (Poema aclaratorio de varias actitudes)"; the title was crossed out on the manuscript and replaced by "Últimos abrazos (Pequeño homenaje a un cronista de salones)" (p. 563). As Gibson suggests (p. 566), parts of "Nadadora sumergida" can be read autobiographically as reflecting Lorca's aesthetic shift: "dejé la literatura vieja que yo había cultivado con gran éxito. Es preciso romperlo todo para que los dogmas se purifiquen y las normas tengan nuevo temblor": Federico García Lorca, *Obras completas*, vol. III, p. 160.

Also noteworthy is the fact that Lorca composed the provocatively modernistic prose text "La muerte de la madre de Chariot" on 7 September 1928; in his study of this piece, "Millonario de lágrimas," Christopher Maurer calls attention to the resonances between what Chaplin symbolized as an actor and his current personal circumstances of bereavement and the situation in which Lorca found himself in the summer of 1928.

    10   Cf. the comments contained in *E* II, 117, 108. In the midst of his crisis, the first of these odes represents a turning (back) to religion, the (unfinished) second an

with "Santa Lucía y San Lázaro."[11] But it was really only in September 1928 that Lorca seems to have adopted a new aesthetic and got things rolling: in that month, referring to his prose poems, he wrote to Jorge Zalamea that "ahora tengo una poesía de *abrirse las venas,* una poesía *evadida* ya de la realidad" *(E* II, 108), he sent off both "Nadadora sumergida" and "Suicidio en Alejandría" to *L'Amic de les Arts,* and by year's end he had probably composed all six extant *Poemas en prosa.*[12]

The existing correspondence between Dalí and Lorca begins in 1925, and through it we can trace several important shifts in the painter's aesthetics.[13] Individual ideas which were to be synthesized in the key letter mentioned above started to appear from October 1927 onwards,[14] and likewise many

---

expression and exploration of his homosexual preoccupations.

11   Christopher Maurer has pointed out how the first part of the text—corresponding to Santa Lucía—looks back to an aesthetic derived from Gómez de la Serna's *greguería* and Dalí's Cubist phase, while the second—San Lázaro—looks forward to *Poeta en Nueva York:* "García Lorca y el ramonismo," p. 58.

12   "Santa Lucía y San Lázaro" was published in *Revista de Occidente,* November 1927; "Suicidio..." and "Nadadora..." in *L'Amic...,* no. 28, 30 September 1928; and "Degollación de los Inocentes" in *La Gaceta Literaria,* 15 January 1929. "Degollación del Bautista" and "Amantes asesinados por una perdiz" were sent off in December 1928 to Juan Guerrero Ruiz to be published in *Verso y Prosa (E* II, 124), a plan thwarted only by the demise of the magazine, whose last number came out in October of that year. "Degollación del Bautista" was ascribed to August 1928 in its eventual first publication in *Revista de Avance* (La Habana), V, no. 45 (15 April 1930), 104-06. The title of "Amantes asesinados..." (eventually published in *Ddooss* [Valladolid], no. 3 [March 1931]) is clearly modelled after Dalí's prose text "Peix perseguit per un raïm" which appeared alongside "Suicidio" and "Nadadora" in the same number of *L'Amic* (September 1928); Dalí had sent a Castilian version to Lorca earlier, perhaps as a putative contribution to *gallo* and accompanying his letter of November 1927: "Salvador Dalí escribe...," p. 141.

13   The edition of "Salvador Dalí escribe..." contains some thirty-four texts, ranging from telegrammatic postcards to lengthy letters all written over the period June 1925-August 1928, plus a couple of less interesting notes from the 1930s. The epistolary material dating from 1925-26 reflects a distinctly Cubist orientation. Only one letter from Lorca to Dalí is known: it is reproduced by Mario Hernández in "García Lorca y Salvador Dalí: del ruiseñor lírico a los burros podridos (poética y epistolario)," pp. 277-78.

14   "Salvador Dalí escribe...": pp. 67 (mid-October 1927); 71 (October/November 1927); 74 (November 1927); and 82 (mid-January 1928). Dalí waxed lyrical about Miró, opining that "es una cosa de una *Pureza* (1) enorme, y de una gran *alma* [...] (1) Todo lo contrario de lo que esa palabra significa para Juan Ramón." He char-

of these were repeated (sometimes verbatim) and further elaborated in an article which Dalí published in *La Gaceta Literaria* on 15 October 1928, entitled "Realidad y sobrerrealidad."[15] By the same token, a number of Dalí's points and even the occasional identical phrase were incorporated in the "Imaginación, inspiración, evasión" lecture.[16] For instance, from earlier Dalí letters Lorca picked up a comment such as "la metáfora y la imagen han sido hasta hoy anecdóticas; tanto es así, que hasta las más puras e incontrolables pueden ser explicadas como un acertijo," which was carried over into his allusion to modern poets who "pretenden libertar la poesía no sólo de la anécdota, sino del acertijo de la imagen y de los planos de la realidad."[17] From the letter of late August 1928, besides the central concept of "evasión," Lorca returned to Dalí's point that modern art transcended the traditional categories of the beautiful and the ugly.[18] It would be easy, and tidy, to conclude that Dalí's arguments and criticism had finally won Lorca over, that this lecture reflected the poet's new pro-Surrealist stance, and that creatively the *Poemas en prosa*—now quite frequently cited, rather than *Poeta en Nueva York,* as the nearest Lorca ever came to Surrealism[19]—were the direct and immediate result.

However, there are a number of compelling objections to such a scenario. First of all, Dalí himself had not yet, in the autumn of 1928, fully espoused Surrealism.[20] Although the letter and the article show his fascination

---

acterized his own current painting as "evasión de lo acostumbrado, de la realidad anti-real y convencional a que nos ha acostumbrado el arte puerco," and in a postscript added that "Bretón es *muy* inteligente, cada día más quizá, pero no sirve para la poesía" (all p. 67).

Compare also his articles in *L'Amic de les Arts* of September and October 1927 and February/April/May 1928: "La fotografia, pura creació de l'esperit," "Els meus quadros del Saló de Tardor" and "Nous límits de la pintura," reprinted in *Manifiestos, proclamas, panfletos y textos doctrinales...,* ed. Jaime Brihuega, pp. 123-26, 126-28, 129-43.

15   Reprinted in Brihuega, pp. 295-302; cf. Gibson, p. 573.

16   Gibson, p. 575; Christopher Maurer, "Introduction," in Federico García Lorca, *Poet in New York,* p. xvi. Lorca would not have seen the article until *after* he had written his lecture.

17   "Salvador Dalí escribe...," p. 71; *C* II, 17.

18   "Salvador Dalí escribe...," p. 91; *C* II, 13-14, 18, 28.

19   E.g. by García-Posada, p. 9; Rafael Martínez Nadal, *"El público." Amor y muerte en la obra de Federico García Lorca,* p. 106; Hernández, passim.

20   The first sign that he was moving towards it comes in June 1927; the process was not complete until the very *end* of 1928: see Marie Laffranque, *Les Idées*

and considerable sympathy for the French movement, the aesthetic stance taken still derives essentially from that laid out in the "Manifest antiartistic català," published as a pamphlet in Barcelona in March 1928 and reproduced in Castilian in *gallo* no. 2 (April/May 1928).[21] Secondly, there are Lorca's own, oft-quoted words in the September 1928 letter to Gasch which accompanied his submission of "Nadadora sumergida" and "Suicidio en Alejandria" to *L'Amic de les Arts:* "Ahí te mando los dos poemas. [...] Responden a mi nueva manera *espiritualista,* emoción pura descarnada, desligada del control lógico, pero, ¡ojo!, ¡ojo!, con una tremenda lógica poética. No es surrealismo, ¡ojo! la conciencia más clara los ilumina" (*E* II, 114). Finally, there is the lecture "Imaginación, inspiración, evasión" itself, first delivered on 11 October and prepared in the days and weeks immediately preceding, a text which repays a closer, more pondered, and more discriminating reading than it has often received.[22]

One reason for this relative neglect is the fact that we do not actually have Lorca's manuscript, but rather only a series of newspaper accounts of the talk. A close collation of the journalistic reports from October 1928 (Granada), February 1929 (Madrid), February 1930 (New York) and March 1930 (La Habana) reveals that although Lorca tinkered a good deal with his opening and closing remarks, the body and substance of the lecture remained almost unchanged, and this observation allows us to proceed with an analysis on the basis of a conflation of the "second-hand" texts at our disposal.[23]

Despite its tripartite title, the thrust of "Imaginación, inspiración, evasión" actually sets up a major binary opposition between the first two terms, while "evasión" floats rather uncomfortably as both the means to and product

---

esthétiques de Federico García Lorca, pp. 155, 169, n. 82; Gibson, p. 569; Dawn Ades, *Dalí,* pp. 46-48.

21   Lorca had collaborated with the triumvirate of authors—Dalí, Gasch and Lluís Montanyà—on first drafts of the manifesto during his stay in Catalonia in the summer of 1927 (Gibson, p. 542; postcard of July 1927 from Dalí to Gasch, cited by Hernández, p. 303). Brihuega reproduces the Catalan original of the manifesto on pp. 157-61.

22   Three exceptions are Philip W. Silver, who dedicates several pages to it in his *La casa de Anteo...,* pp. 164-69; Hernández, who likewise devotes a section of his article, pp. 290-93; and Jesús Villegas Guzmán, "Lorca y la vanguardia: lectura de cuatro conferencias," whose discussion of it (pp. 51-58), however, is rather less original.

23   Numerous phrases, sentences, and even paragraphs are repeated verbatim from one newspaper report to the next, suggesting that in those passages we have a more or less perfect transcription—or indeed extract—of Lorca's own text.

of "inspiración."[24] According to Lorca's definitions, imagination—the apti-
tude to discover unsuspected connections—spawns metaphors, which bring
together elements drawn from the real world in a process governed by human
logic or reason. But the imagination is inadequate to the poet's ultimate task:
it does not permit him to plumb the depths or to capture all the nuances
of external reality. In contrast, by shunning—or even subverting—mimetic
conventions and leaving the real world behind (one sense of "evasión"), the
"gift" of inspiration liberates the poet and enables him to discover or invent
mysterious and inexplicable "hechos poéticos," free-standing images devoid
of any analogical meaning whose creation, internal functionings, and inter-
relations are now determined only by a "lógica poética."[25] These "hechos poéticos," furthermore, produce fresh, intense, poetic emotions, and serve as a
kind of springboard thanks to which the poet/poem can escape from the real
world and achieve a certain transcendence (the other sense of "evasión") on
the plane of "una asombrosa realidad poética."[26]

Imagination and the metaphor are exemplified in the work of Góngora;
inspiration and the "hecho poético" in that of San Juan de la Cruz (C II,
21, 26, 31).[27] The now superseded "Góngora phase" of Spanish poetry corresponds to "la madurez del cubismo, pintura de raciocinio puro" (C II, 26),
while Larrea, Diego, Alberti, Guillen, and Salinas—"los nuevos valores de
la poesía española"—are leading lights in "un renacimiento, una 'vuelta a la
naturaleza' en reacción contra los academicismos de la época madura del cubismo," a new poetic movement paralleled by Miró and "los jóvenes pintores
españoles" (C II, 23, 27).[28] Furthermore, it follows that "las últimas generacio-

---

24   Cf. Laffranque, pp. 171-72, 250-51; the later lecture, "Juego y teoría del
duende," is also apparently ternary, though eventually "ángel" and "musa" are set in
binary opposition to "duende."

25   Maurer, "Introduction," *Poet in New York*, p. xvi. The mode of operation
of the "hecho poético" is therefore comparable to that of the *collage,* that is, a "yux-
taposición de dos entidades cuya relación *no* puede explicarse mediante la analogía":
Maurer, "García Lorca y el ramonismo," p. 59. *Collage* in art had of course been pio-
neered by Picasso and Braque in the second—"Synthetic"—phase of Cubism.

26   This account is synthesized from all five newspaper reports, C II, 13-31, *passim.*

27   The distinction brings to mind a review, "Panorama–*Canciones,* de Federico García Lorca," which Lluís Montanyà published in *L'Amic de les Arts* (July 1927).
For him Lorca's book brought together two strands of pure poetry, typified respectively by Góngora and San Juan de la Cruz.

28   Here Lorca is seeking to establish an analogy between modern poets and
painters: "en general pintores y poetas, después de la brisa pura del cubismo, vuelven
los ojos 'al puro instinto, a la creación virginal incontrolada [...]'"; these writers (just

nes de poetas"—again essentially Lorca's contemporaries—"se preocupan de reducir la poesía a la creación del hecho poético y seguir las normas que este mismo impone, sin escuchar la voz del razonamiento lógico ni el equilibrio de la imaginación" *(C* II, 17, and cf. 25).

Closer to home, among his *own* poetry, Lorca strained to find examples of "hechos poéticos" in his already "outmoded" *Romancero gitano (C* II, 22, 25), prompting one journalist to comment that some of the images were "no tan inexplicables en su relación interior como él mismo se figura" (*C* II, 23). It would be plausible to think that one of Lorca's goals here was to rehabilitate (salvage?) the *Romancero* by presenting the mode of operation of its metaphors from a particular perspective that would tend to situate the poetry as more in accord with Dalí's current aesthetic than Dalí himself had found the collection to be.[29] Much later, in the *conferencia-recital* of *Romancero gitano,* whose first known reading was in Barcelona on 9 October 1935, Lorca picked up an identical terminology and, apparently, an almost identical purpose.[30] Here he stated that he was not going to "mostrar la mecánica de sus imágenes," perhaps because "el misterio poético es también misterio para el poeta que lo comunica"; the whole collection was in a sense "un hecho poético" and hence in particular the "Romance sonámbulo" "es un hecho poético puro del fondo andaluz, y siempre tendrá luces cambiantes, aun para el hombre que lo

---

identified) are members of the "grupo de poetas puros españoles," while the artists are "los jóvenes pintores españoles, con Juan Miró a la cabeza, [que] siguen la misma trayectoria, venciendo las dificultades del poema plástico" *(C* II, 26-27). The analogy really only holds true in the broadest of terms, but few others can have attempted to establish any kind of parallel between Salinas and Miró!

A more detailed analysis of Cubism and Surrealism is to be found in the contemporaneous "Sketch de la nueva pintura," which I summarize below.

29   Remember Dalí's comment that "tú quizá creerás atrevidas ciertas imágenes, o encontrarás una dosis crecida de irracionalidad en tus cosas," a false estimation that he went on immediately to explode: "Salvador Dalí escribe...," p. 89.

30   In 1935 Lorca also sought to inject the collection with a stronger sociopolitical significance, stressing such poems as the "Romance de la Guardia Civil española." García-Posada comments that "la conferencia-recital efectúa una lectura irracionalista o surrealista, o surrealizante, si se quiere, del *Romancero*" (p. 7), and even goes so far as to say that the *conferencia-recital* represents a "falseamiento de los postulados sobre los que había elaborado [Lorca] el *Romancero gitano*" (p. 8). It *is* true that the picture which Lorca gives of the composition of the *Romancero* is, at the very least, anachronistic, when measured against what we know of the actual development of his poetic practice. By coincidence, Lorca had seen Dalí again—for the first time in eight years—just eleven days before the lecture-recital.

ha comunicado, que soy yo. [...] no sabré decir más, ni mucho menos explicar su significado."[31]

Between these two dates—1928 and 1935—Lorca invoked "hechos poéticos" more justifiably with regard to *Poeta en Nueva York*.[32] In Cuba in 1930, for instance, he reflected on the recent composition of *Poeta*... "donde el hecho poético se produce como un hecho propio" and "el hecho poético se produce por la reunión de elementos de belleza dentro de un asunto en donde sólo interviene la ficción del poeta."[33] Similarly, in his *conferencia-recital* of *Poeta en Nueva York,* first given in Madrid on 16 March 1932, he made direct allusion to "esta clase de poemas que voy a leer que, por estar llenos de hechos poéticos dentro exclusivamente de una lógica lírica y trabados tupidamente sobre el sentimiento humano y la arquitectura del poema, no son aptos para ser comprendidos rápidamente."[34]

Although the notions of "evasión" and "hecho poético" do not appear by name in the "Sketch de la pintura moderna," this lecture, first delivered only a little over two weeks after "Imaginación..." and at the same locale, nevertheless offers a complementary and neatly interlocking body of aesthetic ideas. Turning his attention from poetry to painting, Lorca found the most fundamental divide in the whole history of (European) art to be that separating all "realistic," representational painting (up to and including Impressionism) from modern, anti-representational painting, which had been ushered in by Cubism and continued by Surrealism. Thus modern art possessed a "modo

---

31   *Obras completas,* III, pp. 340-43.

Barely five weeks later, in an interview given in Valencia, Lorca stated that "yo pretendo hacer de mis personajes [teatrales] un hecho poético, aunque los haya visto alentar alrededor mío. Son una realidad estética." Pressing the point, he proposed rather fancifully that "por esa razón gustan tanto a Salvador Dalí y a los surrealistas": see Ricardo G. Luengo, "Conversación de Federico García Lorca."

32   A collection where "lo inexplicable de la imagen prevalece sobre la lógica de la metáfora," perhaps because Lorca había lost "su confianza en el poder epistemológico de la metáfora" and had become "mucho menos convencido de la capacidad del ingenio y de la metáfora para iluminar zonas desconocidas de la realidad": Maurer, "García Lorca y el ramonismo," p. 59.

33   Germán Arciniegas, "Federico García Lorca," quoted by Daniel Eisenberg, "Dos conferencias lorquianas (Nueva York y La Habana, 1930)," p. 200, n. 10. We should note that "Imaginación, inspiración, evasión" was given before, during, and after the essential composition of the poems in *Poeta en Nueva York,* and that the concept of the "hecho poético" is an important aesthetic key to the collection: Maurer, "Introduction," *Poet in New York,* p. xvi.

34   *Obras completas,* III, p. 348.

espiritualista en el cual las imágenes ya no son dadas por la inteligencia, sino por [el] inconsciente, por la pura inspiración directa" *(C* II, 38); having undertaken "la obra más purificadora, mas libertadora," it was no longer tied by any mimetic imperative but rather self-sufficient, pure, divorced from reality, auto-referential, and in it "lo mismo que el poeta crea la imagen que define, el pintor crea la imagen plástica que fija y orienta la emoción" (*C* II, 39, 42).

However, despite this overall enthusiasm, the later stages of Cubism Lorca characterized as falling into "un triste cerebralismo" (*C* II, 44). Consequently, he found a secondary division within the modern period, and what followed Cubism—essentially Surrealism—was now to be set in opposition against it. Surrealism was informed by "[el] instinto, [...] [el] acaso, [...] la inspiración pura, [...] la fragancia de lo directo," and had heralded "un período místico, incontrolado, de suprema belleza [en que] se empieza a expresar lo inexpresable" *(C* II, 45). In particular, Lorca singled out Miró's recent work as representing the finest manifestation of "arte [...] puro," for his canvases "vienen del sueño, del centro del alma, allí donde el amor esta en carne viva" *(C* II, 47, 48).

As will have become clear, "Imaginación, inspiración, evasión"—and, for that matter, "Sketch de la pintura moderna"—are veritable compendia of avant-garde aesthetic theories and currents, and in them a number of different tendencies surface and often intersect. Furthermore, many of the basic ideas are not—nor could they be expected to be—entirely original. The "Sketch..." shows that Lorca was clearly well-informed about the contemporary art scene and had mastered its complexities, but he was obviously not aiming at novelty in this essentially expository survey. Here Lorca praised Cubism as representing "una *superación* de la pintura y una *creación* dentro de los límites plásticos, insólita y absolutamente nueva" (*C* II, 43; my italics), and in using those particular words he could almost have been thinking of Apollinaire himself, or else of Guillermo de Torre, who, in 1920, had quoted the French writer on Cubism as an art "de concepción, que puede elevarse hasta la creación" and had gone on to vaunt "el vértice de creación o superación realista."[35] Likewise a number of Lorca's other opinions coincide with those of the professional art critic Sebastián Gasch, though in the autumn of 1927 Gasch had tended to judge Surrealist painting much more negatively than Lorca did exactly a year later.[36] In fact, in the "Sketch..." and likewise in

35   "Alquimia y mayéutica de la imagen creacionista," reprinted in Juan Manuel Rozas, *La generación del 27 desde dentro*, pp. 221-25 (224).

36   See, for instance, "Del cubismo al superrealismo," *La Gaceta Literaria* (October 1927), reprinted in Rozas, pp. 144-53.

"Imaginación, inspiración, evasión," as will be demonstrated in greater detail in the paragraphs which follow, Lorca inevitably employed concepts, terms, and lines of argument which had already enjoyed a considerable and fairly widespread use during the earlier part of the decade in France and in Spain, ideas which were much "in vogue" in certain circles but which he redefined, "fine-tuned" or recombined for his own particular purposes.[37]

To begin with, at several junctures in "Imaginación..." the opinions expressed by Lorca recall observations made several years earlier by Jean Epstein in *La Poésie d'aujourd'hui...*[38] Here Epstein quotes one Edouard Abramowski on the subject of the "fait esthétique" (p. 43) (which might be translated literally as "hecho estético"), while he himself later writes that "la logique rationnelle et grammaticale n'a plus rien à voir ici. L'enchaînement des idées, si on peut appeler cela des idées, se fait selon des associations partielles et absolument illogiques" (pp. 101-02) (i.e. the rejection of "lógica humana"). The French critic continues: "Néanmoins il est difficile d'imaginer que ces enchaînements n'admettent aucune loi, ni règle [...] Il est au contraire infiniment probable que la pensée-association connaît un ordre assurément très compliqué mais tout de même compréhensible [...] la logique rationnelle ne sera plus qu'une partie de cette logique dont nous pouvons chercher à comprendre cette autre partie qui a trait à la pensée-association" (p. 108) (i.e. the existence of a "lógica poética"). Finally, we may note that several years before the official birth of Surrealism, Epstein had found that modern writers were "cherchant à se rapprocher de plus en plus de leur subconscient" (p. 68), and he went on to propose that "la logique de la pensée-association [...] et celle du rêve auront beaucoup de chances de coïncider sur plus d'un point" (p. 109) ("evasión" linked with the "subconsciente"—*C* II, 18).

In a rather similar fashion, the crucial notion of "evasión" boasts quite a long and distinguished heritage in recent aesthetic criticism. As far back as 1920, for instance, in full *ultraísta* flood, Guillermo de Torre pontificated that "por escalas sucesivamente ascensionales, el poeta llega a obtener así la

---

37   Laffranque suggests that he was as much reacting against aesthetic doctrines—in order to establish his own position—as aligning himself with them (p. 159).

38   Lorca knew this rarely mentioned work and had quoted from it in "La imagen poética de don Luis de Góngora": see *C* I, 102 and Maurer's annotation in n. 15. Paul Ilie has studied the relationship between a second book by Epstein—*La Lyrosophie*—with Spanish avant-garde movements of the 1920s, in "La lirosofía, entre poesía pura y deshumanización." *La Poésie d'aujourd'hui...* also seems to have had a strong influence on Ortega, as will be noted below.

purificación total en la libre cerebración sugeridora y la evasión telúrica de la imagen, que asciende aviónicamente a un plano hiperespacial."[39] In 1921, Jean Epstein commented extensively on "l'illogisme des lettres modernes," and observed that "pour s'évader de la logique, il fallait donc s'évader de la grammaire. C'était une fuite difficile."[40] A notably similar formulation occurs in Ortega y Gasset's *La deshumanizacion del arte,* the essays of which were partially published as newspaper articles during 1924 and in book form in 1925.[41] Here Ortega notes that "la 'realidad' acecha constantemente al artista para impedir su evasión. ¡Cuánta astucia supone la fuga genial!" (p. 36), and later that "sólo la metáfora nos facilita la evasión [de lo real, de lo que ya es]" (p. 46). Of all this he concludes: "Un mismo instinto de fuga y evasión de lo real se satisface en el suprarrealismo de la metáfora y en lo que cabe llamar infrarrealismo. A la ascensión poética [remember de Torre's words] puede sustituirse una inmersión bajo el nivel de la perspectiva natural" (p. 49).[42]

In the light of these examples, it is hard to believe that Dalí's references to "evasión" in his letter of late August 1928 were not influenced by contemporary aesthetic ideas and usage. On the other hand, he does push the concept further: the "escape" now is of a perceptual—almost phenomenological or epistemological—order. By means of "la evasión de las ideas que nuestra inteligencia ha ido forjando artificialmente," that is, by refusing the conventional, the commonly accepted, and the unquestioning, and by adopting a new, determinedly intrinsic vision of things, the artist can capture "su exacto sentido real."[43] As a sample of this radically different perception of objects in

---

39   "Alquimia y mayéutica de la imagen creacionista," p. 222. I offer this as a representative "early" occurrence; the use of the term no doubt goes back a lot further.

40   *La Poésie d'aujourd'hui...,* pp. 95, 97.

41   Quotations are taken from the 10th ed. of 1970.

42   In addition, Juan Larrea's first *poem* was entitled "Evasión," dating from 1919: David Bary, *Larrea: poesía y transfiguración,* p. 42; and the first section of Gerardo Diego's collection *Imagen* (published 1922) was entitled *Evasión* (1918-19). With no specific date attached, Ramón Gómez de la Serna is quoted as writing in a similar vein: "Coincidiendo con la actitud primera de la generación poética que nace hacia 1920, dice: 'La nueva literatura es evasión'"; see Luis Cernuda, *Estudios sobre poesía española contemporánea,* p. 132. Note also José María Hinojosa and his "Texto onírico VI" from *La flor de California* (published April 1928): "Y ahora que somos libres, ¿cuál es nuestra verdad? ¿Podremos evadirnos de nuestros límites en esta limitada evasión? ¿Dónde comienzo y dónde termino?"; quoted from Julio Neira's modern edition, pp. 131-32.

43   "Salvador Dalí escribe...," p. 89. In one sense Dalí pushes beyond the Futurist concept of *parole in libertà* and asserts the need for *cosas en libertad*: "Hay que

their unvitiated and inherent reality or being—"su real y *consustancial* manera de ser," Dalí proposes that "los minuteros de un reloj [...] empiezan a tener un valor real en el momento en que [...] se *evaden* de tal reloj para articularse al sitio al que correspondería el sexo de las miguitas del pan" (pp. 91, 90).[44]

It is almost certain that Dalí's letter was the immediate stimulus for Lorca's utilization of the term "evasión" in the formulation of his new aesthetic, but Ortega's use of it—and others' before him—must also have weighed upon Lorca and made their own direct or indirect contribution.[45] As we have seen, the rather amorphous definition of the notion offered by Lorca went further than Ortega but not as far as Dalí: the "hecho poético" pushed significantly beyond the purely metaphorical, but did not transform (and disrupt) the very perception of reality to the extent that Dalí proposed.

---

dejar las cositas *libres* de las ideas convencionales a que la inteligencia las ha querido someter. [...] ¡Que ellas mismas decidan la dirección del curso de la proyección de sus sombras!" (p. 91). In very similar fashion, he goes beyond the Cubist/*creacionista* notion of the work of art being in and of itself, and wants to endow that quality (also) on outside physical reality. Note, however, that already present in Cubist theory is the desire to "llegar a la esencia de los objetos," and to capture not a superficial reality but rather a profound one: Juan Cano Ballesta, "Sobre cubismo y creacionismo poético (Ecos de una controversia)," pp. 5, 8. Ozenfant's and Jeanneret's Purism sought to take Cubism to its "logical" conclusions, and some of their central tenets—the precise, objective stress on the thing *(objet type)* in and of itself—are clearly present in Dalí. Cf. also Lorca's "Sketch...": "Con unos cuantos objetos le basta [al pintor]. Parte de ellos y los crea de nuevo, mejor, descubre su intimidad, su meollo pictórico, que no ve el copista" *(C* II, 42).

44   A somewhat fuller recasting of the same essential notions is contained in his contemporaneous article, "Realidad y sobrerrealidad": see Brihuega, especially pp. 296, 298-300. Here it becomes clear that the "dato estrictamente objetivo obtenido anti-artísticamente por un riguroso método analítico" ("Salvador Dalí escribe...," p. 92) is actually obtained through a fundamental shift of *gestalt* in which automatism, forgetfulness, passivity, or day-dreaming may all play a part, and from which all rational, intellectual, and imaginative participation have been banished (cf. Dalí's example of a horse and a rider—of all that people unreflectingly assume and what they should really *see,* pp. 90-91). This new vision enables the artist to achieve true objectivity and total immediacy; by taking art out of its cultural context, things can simply *be,* they no longer have to be rendered through cultural codes that are variable both historically and geographically. Thus modern painters attain a "lenguaje absoluto [i.e. universal]" (Brihuega, p. 300).

45   García-Posada oversimplifies by asserting baldly that "el concepto de *evasión* manejado deriva de esta carta" (p. 7).

Significantly enough, Lorca probably derived the term and the concept of the "hecho poético" from Dalí as well, though once more the phrase had already appeared in a number of earlier writings. We have noted Epstein's use of "fait esthétique," while Dalí, in an epigraph to one of his articles, approvingly reproduces a passage from Le Corbusier: "plus forte est la poésie des faits. Des objets qui signifient quelque chose et qui sont disposés avec tact et talent créent un *fait poétique*."[46] Dalí's direct translation into Catalan—"fet poètic"—appears in his own writings as early as September 1927 and again in October,[47] although before or by that date he may also have discussed the notion with Lorca in person or alluded to it in a letter now lost.[48]

In contrast, what are we to make of phrases such as "el sentido espiritual y hondo del poema puro" (*C* II, 15, 19, 30), "llevar la poesía a un último plano de pureza y sencillez" (*C* II, 17, 25), and "arte que persigue la pureza" (*C* II, 18)? One could be forgiven for thinking that these were extracts, not from Dalí's letters or articles, but rather from the "carta-prólogo" and "notas-epílogo" to Jiménez's *Segunda antolojía poética* (Madrid: Calpe, 1922), though in fact they are all phrases once more excerpted from the text of "Imaginación...." In fact, "purity" was a much invoked ideal throughout the 1920s with several different strands of the avant-garde laying claims to it, and the resulting overlap in terminology may account in part for the apparent coincidence or confusion of ideas.[49] Nonetheless, it should be noted that Jiménez is quoted

---

46   "Poesia de l'util standarditzat," *L 'Amic de les Arts* (March 1928), reprinted in Paul Ilie, ed., *Documents of the Spanish Vanguard,* p. 277 (my italics). The quotation, which I have not been able to trace, presumably comes from *Après le Cubisme* (1918), *Vers une architecture* (1923), *La Peinture moderne* (1925) or an article in *L'Esprit nouveau* (1920-25).

47   "La fotografia, pura creació de l'esperit," in Brihuega, p. 123; "Els meus quadros del Saló de Tardor," in Brihuega, p. 128. In "Film-arte, film-antiartístico," *La Gaceta Literaria* (December 1927), Dalí extolls "la emoción poética completamente nueva de todos los hechos más humildes e inmediatos."

48   Silver points out that Lorca mentions Ozenfant, Jeanneret (Le Corbusier), and the Purists by name in his "Sketch..." (*C* II, 38, 44), while "Imaginación..." contains an aside to Le Corbusier (*C* II, 18, 22), and he goes on to suggest quite persuasively that Purism played a major role in the elaboration of Lorca's new aesthetic (pp. 165-67).

49   Ilie has pointed out Guillermo de Torre's frequent early use of terms such as "puro," "purista," "purificación," "depurado" (and, we might note, "límpido," "desnudo" and "sencillez"), at a time before the Abbé Brémond controversy and well before the description of Generation of '27 poets as "poetas puros": see "La lirosofía, entre poesía pura y deshumanización." Huidobro employs a similar vocabulary—

in Lorca's lecture by name, Jiménez who for Dalí was "el jefe máximo de la putrefacción poética,"[50] but who for Lorca was still (and despite Dalí's repeated attacks) the "inspirador ilustre e indudable de este [nuevo] movimiento poético" *(C* II, 23).[51] Clearly the aesthetic values and goals of Jiménez's brand of *poesía pura* still held some sway with Lorca in 1928, even if by that date he had moved well away from any direct imitation or influence.

Similarly, but even more strikingly, still other ideas and propositions in the "Imaginación..." lecture are strongly reminiscent of the theories of Huidobro's *creacionismo,* in particular as they are laid out in his various writings gathered together in the book *Manifestes* (1925).[52] Dedicated copies of both *Ecuatorial* and *Poemas árticos* are preserved in Lorca's library, and the former bears an inscription where Huidobro recalls "tantas veladas musicales y poéticas inolvidables."[53] On the evidence of the dates, it seems probable that

---

"puro," "depurado," etc.; Ozenfant and Jeanneret sought to continue and "correct" Cubism in the movement which they called Purism; Dalí talks of *Mariana Pineda* as "depurada" and as possessing "sencillez," and later of Miró's work in terms of "pureza"; Lorca himself adduced Juan Larrea as an example of the "poetas modernos" who aspire to "llegar al plano de pureza y sencillez" (*C* II, 25); while in his review of Lorca's *Canciones* (1927), Montanyà characterized the verse as essentially "poesía pura," but of a kind which presented two different facets: one suggested "inteligencia," "álgebra," "geometría," and the poetry of Mallarmé, Valéry and Góngora, the other "intuición," "sueño," "subconsciente," and the poetry of Rimbaud, Lautréamont, Éluard and San Juan de la Cruz.

50   "Salvador Dalí escribe...," p. 71. Dalí was no less critical of Valéry: see p. 84 and "Realidad y sobrerrealidad," p. 300.

51   In context the passage runs as follows: "Dijo que debían teñirse los poemas de un sentimiento planetario y procurar que huyan de toda estética establecida. Citó a Juan Ramón Jiménez como inspirador ilustre e indudable de este movimiento poético—no lo llamaremos 'escuela' por no estatizarlo—, y explicó sus diferencias con los superrealistas, que buscan su inspiración en el mundo de los sueños y lo subconsciente" *(C* II, 23). If Lorca went to the trouble of differentiating Jiménez from the Surrealists, then there may be some grounds for supposing that he believed that they shared certain basic things in common.

52   The work collects ten texts, some printed previously between 1921 and 1924; however, *"Non serviam"* (1914), "La Création pure" (1921), and one or two other pieces were not included. All my quotations are taken from Vicente Huidobro, *Obras completas,* ed. Hugo Montes; vol. 1 contains a comprehensive section of "Manifiestos" (incorporating a Spanish translation of *Manifestes),* to which page numbers refer.

53   Manuel Fernández-Montesinos, "Descripción de la biblioteca de Federico García Lorca (Catálogo y estudio)," pp. 54-55.

before the 1930s Huidobro and Lorca can only have coincided in Madrid once, in 1919,[54] but there were many other channels through which Lorca would have become perfectly familiar with the Chilean's aesthetics.[55]

Huidobro rejected representational art, and sought to invent new worlds or realities wherein the poem would exist purely on its own terms (pp. 715, 716, 719, 733). To do this the poet had to rise up from the level of the everyday to "un plano superior," where the aim was to "expresar sólo lo inexpresable" (pp. 716, 717, 725). Furthermore, if "toda poesía válida tiende al último límite de la imaginación," when it reaches there "el encadenamiento habitual de los fenómenos" will break down and be replaced by a "lógica nueva" in which all limits and opposites are transcended (p. 717). Elsewhere Huidobro describes the elaboration of the poet's discourse "en donde lo arbitrario pasa a tomar un rol encantatorio" (p. 717). Concomitantly, if poetry ultimately remains under "el control de la razón," this cannot be a "fría razón" but rather "otra razón," a "razón elevada" which corresponds uniquely to poets (pp. 723, 725). Finally, Huidobro writes insistently of the selection, combination, and transformation of elements derived from the objective world which, in the new form given to them by the poet, reemerge as "hechos nuevos" (p. 720);[56]

---

54   As far as we know, Huidobro was in Madrid in November/December 1916, July-November 1918, November 1919, August/September 1920, April (?) and December 1921, and thereafter in 1931 and 1932; see Gloria Videla de Rivero, "Huidobro en España," and René de Costa, *Vicente Huidobro. The Careers of a Poet, passim.* During all these periods save for that in 1919 (and the conjectural stay in April 1921 for the publication of the first number of *Creación*), Lorca was living down in Granada. René de Costa's article "La poesía y sus circunstancias: un inédito de García Lorca," and Mario Hernández's speculations in his Introduction to Federico García Lorca, *Libro de poemas*, pp. 23-26, both contain chronological inaccuracies.

55   Several critics have found "huellas creacionistas" in Lorca's poetry, particularly his early production: Gerardo Diego, writing in *Atenea* (Santiago de Chile), nos. 295-96 (January-February 1950), quoted by Robert E. Gurney in "Vicente Huidobro y Juan Larrea"; Juan Larrea, in a letter of 1953 quoted by David Bary, *Nuevos estudios sobre Huidobro y Larrea*, p. 23; Antonio de Undurraga, "Teoría del creacionismo," in Vicente Huidobro, *Poesía y prosa. Antología*, pp. 98-102; and Santiago Ontañón, with José María Moreiro, *Unos pocos amigos verdaderos*, pp. 131-32.

56   I have counted thirteen occurrences of this phrase between pp. 718-53. The "hecho nuevo" is obviously a special kind of image—"una imagen pura creada" (p. 733); of its creation Huidobro wrote that "el poeta es aquel que sorprende la relación oculta que existe entre las cosas más lejanas, los ocultos hilos que las unen. Hay que pulsar aquellos hilos como las cuerdas de un arpa, y producir una resonancia que ponga en movimiento las dos realidades lejanas. La imagen es el broche que las une,

as a result, "el conjunto de los diversos hechos nuevos unidos por un mismo espíritu es lo que constituye la obra creada" (p. 750). The similarities with Lorca's position are startling, and once more we should not be surprised to find him commenting in his lecture that "Juan Larrea y su discípulo Gerardo Diego construyen poemas a base de hechos poéticos encadenados, cada vez más limpios de imagen y de vuelo más cristalino" (*C* II, 26), Larrea and Diego who had precisely been named a few years earlier, and by none other than Huidobro, as "los dos poetas creacionistas españoles" (p. 735).[57]

And so finally to Surrealism proper, which, in a gross simplification, might be said also to have identified two worlds, the waking, conscious, external world and the inner psychic world of the subconscious, and one of whose primary goals was to unite the two, by whatever means possible, on a plane of absolute reality or surreality—the concept which gave the movement its name.[58] In his letter Dalí had stressed that "evasión" was the thing, while adding in a postscript that "el surrealismo es *uno* de los medios de Evasión" and that "yo voy teniendo mis maneras al margen del surrealismo."[59] In the October 1928 version of his lecture, Lorca seems to have referred bluntly to "'evasión' de la realidad por el camino del sueño, por el camino del subconsciente, por el camino que dicte un hecho insólito que regale la inspira-

---

el broche de luz. Y su poder reside en la alegría de la revelación. [...] la imagen constituye una revelación. Y mientas más sorprendente sea esta revelación, más transcendente será su efecto" (p. 726).

57   The links between *ultraísmo, creacionismo, deshumanización* and *poesía pura* are well established: see Juan Cano Ballesta, *La poesía española entre pureza y revolución (1930-1936)*, pp. 34-40; Gustav Siebenmann, *Los estilos poéticos en España desde 1900*, pp. 225-32; and Antonio Blanch, *La poesía pura española. Conexiones con la cultura francesa*, pp. 114-16. Consequently, it is not that surprising to discover Ortega writing on occasions as if he had Huidobro's manifestos at his side: cf. *La deshumanización del arte...*, pp. 36, 44-45, 50, 67.

Because of chronological and theoretical overlapping, it is also understandable that, as the examples and testimonies accrue, one "ism" threatens to collapse into another. Beyond the scope of the present article lie a number of other noteworthy "points in common" between Guillermo de Torre (writing in 1920), Jean Epstein (1921) and Ortega (1924); all three resort to mathematical language (equation, theorem, algebra) in referring to images and metaphors; all three stress the elimination of sentiment(ality) from modern literature; and Ortega follows Epstein in asserting that modern art represents (or should represent) not external reality but the artist's response to that reality (cf. in particular Epstein pp. 148-49).

58   C.W.E. Bigsby, *Dada and Surrealism*, p. 75.
59   "Salvador Dalí escribe...," pp. 89, 94.

ción" (C II, 18). By February 1929, his fuller treatment recognized that in "el realísimo mundo de los sueños, se encuentran indudablemente normas poéticas de emoción verdadera," but added the rider that "esta evasión poética puede hacerse de muchas maneras," of which Surrealism was but one (C II, 20-21, 25). Indeed, it was, "aunque muy pura, poco diáfana," and hence likely to be rejected by Spaniards, for which reason "la evasión poética en España se resuelve a base del hecho poético puro" (C 11, 21, 25-26).

If Dalí had no love for Jiménez, if Jiménez was scornful of Huidobro,[60] if Huidobro was a staunch anti-Surrealist,[61] if, indeed, the multiplication of "isms" only made more pressing the need for their respective proponents to stress the differences between one and another, then nevertheless the material just reviewed invites us to a comparison of the *creacionista* image, the Surrealist image, and Lorca's "hecho poético." All three inevitably used components drawn from the world, from reality; all three yoked together disparate elements (with no apparent—and perhaps no real—connection), from whose startling or shocking juxtaposition the poets intended quite similar things. In the case of Huidobro, this was a flash of inspiration or enlightenment—"revelación" (pp. 726-27), something completely new, different, original, and beautiful; in that of the Surrealists, a disruptive or subversive clash, jolting the reader, undermining ("common") sense, and perhaps enabling him or her to break through to that new—higher—realm of reality or perception;[62] and, in the case of Lorca, some pure, emotional—and irreducible—form of aesthetic experience.[63] Given their substantial common origins in Pierre Reverdy's famous definition of the image in the March 1918 number of *Nord-Sud*,[64] it is understandable that the images themselves and their im-

60   Gerardo Diego, "Poesía y creacionismo de Vicente Huidobro," in *Vicente Huidobro y el creacionismo,* ed. René de Costa, p. 211.

61   Costa, *Vicente Huidobro. The Careers of a Poet,* pp. 3, 76-77, 85; Huidobro's own comments on the impossibility of pure psychic automatism (pp. 722-24, 728, 740).

62   Bigsby, p. 61.

63   Epstein writes of "la nonparticipation de la volonté, du jugement, du libre choix, etc. à l'émotion esthétique," and hence "il reste donc à considérer l'émotion esthétique comme une sorte de réflexe intellectuel, ou plutôt comme un réflexe émotionnel s'accompagnant d'un état intellectuel agréable, pour faire la part du subjectif" (p. 32). Johnnie Gratton finds literalness, irreducibility, and arbitrariness to be characteristics of the Surrealist image: "Poetics of the Surrealist Image," pp. 106-08.

64   Cf. Guillermo de Torre, "Alquimia y mayéutica de la imagen creacionista," pp. 221-22. Breton openly acknowledged his indebtedness to Reverdy: Gratton, pp. 106-07.

mediate workings and effects are often difficult to tell apart, but the actual means of bringing them into being and their eventual goals were really very different.[65]

Huidobro extolled the poet as a man of special vision and as a highly conscious and controlling creator, bringing poems into the world as Nature did roses; the Surrealists, on the other hand, employed automatic writing, free association, formal and acoustic similarities, clichés, quotations, puns, any method in fact that would liberate them and the poem from the careful guiding mind and hand of the poet,[66] and in doing so their aims were ultimately metaphysical and epistemological in scope.[67] Lorca and his "hecho poético" can be located somewhere in between these two extremes, neither as controlled as *creacionismo* nor as uncontrolled as Surrealism, rejecting "lógica humana" but replacing it with "lógica poética," shunning the imperative to decode or interpret images such as the traditional metaphor or conceit, and espousing instead an intuitive and emotional response to the

---

In his brief but seminal text entitled simply "L'Image," Reverdy had written that "l'Image est une création pure de l'esprit. Elle ne peut naître d'une comparaison mais du rapprochement de deux réalités plus ou moins éloignées. Plus les rapports des deux réalités rapprochées seront lointains et justes, plus l'image sera forte—plus elle aura de puissance émotive et de réalité poétique. [...] L'émotion ainsi provoquée est pure, poétiquement, parce qu'elle est née en dehors de toute imitation, de toute évocation, de toute comparaison. Il y a la surprise et la joie de se trouver devant une chose neuve. [...] La création de l'image est donc un moyen poétique puissant et l'on ne doit pas s'étonner du grand rôle qu'il joue dans une *poésie de création*. Pour rester pure cette poésie exige que tous les moyens concourent à créer une *réalité poétique*." A notably similar articulation of ideas on the modern image is to be found in Epstein, pp. 65, 131, 133-34.

65   Cf. Cernuda's comment that "la metáfora creacionista y la superrealista, aunque diferentes entre sí, son ambas libres e ilógicas, y no tienen el aire de 'adivina, adivinanza' que tenían las de los susodichos movimientos literarios anteriores" (p. 147). Cernuda's somewhat derogatory reference to the "riddle image" brings closely to mind Dalí's—and then Lorca's—dismissal of "el acertijo de la imagen" (cf. note 17).

66   Michael Riffaterre, "La Métaphore filée dans la poésie surréaliste." In his letter of end-August 1928 Dalí invoked rage, horror, and "evasión"; in the succeeding article he advocated the techniques of automatism, forgetfulness, passivity, daydreaming, and soundings in irrationality and the subconscious.

67   If for the Symbolists the image was still an expression of the ineffable, for the Surrealists it was not an *expression* of the ineffable, rather it *created* the ineffable: Bigsby, pp. 60-62, and cf. pp. 59, 66.

"hecho poético."[68] This free-standing "poetic fact," "act" or "event," then, was comparable to a miracle *(C* II, 22, 27), in that it was charged with mystery and had to be responded to accordingly; its ultimate function was to express what Lorca sibyllinely called "la verdad poética" (C II, 13, 16), but he made no farther-reaching artistic or philosophical claims for it than that.[69]

In the survey offered by "Sketch de la pintura moderna," Lorca found that "una multitud de *ismos* impera" (*C* II, 44); "Imaginación, inspiración, evasión" shows him seeking to understand, delineate, order, and synthesize many of those very "isms" while at the same time trying to plot a way forward for himself. In our attempt to triangulate Lorca's aesthetic position as it emerges in this lecture, therefore, it has become evident that a large variety of crosscurrents do indeed coincide—and sometimes collide—in its lines: the complex mesh of tendencies and influences show him to have been simultaneously a man of his age and an independent thinker, highly receptive to the most recent aesthetic developments, but at the same time ever sensitive and faithful to the evolving dictates of his own individual poetic voice and credo. The decisions which he made as to the relative merits of all these pulls on him—decisions made, or at least envisaged, in September 1928—would radically affect all of his subsequent poetic production.[70]

Works Cited

Ades, Dawn. *Dalí.* London: Thames & Hudson, 1988.

Arciniegas, Germán. "Federico García Lorca." *Diario de la Marina* (1 April 1930): 16.

Bary, David. *Larrea: poesía y transfiguración.* Barcelona: Planeta, 1976.

---

68   Cf. Maurer: "Lorca estuvo en todo momento lejos de creer que cualquier imagen de origen subconsciente mereciera formar parte del poema. Pero, por otra parte, no quería que se le escapara, por un exceso de autocrítica, el 'hecho insólito que regale la inspiración.' Para recibir ese 'hecho' [...] está, en 1930, más dispuesto a 'entregarse'" *(C* I, 26). Cf. also García-Posada, who rightly insists on the underlying (symbolic) coherence found in all of his works (p. 8).

69   Irreducibility and perhaps a measure of arbitrariness therefore link the "hecho poético" and the Surrealist image; however the means taken and paths followed to fashion them, and the wider purposes of their very fashioning, are radically different. There exists a whole Surrealist ethos which Lorca was always very far from sharing (cf. Laffranque, p. 175).

70   I am indebted to Christopher Maurer, who read this article in draft form and made a number of valuable suggestions for its improvement.

————. *Nuevos estudios sobre Huidobro y Larrea*. Valencia: Pre-Textos, 1984.

Bigsby, C.W.E. *Dada and Surrealism,* The Critical Idiom. London: Methuen, 1972.

Blanch, Antonio. *La poesía pura española. Conexiones con la cultura francesa.* Madrid: Gredos, 1976.

Brihuega, Jaime, ed. *Manifiestos, proclamas, panfletos y textos doctrinales (Las vanguardias artísticas en España: 1910-1931).* Madrid: Cátedra, 1979.

Buñuel, Luis. *Obra literaria.* Ed. Agustín Sánchez Vidal. Zaragoza: Heraldo de Aragón, 1982.

Cano Ballesta, Juan. *La poesía española entre pureza y revolución (1930-1936).* Madrid: Gredos, 1972.

————. "Sobre cubismo y creacionismo poético (Ecos de una controversia)." *Ojáncano* 1 (October 1988): 5-13.

Cernuda, Luis. *Estudios sobre poesía española contemporánea.* 4th ed. Madrid: Guadarrama, 1975.

Costa, René de. "La poesía y sus circunstancias: un inédito de García Lorca." *Hispania* LXIX (1986): 761-63.

————. *Vicente Huidobro. The Careers of a Poet.* Oxford: Clarendon Press, 1984.

Dalí, Salvador. "Film-arte, film-antiartístico." *La Gaceta Literaria* 24 (15 December 1927): 8.

————. "La fotografia, pura creació de l'esperit." *L'Amic de les Arts* 18 (31[*sic*] September 1927).

————. "Els meus quadros del Saló de Tardor." A loose-leaf insert in *L'Amic de les Arts* 19 (31 October 1927).

————. "Nous límits de la pintura." *L'Amic de les Arts* 22, 24 & 25 (29 February, 30 April & 31 May 1928).

————. "Poesia de l'útil standarditzat." *L'Amic de les Arts* 23 (31 March 1928).

————. "Realidad y sobrerrealidad." *La Gaceta Literaria* 44 (15 October 1928).

————. "Salvador Dalí escribe a Federico García Lorca." Ed. Rafael Santos Torroella, special double number of *Poesía* 27-28 (1987).

Diego, Gerardo. "Poesía y creacionismo de Vicente Huidobro," in *Vicente Huidobro y el creacionismo.* Ed. René de Costa. Madrid: Taurus, 1975. 209-28.

Eisenberg, Daniel. "Dos conferencias lorquianas (Nueva York y La Habana, 1930)." *Papeles de Son Armadans* LXXIX, 236-37 (1975): 197-212.

Epstein, Jean. *La Lyrosophie.* 2nd ed. Paris: Éditions de la Sirène, 1922.

————. *La Poésie d'aujourd'hui: un nouvel état d'intelligence,* suivi d'une lettre de Blaise Cendrars. Paris: Éditions de la Sirène, 1921.

Fernández-Montesinos, Manuel. "Descripción de la biblioteca de Federico García Lorca (Catálogo y estudio)." unpublished M.A. Thesis (Madrid: Universidad Complutense, 1985).

García Lorca, Federico. *Conferencias.* Ed. Christopher Maurer. 2 vols. Madrid: Alianza, 1984.

————. *Epistolario.* Ed. Christopher Maurer. 2 vols. Madrid: Alianza, 1983.

————. "Federico García Lorca escribe a su familia desde Nueva York y La Habana (1929-1930)." Ed. Christopher Maurer, special double number of *Poesía,* nos. 23-24 (1985).

————. "La muerte de la madre de Charlot." *El País* (3 December 1989): 14-15.

————. *Obras completas.* Ed. Arturo del Hoyo. 22nd ed. 3 vols. Madrid: Aguilar, 1986.

García-Posada, Miguel. "Lorca y el surrealismo: una relación conflictiva." *Ínsula* XLIV, 515 (1989): 7-9.

Gasch, Sebastián. "Del cubismo al superrealismo." *La Gaceta Literaria* 20 (15 October 1927).

Gibson, Ian. *Federico García Lorca.* Vol. 1. *De Fuente Vaqueros a Nueva York (1898-1929).* Barcelona: Grijalbo, 1985.

Gratton, Johnnie. "Poetics of the Surrealist Image." *Romanic Review* LXIX (1978): 103-14.

Gurney, Robert E. "Vicente Huidobro y Juan Larrea." *Ínsula* XXIX, 337 (1974): 1, 14.

Hernández, Mario. "García Lorca y Salvador Dalí: del ruiseñor lírico a los burros podridos (poética y epistolario)." *L'"imposible/posible" di Federico García Lorca.* Ed. Laura Dolfi. Naples: Edizioni Schientifiche Italiane, 1989. 267-319.

————. "Introducción." Federico García Lorca, *Libro de poemas.* Madrid: Alianza, 1984. 11-40.

Hinojosa, José María. *La flor de California.* Ed. Julio Neira. Santander: La Isla de los Ratones, 1979.

Huidobro, Vicente. *Manifestes.* Paris: Éditions de la Revue Mondiale, 1925.

————. *Obras completas.* Ed. Hugo Montes. 2 vols. Santiago de Chile: Andrés Bello, 1976.

Ilie, Paul, ed. *Documents of the Spanish Vanguard.* Chapel Hill: U of North Carolina P, 1969.

————. "La lirosofía, entre poesía pura y deshumanización." *Ojáncano* 1 (October 1988): 23-36.

Laffranque, Marie. *Les Idées esthétiques de Federico García Lorca*. Paris: Centre de Recherches Hispaniques, 1967.

Luengo, Ricardo G. "Conversación de Federico García Lorca." *El Mercantil Valenciano* (15 November 1935); reproduced (with some cuts) as "Una entrevista olvidada con García Lorca sobre su teatro." *El País* (4 March 1987): 28.

Martínez Nadal, Rafael. *"El público." Amor y muerte en la obra de Federico García Lorca*. 3rd ed. Madrid: Hiperión, 1988.

Maurer, Christopher. "García Lorca y el ramonismo." *Boletín de la Fundación Federico García Lorca* III, 5 (1989): 55-60.

————. "Introduction." Federico García Lorca, *Poet in New York*. Trans. Greg Simon & Steven F. White. New York: Farrar, Straus, Giroux, 1988.

————. "Millonario de lágrimas." *El País* (3 December 1989), p. 15.

Montanyà, Lluís. "Panorama–*Canciones,* de Federico García Lorca." *L'Amic de les Arts* 16 (31 July 1927): 55-56.

Ontañón, Santiago, with José María Moreiro. *Unos pocos amigos verdaderos*. Madrid: Fundación Banco Exterior, 1988.

Ortega y Gasset, José. *La deshumanización del arte y otros ensayos estéticos*. 10th ed. Madrid: Revista de Occidente, 1970.

Reverdy, Pierre. "L'Image." *Nord-Sud* 13 (March 1918): 3-5.

Riffaterre, Michael. "La Métaphore filée dans la poésie surréaliste." *Langue Française* 3 (September 1969): 46-60.

Rozas, Juan Manuel. *La generación del 27 desde dentro*. 2nd ed. Madrid: Istmo, 1986.

Sánchez Vidal, Agustín. *Buñuel, Lorca, Dalí: El enigma sin fin*. Barcelona: Planeta, 1988.

Siebenmann, Gustav. *Los estilos poéticos en España desde 1900*. Madrid: Gredos, 1973.

Silver, Philip W. *La casa de Anteo. Estudios de poética hispánica. (De Antonio Machado a Claudio Rodríguez)*. Madrid: Taurus, 1985.

Torre, Guillermo de. "Alquimia y mayéutica de la imagen creacionista." *Cosmópolis* 21 (1920).

Undurraga, Antonio de. "Teoría del creacionismo." Vicente Huidobro, *Poesía y prosa. Antología*. Madrid: Aguilar, 1957: 19-186.

Videla de Rivero, Gloria. "Huidobro en España." *Revista Iberoamericana* XLV, 106-07 (1979): 37-48.

Villegas Guzmán, Jesús. "Lorca y la vanguardia: lectura de cuatro conferencias." Honorata Mazzotti Pabello, Gabriel Rojo Leyva, Jesús Villegas Guzmán, *Tres ensayos sobre Federico García Lorca*. Mexico City: Universidad Autónoma Metropolitana, 1990: 25-75.

2
Sebastià Gasch y Federico García Lorca: influencias recíprocas y la construcción de una estética vanguardista

S EBASTIÀ GASCH I CARRERAS nació en Barcelona el 9 de octubre de 1897, y murió allí el 9 de diciembre de 1980; en efecto, aparte de unos tres años en París, pasó casi la totalidad de su vida en la Ciudad Condal. Después de terminar el bachillerato no siguió a la universidad; más bien, por circunstancias familiares, se fue directamente a trabajar con un mayorista de algodón. Soportó este empleo, que encontraba sumamente desagradable, durante algunos años, pero su vocación de artista era más fuerte, y cuando tenía veintiún años abandonó el comercio y se inscribió en las clases libres del Cercle Artístic de Sant Lluc. Un par de años más tarde, el fracaso de un dibujo suyo colgado en la Exposición de Primavera de dicho Cercle le hizo abandonar la creación artística. Presionado por la precaria situación económica de su madre viuda, volvió al trabajo comercial, primero en una sastrería y luego en una agencia marítima que albergaba el consulado japonés, donde se quedó hasta 1931, año en que empezaría a vivir exclusivamente de la escritura. A pesar de que había dejado de asistir a las clases del Cercle de Sant Lluc, no rompió con el lugar; siguió frecuentándolo y utilizando su biblioteca, la cual recibía muchas revistas de arte moderno, especialmente de Francia. En 1923 fue nombrado oficialmente bibliotecario del Cercle. A finales de 1925 publicó su primer artículo de crítica de arte, y durante los cuatro años siguientes llegó rápidamente a ser considerado el más documentado e influyente crítico de arte moderno en Cataluña.

A finales de 1929, a raíz de una amarguísima polémica sostenida con el pintor y crítico Rafael Benet, se desanimó con la crítica de arte y, aunque siguió escribiendo y publicando durante los años de la República, a partir de

1930 se preocupó más bien por los espectáculos populares modernos, como el *music-hall*, el cine, el circo, el jazz y la danza. Entre 1926 y 1936, pues, colaboró en los periódicos *La Veu de Catalunya, La Publicitat* y *L'Opinió* y en las revistas *Gaseta de les Arts, L'Amic de les Arts, D'Ací i d'Allà, La Nova Revista, Ciutat (Revista Mensual), Mirador (Setmanari de literatura, art i política), Helix, Òc, Butlletí de l'Agrupament Escolar de l'Acadèmia i Laboratori de Ciències Mèdiques de Catalunya, Anti (Full mensual d'arts i lletres), Sol Ixent, Art (Revista de les Arts), A.C. (Documentos de Actividad Contemporánea), Brisas, L'Horitzó (Política, Economia, Lletres...), Quaderns de Poesia, Verso y Prosa, La Gaceta Literaria, Atlántico, Mediodía, Papel de Aleluyas, Murta* y *Meridiano.*

Durante la guerra trabajó en la Generalitat de Catalunya; a finales de 1938 cruzó la frontera y se exilió en Francia. Volvió a Barcelona en 1942, y después de pasar dos meses y medio en la cárcel, empezó lenta y penosamente a reintegrarse en la vida cultural catalana. Mientras que había publicado hasta la fecha sólo dos libritos—uno antes de la guerra y otro durante—, a partir de 1946 empezó a escribir bastante prolíficamente, llegando a tener casi una treintena de volúmenes sobre el ballet y la danza, el circo, el cine, los títeres, el *music-hall* y, por cierto, el arte moderno.[1]

Los años que nos interesan, pues, para el presente estudio—sobre todo 1927 y 1928—caen de lleno dentro del lustro de crítica de arte moderno que ocupa la segunda mitad del decenio de los veinte. Como todo el mundo sabe, Gasch y Lorca se conocieron en 1927, durante la estancia de éste en Cataluña para el estreno de *Mariana Pineda.* Gasch sólo acababa de asomarse a la escena madrileña con su primer artículo en *La Gaceta Literaria,* que apareció en el número del 15 de abril, y por otro lado ni había oído hablar del joven escritor andaluz hasta serle presentado por un amigo en común, el pintor uruguayo Rafael Pérez Barradas. El encuentro debe de haber ocurrido hacia finales de mayo de 1927, ya que la amistad pudo estrecharse durante junio, antes de que Lorca se fuera a pasar el mes de julio con Salvador Dalí en Cadaqués y luego volviera a Granada en agosto. Parece que no se vieron otra vez en persona hasta diciembre de 1935, cuando ya la relación amistosa se había enfriado por completo, pero en los meses y años inmediatamente después del primer encuentro mantuvieron una animada y nutrida correspondencia, la

---

1   Para este resumen biográfico, he utilizado las siguientes fuentes: Alexandre Cirici, "L'aportació de Sebastià Gasch"; Sebastià Gasch, *Expansió de l'art català al món;* Sebastià Gasch, "Un 'manifest' i un 'full groc'"; Joan M. Minguet i Batllori, "Sebastià Gasch, entre l'art i l'espectacle"; Joan M. Minguet i Batllori, "Joan Miró i Sebastià Gasch. La ressonància d'una amistat."

cual constituye el máximo dato para el estudio de sus relaciones intelectuales.[2]

Mientras Gasch se quedó muy impresionado por la deslumbrante personalidad de Lorca, creo que Gasch ejerció una influencia igualmente—o quizás más—importante en Lorca. En sus conversaciones durante junio de 1927, en el intercambio de cartas, y en la lectura de los artículos de Gasch en revistas como *L'Amic de les Arts* y *La Gaceta Literaria,* que Lorca recibía con regularidad, éste se habría familiarizado con las ideas y los juicios del crítico catalán relativos al arte moderno. Mi tesis es, por ende, doble: primero, que podemos rastrear una fuerte influencia de Gasch en la conferencia de Lorca, "Sketch de la nueva pintura," que Lorca dictó en una sola ocasión, la llamada "noche del *gallo*" celebrada en el Ateneo de Granada el 27 de octubre de 1928, y, segundo, que los comentarios—a veces bastante abstractos, a veces algo oscuros—que Lorca hizo acerca de la composición de sus dibujos y poemas en prosa que hallamos en sus cartas de los años 1927 y 1928, se pueden comprender mucho mejor a la luz de la estética formulada por Gasch.[3]

Para los propósitos de este estudio, entonces, he leído todos los artículos publicados por Gasch en *L'Amic de les Arts* entre 1926 y 1929 (las fechas de la existencia de la revista), todos los publicados en *La Gaceta Literaria* entre 1927 y 1929, más una selección de otras revistas (*Gaseta de les Arts, D'Ací i d'Allà, La Nova Revista*) que se incluyó en la recopilación de artículos de Gasch titulada *Escrits d'art i d'avantguarda.* Tomados en su conjunto, estos artículos llegan a constituir un *corpus* de más de cincuenta textos que nos brindan una visión perfectamente coherente de las posturas estéticas de Gasch durante el segundo lustro de los años veinte.

Antes de entrar en materia, hace falta una nota aclaratoria. Algunos se habrán fijado en el hecho que, hasta ahora, sólo me he referido muy de paso a Salvador Dalí. En efecto, Dalí, con quien Gasch había entrado en contacto sólo unos meses antes de conocer a Lorca, y quien a su vez conocía a Lorca desde su encuentro en la Residencia de Estudiantes a principios de 1923, forma el tercer punto de otro triangulo de amigos casi tan interesante como ese otro, mucho más notorio, constituido por Lorca, Dalí y Buñuel. No obstan-

---

2   Gasch, "Mi Federico García Lorca," 13-14. Sobre su amistad, véase Anderson, "Federico García Lorca y Sebastià Gasch: escenas de una amistad epistolar."

3   Por ejemplo, un artículo reciente, cuyo título podría parecer, a primera vista, prometedor, resulta ser poco útil, y no es casual, creo, la falta allí de toda referencia a los escritos de Gasch: véase Medina, 85-111. Por otro lado, Cecelia Cavanaugh, en su libro sobre los dibujos lorquianos, recurre precisamente a Gasch para contextualizar las afirmaciones y opiniones de Lorca.

te, he optado por no incluir a Dalí en la presente discusión por dos razones de peso: un estudio triangular adecuadamente documentado y elaborado no cabría en el espacio y el tiempo que tengo a mi disposición y, además, todavía no se han publicado las cartas, unas doscientas según el mismo Gasch, que Dalí le dirigió y que serían fundamentales para el análisis de sus relaciones.[4]

Ahora bien, como ya he sugerido, se desprenden de los artículos de Gasch una versión consecuente de la evolución del arte moderno desde finales del siglo diecinueve y también una visión nítida del momento actual del arte en la segunda mitad del decenio de los veinte. Solía empezar con un ataque violento contra el impresionismo: para Gasch este movimiento francés había impuesto la luz y el color como las supremas, a veces las únicas, preocupaciones del artista, mientras que, para él, las bases de la pintura se hallaban, más bien, en la forma. Un cambio importante había comenzado con Seurat y luego, más visiblemente, con Cézanne y los *fauves;* fue Cézanne en particular el que preparó el terreno para la reacción violenta de los primeros cubistas, quienes hicieron poco menos que salvar la pintura, recuperando la forma y volviendo a establecerla como el pilar fundamental de la composición pictórica. El cubismo, entonces, llegó de nuevo,

> al fondo de la verdad técnica pictórica, y [...] contribuyó eficazmente a hallar nuevamente las leyes fundamentales de toda obra pintada: las leyes de equilibrio, de composición y de construcción, las leyes arquitectónicas insubstituibles que han gobernado siempre el cuadro en todos los grandes momentos de la Historia del Arte, y que el impresionismo había arrinconado hasta olvidarlas completamente. (Gasch, "Francesc Domingo," 5)

Igualmente, asevera Gasch, la pintura moderna, a partir del cubismo,

> es esencialmente realista. El arte actual, en efecto, no imita la parte material, la parte superficial, la parte externa de la realidad, que no interesa a ningún verdadero artista, sino su parte interna, su parte esencial. [...] el arte moderno [...] no copia el aspecto—caótico—de la naturaleza, sino que crea su equivalente—ordenado—con la ayuda de las leyes de uni-

---

4   De gran interés, no obstante, es el capítulo que Gasch dedica a Dalí en su libro *Expansió de l'art català al món* (139-163). Allí da a entender que no conoció personalmente a Dalí hasta que éste vino a Barcelona durante la estancia de Lorca (142); también se transcriben algunos fragmentos de las cartas de Dalí a Gasch.

dad y armonía que la inteligencia ha discurrido en ella. (Gasch, "Arte y artistas," 7)

Pero las cosas no quedaron allí. El cubismo, sano, auténtico, heroico y casi redentor en su primera época, la analítica, tildada así porque analizaba la realidad externa para sacar de ella sus formas y volúmenes, luego evolucionó y entró en su segunda época, la sintética. Aunque Gasch concede que ésta fue "rica en definitivas realizaciones," la creciente desconexión de la realidad y el esfuerzo por crear un "hecho pictórico puro" también acarreaban el riesgo de hacer la meta del arte la Pintura Pura, cosa que Gasch consideraba igual a la Decoración Pura.[5] En otras palabras, también suyas, el ímpetu innovador del cubismo fue finalmente desvirtuado por "los cerebrales y los teorizadores," y la "exaltación formal" de éstos "no tardó en caer en la insuficiencia decorativa" (Gasch, "Salvador Dalí," 5 y "En torno al libro de Franz Roh," 4). La Pintura Pura para Gasch era lo que denominó en otro lugar el "arte completamente abstracto," y él se mostraba especialmente hostil a los pintores asociados con esta tendencia—Mondrian, el grupo holandés "De Stijl," los promotores del Neoplasticismo—, arte que ni merecía ese nombre y que era, para él, nada más que un ejercicio huero de decoración geométrica.[6]

Los sucesores inmediatos de este cubismo excesivo, excesivo y por ende decadente o "degenerado," fueron el purismo y el neoclasicismo, que florecieron a principios de la década de los veinte (Gasch, "Naturaleza y arte," 5). Con el primero se asociaban los pintores Ozenfant y Jeanneret, y con el segundo, Severini; éstos, aunque volvieron a introducir el "asunto" en el cuadro—es decir, reestablecieron cierta dosis de figurativismo—, se adherían, según nuestro crítico, a "concepciones rígidamente dogmáticas y elucubra-

---

5   Sebastià Gasch, "Els pintors d'avantguarda. Joan Miró," 54. Explica Gasch que algunos cubistas sintéticos se salvaron de este peligro inventando "una tercera dimensión sin invadir los dominios de la perspectiva y sin abandonar nunca los terrenos esencialmente pictóricos. Y así establecieron la vecindad de varias superficies de dimensiones y coloraciones diferentes, las cuales se combinan entre ellas y acaban por dar la sensación de profundidad, una 'profundidad cualitativa,' como ha sido llamada." Gasch nombra a Gleizes como un pintor que ejemplifica esta tendencia.

6   Sebastià Gasch, "La moderna pintura francesa: Del cubismo al superrealismo"; cf. también "Naturaleza y arte," "En torno al libro de Franz Roh. Panorama de la moderna pintura europea" y "Dos pintores valencianos."

ciones cerebrales totalmente deshumanizadas," y por eso, inevitablemente, producían obras frías y acartonadas.[7]

En Alemania, el expresionismo había sido una reacción contra el impresionismo, aunque con menos éxito que el cubismo, ya que prestó excesiva atención a los estados anímicos internos y, por eso, se olvidó del mundo exterior (Gasch, "En torno al libro de Franz Roh," 4). Unos años más tarde, la reacción contra el expresionismo y a la vez el equivalente alemán del neoclasicismo francés surgía en el movimiento llamado la Nueva Objetividad, que "cayó en el extremo opuesto [al expresionismo]: la fijación rigurosa de la realidad externa, menospreciando a menudo la realidad interna" (Gasch, "En torno al libro de Franz Roh," 4). Gasch dedicó más de un artículo a rebatir el argumento principal que Franz Roh defendía en su libro *El realismo mágico,* que acababa de publicarse en España. Roh sostenía que la Nueva Objetividad jugaba un papel dominante entre los movimientos artísticos de vanguardia, pero Gasch la creía no sólo bastante marginal sino también ya superada.[8]

Siempre según esta versión de la historia del arte moderno, la próxima reacción, paralela al neoclasicismo pero muy distinta de éste, ocurrió hacia 1922, y se plasmó en el movimiento del neorromanticismo. En la definición escueta de Gasch: "El neoclasicismo había realizado el retorno al asunto de manera intelectual. Unos cuantos iban a intentar el retorno al asunto de manera instintiva" (Gasch, "La moderna pintura francesa," 5). Con el nuevo énfasis en la emoción y en la expresión de ésta mediante el color vibrante, resultó en lo que él llamaba "un arte de paroxismo"; los artistas principales asociados con esta tendencia eran Vlaminck, Rouault, Utrillo y Modigliani.[9] Al lado del neorromanticismo se situaba el visionarismo alemán, que Gasch estudió en menos detalle. Finalmente, una de las tendencias entonces más recientes, y tendencia que estaba relacionada tanto con el neorromanticismo como con el expresionismo, era el surrealismo, y tendremos ocasión más tarde para volver sobre las ideas de Gasch acerca de este último movimiento y estudiarlas en más detalle.

---

7   Sebastià Gasch, "Salvador Dalí." Cf. también "Els pintors d'avantguarda. Joan Miró," 56, "La moderna pintura francesa," "En torno al libro de Franz Roh," y "Libros. A. Ozenfant: *L'art.* Budry & Cie. *París.* André Level: *Picasso.* G. Crès & Cie. *París.*"

8   Aparte del artículo de Sebastià Gasch, "En torno al libro de Franz Roh," véase además "Cop d'ull sobre l'evolució de l'art modern."

9   Sebastià Gasch, "La moderna pintura francesa." Véanse también "Salvador Dalí" y "En torno al libro de Franz Roh."

Si procedemos ahora a una lectura detenida del "Sketch de la nueva pintura" (García Lorca, OOCC III, 272-281), las múltiples coincidencias de ideas y actitudes son palmarias. Lorca también empieza su "bosquejo" con el impresionismo: afirma que en los pintores de ese movimiento, "la luz y sus sorpresas habían invadido los cuadros agotando la belleza de las formas" y añade que "la naturaleza es torpemente imitada en su gama de colores" (García Lorca, OOCC III, 272). La reacción, empezando con Cézanne, luego crece, ya que "había que volver por el volumen, por la forma, fundamento esencial de un cuadro" (García Lorca, OOCC III, 272). Opina que Picasso, Braque y los otros cubistas,

> estaban realizando la obra más grande, la obra más purificadora, más libertadora que se había hecho en la historia de la pintura. Estaban salvando a la pintura, que era un arte de representaciones, y la estaban convirtiendo en un arte en sí mismo, en un arte puro, desligado de la realidad. [...] en la pintura moderna color y volumen empiezan, ¡por vez primera en el mundo!, a vivir sus propios sentimientos y a comunicarse y entrelazarse sobre el lienzo obedeciendo a leyes dictadas por sus esencias. (García Lorca, OOCC III, 273-274)

Y resume las metas del cubismo de esta manera:

> Hay que libertarnos de esta realidad natural para buscar la verdadera realidad plástica. No ir en busca de las calidades efectivas de los objetos, sino de sus naturales equivalencias plásticas. No buscar la representación real de un objeto, sino encontrar su expresión pictórica, su expresión geométrica o lírica y la calidad apropiada de su materia. (García Lorca, OOCC III, 274)

Pasada esta primera época heroica del cubismo, el arte continúa evolucionando, puesto que sigue en vigor "el afán constructivo que ha de renovar la pintura," y "[es] llevado el andamiaje a un extremo agudo por Ozenfant y Jeanneret con el modo titulado 'purismo,' y a un extremo científico por los constructivistas" (García Lorca, OOCC III, 272). O sea:

> después de la guerra, los pintores, o siguen la disciplina cubista llevándola a extremos científicos, como los *puristas* o constructivistas, [...] o bien hacen de la pintura una exaltación expresiva de las cosas, [...] como

los expresionistas que animaron y animan la ciudad de Berlín. (García
Lorca, OOCC III, 277)

Los pintores que siguen la primera de estas opciones, los que comienzan, hacia 1920, a adherirse a "un objetivismo agudo" que está, sin embargo, despro-
visto de toda emoción, llegan finalmente a agotar completamente las posibilidades del movimiento:

> Llega el 1926. La lección cubista ya está bien aprovechada. Pero un triste
> cerebralismo, un cansado intelectualismo invade la pintura. Severini y
> Gris saben de memoria un cuadro antes de haberlo realizado. (García
> Lorca, OOCC III, 278)

Precisamente como Gasch, Lorca tacha las postrimerías del cubismo de "cerebrales," y este cansancio o agotamiento es lo que ocasiona otra reacción significativa hacia lo instintivo y lo inspirado, reacción que, como era de esperar,
produce el surrealismo (García Lorca, OOCC III, 278).

Ahora bien, las opiniones de Gasch acerca del surrealismo, expresadas en
diversas ocasiones, son, de entre todos los movimientos de arte moderno que
él comenta, las más interesantes—y las más curiosas—. En efecto, el crítico
catalán, uno de los principales apologistas del cubismo, arremete contra el
surrealismo de una manera auténticamente feroz. Su actitud se delinea claramente desde el momento en que traza la genealogía del movimiento:

> El superrealismo puede ser considerado como un arranque desesperado,
> como una convulsión delirante, como un chillido frenético del nuevo
> romanticismo [...]. No precisamente del neorromanticismo propiamen-
> te dicho, sino del estado de espíritu romántico que caracteriza la época
> pictórica presente.[10]

Su objeción principal estriba en su entendimiento de cómo crean sus
obras los surrealistas, con un énfasis total en la expresión y un consiguiente olvido total de la plástica. De allí que pueda referirse repetidamente a "la
expulsión total de la inteligencia de los dominios artísticos," al olvido del
"fondo plástico imprescindible en toda obra pintada," al surrealismo que es

---

10   Sebastià Gasch, "La moderna pintura francesa." También relaciona
el movimiento con Alemania: "Els francesos han agafat una cosa desueta—
l'expressionisme—i n'han fet una degeneració—el superrealisme—" ("Cop d'ull sobre l'evolució de l'art modern").

"huérfano de valores plásticos," a los surrealistas "libertados de toda traba de la razón," a "obras 'sin preocupaciones estéticas,' huérfanas de calidades plásticas," a pinturas hechas "sin el control de la inteligencia," a lienzos pintados "sin ningún control ni preocupación," a "la negación de la regla," y a "la supresión de toda conciencia plástica, de toda inteligencia pictórica."[11] Y por eso, dada la orientación teórica del surrealismo que viene definida en el primer manifiesto de Breton—"doctrina ilógica hecha totalmente de elementos instintivos e incontrolables"—, encontramos "la instauración más absoluta del instinto desenfrenado," "los pintores superrealistas, esclavos de sus instintos," "las pinturas superrealistas [que] son hijas absolutas de la imaginación," "la imaginación llevada a las últimas consecuencias," "la plasmación del mundo interior más recóndito," y "la inspiración, el automatismo, la alucinación."[12] En particular, observa que:

Entregados a sus instintos, esclavos de su inspiración, los superrealistas intentan plasmar las imágenes aparecidas en estados inconscientes, en aquellos momentos de sueño despierto en que la imaginación [...] flota libremente al azar y ve las maravillosas representaciones que engendra la fantasía.

Algunos superrealistas explotan las imágenes nacidas en los momentos que preceden inmediatamente al acto de dormirse, y permanecen atentos a las sugestiones de la imaginación, que se manifiestan en lo que el poeta superrealista catalán J.V. Foix ha llamado "los andenes subterráneos del presueño."
Otros, aun comparan sus telas con los dibujos de los salvajes, de los niños, de los locos, que producen instintivamente, sin ningún control ni preocupación. (Gasch, "La moderna pintura francesa," 5)

---

11   Sebastià Gasch, "Salvador Dalí," "La moderna pintura francesa," "En torno al libro de Franz Roh," y "André Breton: *Le surréalisme et la peinture*," 101-102. Curiosamente, en su "Sketch de la nueva pintura," Lorca hace una crítica muy parecida del impresionismo: "Los pintores se recrean en sus lejanías y en sus humos, sin que el menor control inteligente intervenga en esta borrachera de copiar los espectáculos naturales."
12   Sebastià Gasch, "Salvador Dalí," "La moderna pintura francesa," "En torno al libro de Franz Roh" y "André Breton: *Le surréalisme et la peinture*," 101.

Por consiguiente, el movimiento es "en el fondo absolutamente pueril" y produce obras que son "completamente insuficientes," "obras delincuentes, frágiles e inconsistentes, antiplásticas por excelencia."[13]

Como contrapartida al surrealismo, Gasch señala en primer lugar a Picasso, específicamente el Picasso reciente tal como se definió en una importante exposición celebrada en París en junio-julio de 1926 (Gasch, "En torno al libro de Franz Roh," 4).[14] Según ya hemos visto, Gasch tenía una concepción binaria de la pintura moderna, con elementos básicos de expresión y plástica, o, más bien, con lo que él llama la "deformación expresiva" y la "deformación plástica" de la Naturaleza (Gasch, "Naturaleza y arte," 5). La deformación *expresiva* conlleva nociones de: sensibilidad, emoción, patetismo, lirismo, fantasía, imaginación, inspiración, intuición, instinto y alma, que son todos conceptos que esgrime en sus artículos. Por ejemplo, relaciona explícitamente el atributo de la sensibilidad con Picasso, Miro y Dalí, y habla de "la intensa emoción que le produce la naturaleza" con referencia a otro pintor admirado, Francesc Domingo.[15] La deformación *plástica,* en cambio, implica la intervención en el acto creador de varios de los elementos siguientes: organización, composición, construcción, proporción, orden, equilibrio, ritmo, armonía, economía, claridad, inteligencia, razón, voluntad y entendimiento.

Los términos que Gasch utiliza más frecuentemente para referirse a los dos polos de esta dicotomía son: *poesía* y *plástica,* términos que, según el mismo crítico, ha tomado prestados de Jean Cocteau (Gasch, "Una exposició i un decorat," 56):

> Plástica y poesía. Esas palabras resumen maravillosamente las intenciones de los mejores artistas actuales. Tendencia plástico-poética. Es decir,

---

13   Sebastià Gasch, "La moderna pintura francesa" y "André Breton: *Le surréalisme et la peinture*," 102. Gasch tiene otra objeción, esta vez más personal: además de producir obras "sin preocupaciones estéticas," también produce el surrealismo "obras 'sin preocupaciones morales': más claramente: obras absolutamente inmorales, en las que—Freud no ha atravesado en vano la estética superrealista—los símbolos oníricos y las imágenes sexuales abundan. No es éste el momento de exteriorizar nuestra absoluta disconformidad con las obras de arte inmorales" ("La moderna pintura francesa").

14   Con una ligera equivocación, Gasch atribuye al mes de mayo la exposición celebrada en la Galería Paul Rosenberg.

15   Sebastià Gasch, "Els pintors d'avantguarda. Joan Miró," 56; "El pintor Joan Miró"; "Naturaleza y arte"; carta a García Lorca, mediados de enero 1928, archivo FFGL; "Francesc Domingo."

con un bagaje plástico, hijo del cubismo, "partir en busca del alma de las cosas," como ha dicho el famoso crítico Christian Zervos. O mejor dicho: hablando del papel que juega la realidad en las obras de los artistas actuales, podríamos decir que se la somete a leyes mitad intelectuales y mitad sensibles, mitad plásticas y mitad poéticas. (Gasch, "En torno al libro de Franz Roh," 4)

No nos sorprenderá constatar que Gasch encuentra en la producción más reciente de Picasso el mejor ejemplo de esta tendencia. En efecto, se trata de una fusión o síntesis—a veces la llama una totalización—de "elementos aparentemente contradictorios" (Gasch, "En torno al libro de Franz Roh," 4) que se logra cuando el artista presta más o menos igual atención a ambas "deformaciones":

La tendencia que nace del Picasso actual, en efecto, es una dosificación de los hallazgos de la razón y de los hallazgos del instinto, y se encuentra tan alejada del cubismo cerebral de la inmediata post-guerra como del superrealismo completamente instintivo. A las antípodas, tanto de un polo como de otro, es, no obstante, su sabia fusión, y hacia ella parecen inclinarse los espíritus más selectos de esta generación. Plástica y poética al mismo tiempo, esa tendencia parece ser la lógica resulta de las investigaciones emprendidas en el terreno pictórico desde unos cuantos años hacia acá, y es la verdadera característica del actual momento plástico internacional... (Gasch, "Salvador Dalí," 5)

Evidentemente, la pareja poesía–plástica, la poesía plástica o la plástica poética, representa, *mutatis mutandis,* nada menos que "una fusión del cubismo y del superrealismo" y una síntesis de "la abstracción y la realidad" (Gasch, "En torno al libro de Franz Roh," 4 y "La moderna pintura francesa," 5).

Por eso, el surrealismo se salva de la condena absoluta y definitiva por una mera razón: el surrealismo es, o puede servir como, una fuente de "poesía," entendida siempre en el sentido ya establecido:

El superrealismo es un hecho que no se puede menospreciar. En una época que veía la pintura naufragar lamentablemente en el más árido de los cerebralismos, él la enriqueció con aquella virtud poética que tanta falta le hacía. El superrealismo es una lección de poesía de alta categoría. En el fondo del buen arte de todos los tiempos existió un depósito de superrealismo. El artista no ha de menospreciar la inspiración, la iluminación. El artista no ha de menospreciar los hallazgos realizados en los estados pasivos, en la ausencia del pensamiento, en la liberación del subconsciente. El artista no ha de menospreciar el sueño. El artista, empero, ha de purificarlo, ha de controlarlo, ha de pulirlo, ha de eliminar de él por completo las impurezas que contenga. (Gasch, "André Breton," 102-103)

Por otro lado, Gasch mantiene que el surrealismo a solas nunca será satisfactorio porque la poesía, sin la base o el andamiaje de la plástica, cae irremediablemente en lo que él denomina la mera "literatura" o la "divagación literaria."[16]

Veamos ahora, a la luz de todo lo expuesto hasta aquí, lo que dice Gasch acerca de los dibujos de Lorca.[17] Empieza por situarlos dentro de su tendencia predilecta: "Dibujos de Lorca. He aquí una nueva muestra de esa función de la plástica y la poesía que intentan los mejores artistas actuales," e incluso llega a compararlos con las ilustraciones de Picasso para el *Ragtime* de Strawinsky y con los dibujos de Miró (Gasch, "Lorca dibujante," 4). Explica, a continuación, cómo un artista como Lorca "representa" el mundo:

> Los dibujos de Lorca no imitan al natural. [...] El verdadero artista, con elementos extraídos de la realidad, construye su mundo interior, que alimenta la fantasía. Un mundo interior que guarda almacenados recuerdos de la realidad que se instalan en él, no agrupados según una lógica objetiva, sino según una lógica subjetiva que es la única que interesa al artista. Y estos paisajes interiores son los que plasma el artista en sus obras. (Gasch, "Lorca dibujante," 4)

---

16   Sebastià Gasch, "Salvador Dalí," "Una exposició i un decorat," "En torno al libro de Franz Roh" y "Lorca dibujante." Otra vez, estas ideas pueden compararse fácilmente con las opiniones expresadas por Lorca en su "Sketch," donde escribe:

> Conjuntamente con el cubismo [...] surgen otras, varias escuelas que, utilizando el lenguaje del color han hecho, ¡ojo!, no *plástica*, como se pretende ahora en este bendito momento, sino *literatura* y muchas veces mala *literatura*. (276)

> Una multitud de ismos [artísticos] impera. Unos literarios, de belleza indudable y utilidad artística reconocida; otros puros, plásticos, pictóricos, los que siguen y rodean a la disciplina cubista. (277)

17   Cecelia Cavanaugh estudia los dos artículos de Gasch sobre Lorca en la sección titulada "Drawing Poems in 1927: Gasch and *Totalismo*" (46-72), del segundo capítulo— "Reading Poetry and Plasticity"—de su libro *Lorca's Drawings and Poems*.

Vuelve a insistir, también, sobre la fusión de poesía y plástica en los dibujos, con la presencia de los elementos interdependientes de fantasía y "andamiaje plástico" (Gasch, "Lorca dibujante," 4). Esto posibilita que Lorca alcance su meta:

> Equilibrio de líneas, dimensión, relación de tonos. No armonía querida, sin embargo. Ya que si la voluntad se mezclara en este juego, el juego se volvería impuro. Ya que si el razonamiento tuviera acceso en él, el juego perdería toda su importancia. Armonía instintiva, simplemente. Sentido plástico instintivo que se opone decisivamente a la caída en la divagación literaria. (Gasch, "Lorca dibujante," 4)

Con esto, creo, llegamos a la parte más interesante de los juicios de Gasch. Nótese que los "recuerdos de la realidad" se ordenan en el "mundo interior" del artista "según una lógica subjetiva," o bien, para decirlo con otras palabras, que la "armonía" se consigue gracias a un "sentido plástico instintivo":

> Federico García Lorca el poeta [...] siente a menudo la necesidad [...] de plasmar sus sueños plásticamente, de fijar las relaciones que unen a su alma con el mundo exterior por medios esencialmente plásticos. Y nacen automáticamente sus dibujos. Dibujos presentidos, dibujos adivinados, dibujos vistos en un momento de inspiración, y que pasan directamente de lo más profundo del ser del poeta a su mano. Una mano que se abandona, que no opone resistencia, que no sabe ni quiere saber dónde se la conduce, y que pare sin esfuerzo, sin tortura, con optimismo, con alegría, con la misma alegría del niño que llena de garabatos una pared, esas maravillosas realizaciones que alían la más pura fantasía, el más exacto equilibrio de líneas y colores. (Gasch, "Lorca dibujante," 4)

Aquí debemos tener mucho cuidado, ya que una frase como "y nacen automáticamente sus dibujos" puede fácilmente inducir a error. Gasch entiende y elogia los dibujos de Lorca dentro de exactamente el mismo esquema de valores que aplica a Picasso y a Miró. En cuanto al primero, el "genio andaluz" como le llama, aunque participa plenamente de la inspiración y del sueño de los surrealistas, hay para Gasch una sutil pero importantísima diferencia: Picasso controla esos sueños gracias a su "sólida cultura pictórica," y por ende sus obras no caen en la "literatura" (Gasch, "André Breton," 103). De manera parecida, aunque muchos consideren a Miró surrealista, con todo lo que esto conlleva, Gasch le salva de su condena rotunda de todos los otros pintores afiliados al movimiento porque opina que Miró sí incorpora—instintivamente o incluso *malgré lui*—un fondo plástico en sus lienzos "poéticos" (Gasch, "Cop d'ull" e "Inaugural de les Galeries"). Y lo mismo para Lorca: aunque se subraye la fantasía de sus dibujos, nunca desaparece "el más exacto equilibrio de líneas y colores" (Gasch, "Lorca dibujante," 4).

Al llegar a este punto en nuestra pesquisa, podemos volver finalmente a las cartas de Lorca a Gasch de 1927 y 1928 y las conferencias de 1928, y nos será posible, creo, comprender con mucha más precisión algunos de los términos que maneja allí y algunas de las actitudes que adopta.[18] Empecemos con el propósito estético general que Lorca dice tener. Informa a su amigo que:

> En prosa hago ahora un ensayo en el que estoy interesadísimo. Me propongo dos temas literarios, los desarrollo y luego los analizo. Y el resultado es un poema. Trato de unir mi instinto con el virtuosismo que posea.[19]

La meta de unir instinto y virtuosismo nos remite inmediatamente al ideal de Gasch de combinar lo expresivo y lo plástico. En las mismas fechas, Lorca vuelve sobre el tema un par de veces, ahora con referencia a sus dibujos:

> Ahora pongo toda mi alma y toda *mi tinta china* en hacerlos...

---

18   Otros conceptos estéticos que Lorca y Gasch tienen en común, pero que no he estudiado detenidamente, puesto que son secundarios a los ya analizados, son: pureza, sencillez e intensidad. Gasch elogia las formas puras y sencillas, y asevera que los dibujos de Lorca se dirigen exclusivamente a los puros y los sencillos; para él tanto los dibujos de Lorca como los escritos de Dalí tienen "una intensidad patética" ("Una exposició i un decorat"; carta a García Lorca, mediados de enero 1928, archivo FFGL; "De un orden nuevo"). De manera similar, Lorca afirma que hace dibujos porque vive, al hacerlos, "momentos de una intensidad y de una pureza *que no me da* el poema," y que el "llegar al plano de pureza y sencillez a que conduce el hecho poético, es lo que pretenden los poetas modernos" *(Epistolario completo,* 513, e "Imaginación, inspiración, evasión," OOCC III, 267).

19   García Lorca, *Epistolario completo,* 513-514. Casi todas las cartas de Lorca a Gasch parecen haberse conservado y se hallan en el citado *Epistolario.* De las respuestas de Gasch a Lorca, nueve se encuentran en el archivo de la Fundación Federico García Lorca; a la luz de una reconstrucción de su correspondencia, parece que por lo menos once cartas de Gasch a Lorca se han perdido: para más detalles véase Anderson, "Federico García Lorca y Sebastià Gasch: escenas de una amistad epistolar."

Yo he pensado y hecho estos dibujitos con un criterio poético-plástico o plástico-poético, en justa unión. [...] Estos dibujos son poesía pura o plástica pura a la vez.[20]

Al entrar en más detalle sobre el proceso de conseguir esta fusión, queda evidente que la sensibilidad, es decir, la capacidad receptora y expresiva del poeta o del artista, tiene un papel fundamental. Lorca dice tener "una sensibilidad ya casi física que me lleva a planos donde es difícil tenerse de pie," y por eso:

mis ojos y mis palabras están en otro sitio. Están en la inmensa biblioteca que no ha leído nadie, en un aire fresquísimo, país donde las cosas bailan sobre un solo pie. (García Lorca, *Epistolario completo*, 516)

Otra vez, como ya hemos constatado, la sensibilidad es también un concepto importante manejado por Gasch, quien define el lirismo—otra noción íntimamente relacionada—citando a Pierre Reverdy: es "la chispa saltada al choque de una sensibilidad sólida al contacto de la realidad" (Gasch, "Francesc Domingo," 5).

Para Lorca, la sensibilidad es lo que utiliza, lo que le sirve, para captar "la emoción pura" de su asunto (García Lorca, *Epistolario completo*, 519). Para lograr esto, dice, "he procurado escoger los rasgos esenciales de emoción y de forma, o de super-realidad y super-forma": no los aspectos exteriores que se perciben con los ojos, sino una especie de quintaesencia.[21] Hace de los "rasgos esenciales" "un *signo* que, como llave mágica, nos lleve a *comprender mejor* la realidad que tienen en el mundo" (García Lorca, *Epistolario completo*, 519). La realidad, entonces, no se comprende en su profundidad directamente, sino que hay que atravesar el "signo" que es el dibujo o el poema. Refiriéndose

---

20   García Lorca, *Epistolario completo*, 513 y 519. Como hemos notado, Cecelia Cavanaugh analiza en su libro, en el apartado ya citado, la relación de las cartas de Lorca con sus dibujos y con algunos de los artículos de Gasch. Mientras que mi enfoque y el suyo no son idénticos, y a pesar de algunas pequeñas divergencias, son en gran medida complementarios.

21   García Lorca, *Epistolario completo*, 519. Compárese esta cita del "Sketch de la nueva pintura": "Se ha partido de la realidad para llegar a esta creación. Lo mismo que el poeta crea la imagen que define, el pintor crea la imagen plástica que fija y orienta la emoción. Con unos cuantos objetos le basta. Parte de ellos y los crea de nuevo; mejor, descubre su intimidad, su meollo pictórico, que no ve el copista" (275).

siempre a sus dibujos, Lorca llega a llamarlos "abstracciones," pero con una reserva significativa:

> En estas abstracciones mías veo yo *realidad* creada que se une con la realidad que nos rodea, como el reloj concreto se une al concepto de tiempo de una manera como lapa en la roca. (García Lorca, *Epistolario completo,* 520)

Sensibilidad—emoción pura—rasgos esenciales—signo—abstracción, pero abstracción que no se aparta de la realidad (externa), sino que se funde con ella: "Tienes razón, queridísimo Gasch, hay que unir la abstracción a la realidad" (García Lorca, *Epistolario completo,* 520).[22] En otras palabras: el mundo interno *y* el mundo externo, la expresión *y* las formas, poesía plástica.

Al describir detenidamente cómo hace sus dibujos, Lorca identifica dos maneras que resume así: "Ya me voy *proponiendo* temas antes de dibujar, y consigo el *mismo* efecto que cuando no pienso en nada" (García Lorca, *Epistolario completo,* 516). El segundo método parece atraerle algo más que el primero, ya que dedica una sección bastante larga de una carta a especificar el proceso:

> Abandonaba la mano a la tierra virgen y la mano junto con mi corazón me traía[n] los elementos milagrosos. Yo los descubría y los anotaba. Volvía a lanzar mi mano, y así, con muchos elementos, escogía los característicos del asunto o los más bellos e inexplicables, y componía mi dibujo. (García Lorca, *Epistolario completo,* 518)

La cita contiene indicaciones sólo aparentemente contradictorias, con sugestiones de pasividad y actividad, de abandono y de control. Esto resulta en una "armonía de líneas," pero una armonía "que no había *pensado,* ni *soñado,* ni *querido,* ni *estaba inspirado.*"[23] Lo que Lorca describe, en efecto, concuerda exactamente con la interpretación de Gasch que acabamos de ver: la intuición, la disponibilidad regida discreta o incluso instintivamente por el sentido de la forma, que resulta en la poesía plástica. Además, parece que lo que tenemos aquí es un caso de diálogo teórico o crítico: el primer artículo de

---

22   En su "Sketch de la nueva pintura," Lorca habla de "las abstracciones disciplinadas del cubismo" (278).

23   García Lorca, *Epistolario completo,* 519. En su conferencia "Imaginación, inspiración, evasión" (OOCC III, 258-271), Lorca habla de "poesía en sí misma llena de un orden y una armonía exclusivamente poéticos" (261).

Gasch sobre los dibujos de Lorca, "Una exposició i un decorat," apareció en *L'Amic* el 31 de julio de 1927, las cartas de Lorca citadas son del ¿27? de agosto y del 2 de septiembre de 1927, y el segundo artículo de Gasch, "Lorca dibujante," se publicó en *La Gaceta Literaria* el 15 de marzo de 1928. En todos los textos encontramos ideas y hasta frases parecidas o idénticas, lo que demuestra la estrecha compenetración intelectual de los dos amigos en este momento.

En el curso de la elaboración de esta estética de la creación, Lorca hace un par de puntualizaciones muy importantes, la primera de las cuales tiene que ver con la sensibilidad. A pesar de que ésta le lleva a planos muy elevados o extremos, Lorca asevera que el grado de sensibilidad que alcanza no implica la entrada ni la caída en el "abismo" ni en el "sueño," dos términos que él—y Gasch—utilizan casi de manera intercambiable: "El abismo y el sueño los *temo*."[24] Así, mientras reconoce que en esos planos "casi se vuela sobre el abismo," insiste en que nunca cae en él.[25] De manera paralela, contestando a un reparo de Gasch, escribe que "mi estado no es de *perpetuo sueño*. Me he expresado mal. *He cercado* algunos días al sueño, pero sin caer del todo en él."[26] Glosando el mismo punto, Lorca describe su proceso de composición y luego añade: "Pero *sin tortura* ni *sueño* [...] ni complicaciones" (García Lorca, *Epistolario completo*, 519). Es decir, que ese estado de receptividad emotiva y de búsqueda poética en que entra para encontrar la "emoción pura" y los "rasgos esenciales" de la realidad, sea lo que sea, no es un trance ni una alucinación ni un ensueño ni el sueño, y por eso puede asegurar a Gasch que "abomino del arte de los sueños" (García Lorca, *Epistolario completo*, 519). Le interesa la sensibilidad agudizada, que supere el raciocinio intelectual, pero, claro está, no le interesa renunciar totalmente a la conciencia.

Una segunda y más escueta puntualización se relaciona con esta primera. Como "el arte de los sueños," Lorca también rechaza el puro automatismo, que tanto asco daba a Gasch, que aparece aquí bajo la forma de la "pintura directa":

24　García Lorca, *Epistolario completo*, 520. En otro punto dice que el "soñar" tiene "barrancos," reforzando la equivalencia (520). Cf. Gasch, "Joan Miró."

25　García Lorca, *Epistolario completo*, 516. No traspasa el borde porque, según otra cita pertinente, "Yo nunca me aventuro en terrenos que no son del hombre, porque vuelvo tierras atrás en seguida" (518).

26　García Lorca, *Epistolario completo*, 518. Lo que le protege ("que llevo *defensas*") del abismo/sueño, es la alegría y otras calidades humanas: "Teniendo desde luego un atadero de risa y un seguro andamio de madera"; "un salvoconducto de sonrisas y un equilibrio bastante humano"; "Mi estado es siempre alegre" (518 y 520).

Y me da horror la pintura que llaman *directa,* que no es sino una angustiosa lucha con las formas en la que el pintor sale *siempre* vencido y con obra *muerta.* (García Lorca, *Epistolario completo,* 519)

Como sugiere el término que utiliza, la "pintura directa" no debe implicar más de una fase o faceta, mientras que su estética conlleva por lo menos dos: intuición y plasmación, poesía y plástica.

Un lugar muy apropiado para terminar esta discusión es la tan famosa y controvertida carta que Lorca envió a Gasch en septiembre de 1928 adjunta a los manuscritos de dos poemas en prosa, "Nadadora sumergida" y "Suicidio en Alejandría." Allí precisa que:

Responden a mi nueva manera *espiritualista,* emoción pura descarnada, desligada del control lógico, pero, ¡ojo!, ¡ojo!, con una tremenda *lógica poética.* No es surrealismo, ¡ojo!, la *conciencia más* clara los ilumina.[27]

Como el envío va dirigido a Gasch, no nos sorprenderá descubrir que establece la diferencia, sutil pero crucial, entre estos textos y el surrealismo en términos característicamente gaschianos. La palabra "espiritualista" ocurre también en el "Sketch de la nueva pintura," donde Lorca la utiliza para referirse a la tendencia artística más reciente, una tendencia que abarcaría el surrealismo pero sin restringirse exclusivamente a él:

se abre en la pintura una reacción anímica, un modo espiritualista en el cual las imágenes ya no son dadas por la inteligencia, sino por el inconsciente, por la pura inspiración directa. (García Lorca, OOCC III, 273)

La próxima frase, "emoción pura descarnada," no necesita, creo, más comentario. La oposición "control lógico" vs "lógica poética" responde, claramente, a la distinción hecha por Gasch seis meses antes, en su artículo sobre "Lorca dibujante," y que ya hemos citado: "[recuerdos] no agrupados según una lógica objetiva, sino según una lógica subjetiva que es la única que interesa al

---

27   García Lorca, *Epistolario completo,* 588. Es realmente llamativa la similitud entre este pasaje y lo que escribiría Gerardo Diego en un artículo publicado unos meses más tarde: "Queremos una poesía humana y, por lo tanto, inteligente—pero no intelectual—, razonable—pero por razones no lógicas, sino poéticas—, viva, despierta, consciente (perdonen los superrealistas), activa—pero no política—, apasionada y, por supuesto—es la base—, sensible" ("La nueva arte poética española," 188).

artista."[28] Finalmente, Lorca subraya que "la conciencia los ilumina," es decir, que no ha caído, siempre en términos suyos, ni en el abismo ni el sueño. Para concluir. Si todo esto es así, si Gasch ataca y descarta el surrealismo, si Gasch elogia la última manera de Picasso, que funde el cubismo y el surrealismo para producir una "poesía plástica," y si Lorca claramente se alinea con Gasch, entonces estos resultados nos ofrecen no sólo una instantánea nítida y detallada de la postura estética de Lorca tal como se configuraba hacia el otoño de 1928, sino que nos indican también una pauta, clara y bien definida, para el análisis de los textos compuestos bajo la influencia de esta estética, es decir *Poemas en prosa* y *Poeta en Nueva York*.

Obras citadas

Anderson, Andrew A. "Lorca at the Crossroads: 'Imaginación, inspiración, evasión' and the 'novísimas estéticas.'" *Anales de la Literatura Española Contemporánea* (Boulder, CO), XVI, nos. 1-2 (1991): 149-173.

————. "Federico García Lorca y Sebastià Gasch: escenas de una amistad epistolar." *Boletín de la Fundación Federico García Lorca*, XII, no. 23 (1998): 83-105.

Brihuega, Jaime (ed.). *Manifiestos, proclamas, panfletos y textos doctrinales. Las vanguardias artísticas en España. 1910-1931*. Madrid: Cátedra, 1979.

Cavanaugh, Cecelia J., SSJ. *Lorca's Drawings and Poems. Forming the Eye of the Reader*. Lewisburg: Bucknell UP, 1995.

Cirici, Alexandre. "L'aportació de Sebastià Gasch." *Serra d'Or* (Barcelona), XIII, no. 140 (15-V-1971): 41-43.

————. "No oblidem Sebastià Gasch." *Serra d'Or* (Barcelona), XXIII, no. 257 (febrero 1981): 49-51.

Diego, Gerardo. "La nueva arte poética española." *Síntesis*, año II, VII, no. 20 (enero 1929): 183-199.

García Lorca, Federico. *Obras completas, III: Prosa. Dibujos*. Edición de Arturo del Hoyo, edición del cincuentenario. Madrid: Aguilar, 1986.

————. *Epistolario completo*. Edición de Andrew A. Anderson y Christopher Maurer. Madrid: Cátedra, 1997.

---

28   La "lógica poética" también aparece en la conferencia "Imaginación, inspiración, evasión," donde está relacionada con la inspiración y el "hecho poético" (García Lorca, OOCC III, 261, 263 y 267). Para más sobre estos conceptos, véase mi artículo "Lorca at the Crossroads: 'Imaginación, inspiración, evasión' and the 'novísimas estéticas.'"

Gasch, Sebastià. "Els pintors d'avantguarda. Joan Miró." *Gaseta de les Arts* (Barcelona), II, no. 39 (15-XII-1925): 3-5. *Escrits,* 52-57.

―――. "El pintor Joan Miró." *La Gaceta Literaria* (Madrid), I, no. 8 (15-IV-1927): 3.

―――. "Salvador Dalí." *La Gaceta Literaria* (Madrid), I, no. 14 (15-VII-1927): 5.

―――. "Una exposició i un decorat. Una exposició de F.G. Lorca. Un decorat de S. Dalí." *L'Amic de les Arts* (Sitges), II, no. 16 (31-VII-1927): 56. *Escrits,* 89-91.

―――. "Francesc Domingo." *La Gaceta Literaria* (Madrid), I, no. 16 (15-VIII-1927): 5.

―――. "Cop d'ull sobre l'evolució de l'art modern." *L'Amic de les Arts* (Sitges), II, no. 18 (30-IX-1927) : 91-93. *Escrits,* 92-100.

―――. "La moderna pintura francesa: Del cubismo al superrealismo. I. El cubismo, reacción técnica contra el impresionismo. II. Caída en la abstracción. III. El retorno al asunto. IV. El superrealismo." *La Gaceta Literaria* (Madrid), I, no. 20 (15-X-1927): 5. Ilie, 311-320; Rozas, 144-153; Brihuega, 284-294.

―――. "Naturaleza y arte." *La Gaceta Literaria* (Madrid), II, no. 25 (1-I-1928): 5. Brihuega, 231-235.

―――. "En torno al libro de Franz Roh. Panorama de la moderna pintura europea." *La Gaceta Literaria* (Madrid), II, no. 27 (1-II-1928): 4.

―――. "Lorca dibujante." *La Gaceta Literaria* (Madrid), II, no. 30 (15-III-1928): 4.

―――. "De un orden nuevo." *La Gaceta Literaria* (Madrid), II, no. 32 (15-IV-1928): 4.

―――. "André Breton: *Le surréalisme et la peinture.*" *La Veu de Catalunya* (Barcelona), (15-V-1928): 3. *Escrits,* 101-105.

―――. "Joan Miró." *La Gaceta Literaria* (Madrid), II, no. 39 (1-VIII-1928): 5.

―――. "Inaugural de les Galeries Dalmau." *L'Amic de les Arts* (Sitges), III, no. 30 (31-XII-1928): 236-238. *Escrits,* 106-113.

―――. "Arte y artistas. El realismo de la pintura nueva. Arte decorativo, todavía." *La Gaceta Literaria* (Madrid), III, no. 49 (1-I-1929): 7. Brihuega, 245-247.

―――. "Dos pintores valencianos." *La Gaceta Literaria* (Madrid), III, no. 53 (1-III-1929): 7.

————. "Libros. A. Ozenfant: *L'art.* Budry & Cie. *París.* André Level: *Picasso.* G. Crès & Cie. *París." La Gaceta Literaria* (Madrid) III, no. 53 (1-III-1929): 7.

————. "Mi Federico García Lorca [Prólogo:]." En *Federico García Lorca. Cartas a sus amigos.* Barcelona: Cobalto, 1950. 7-14.

————. *Expansió de l'art català al món.* Barcelona: s.e. [Imprenta Clarasó], 1953.

————. "Un 'manifest' i un 'full groc.'" *Serra d'Or* (Barcelona), X, no. 107 (agosto 1968): 27-30.

————. "El arte de vanguardia en Barcelona." *Cuadernos Hispanoamericanos* (Madrid), nos. 253-254 (enero-febrero 1971): 138-154.

————. *Escrits d'art i d'avantguarda (1925-1938).* Edición de Joan M. Minguet i Batllori. Barcelona: Edicions del Mall, 1987.

Ilie, Paul (ed.). *Documents of the Spanish Vanguard.* Chapel Hill: The U of North Carolina P, 1969.

Medina, Raquel. "'Poesía-plástica' o 'plástica-poética': elaboración metafórica de la conciencia del yo en García Lorca." *Anales de la Literatura Española Contemporánea* (Boulder, CO), XIX, nos. 1-2 (1994): 85-111.

Minguet i Batllori, Joan M. "Sebastià Gasch, entre l'art i l'espectacle." *Revista de Catalunya* (Barcelona), no. 58 (diciembre 1991): 98-110.

————. "Joan Miró i Sebastià Gasch. La ressonància d'una amistat." En *Miró-Dalmau-Gasch: l'aventura per l'art modern, 1918-1937,* catálogo de la exposición. Edición de Pilar Parcerisas. Barcelona: Generalitat de Catalunya–Departament de Cultura, 1993. 79-90.

Roh, Franz. *El realismo mágico.* Madrid: Revista de Occidente, 1927.

Rozas, Juan Manuel (ed.). *La generación del 27 desde dentro.* 2ª edición. Madrid: Istmo, 1987.

3
Dalí y Lorca en diálogo:
"Corazón bleu y coeur azul"

S I TOMAMOS EL CONCEPTO de "conversación" en el sentido más amplio de la palabra, las que mantuvieron Federico García Lorca y Salvador Dalí a lo largo de varios años durante el decenio de los veinte pueden dividirse, esquemáticamente, en cuatro categorías básicas: las que sostuvieron directamente, en persona, en los distintos lugares donde coincidieron; las que se llevaron a cabo en el intercambio de las cartas, cuando se hallaban en sitios apartados; las constituidas por las colaboraciones artísticas; y, por último, el diálogo más figurativo que tuvo lugar a raíz de la redacción de diversos textos y la composición de varios cuadros y dibujos, cuyo destinatario—Lorca o Dalí—a veces iba declarado por una dedicatoria explícita, pero que en otros momentos sólo se sobreentendía en la red de referencias privadas que compartían los dos.

Las conversaciones directas empezarían cuando se conocieron en la Residencia de Estudiantes, a principios de 1923, y continuarían, por ejemplo, durante las visitas de Lorca a Cataluña en 1925 y 1927. Dalí evocó aquel primer momento en una carta dirigida a Sebastià Gasch:

> La primera època de Madrid que comensa la meva gran amistat em L'orca es caracterisa ja per l'antagonisme violent del seu esperit eminentment religiós (eròtic) y el meu anti-religiosisme (sensual). Recordo les inacavables discussions que duraven fins a les 3 i les 5 del dematí y que s'an perpetuat al llarc de la nostra amistat. Llavors a la Residència d'estudians, es devorava Dostoyewski, era el moment del Rusus. Prust venia com terreny encara inexplorat. La meva indiferensia devan d'aquests escritors indignava a Lorca. A mí tot lo que fes referencia al mon interior, em

deixava absolutament indiferent, millor dit me s'oferia com quelcom d'extraordinarament desagradable.[1]

Un testimonio indirecto de sus conversaciones—y discusiones—en Figueres lo hallamos en una carta de Dalí a Lorca:

> *Tontísimo* hijito, por qué tendría que ser yo tan estúpido en engañarte respecto a mi *verdadero entusiasmo* por tus canciones deliciosas; lo que pasa es que se me ocurrieron una serie de cosas seguramente, como tú dices, inadecuadas y vistas a través de una exterior pero pura modernidad (plástica nada más).[2]

Gasch también describe su interacción en Barcelona en 1927:

> Una noche, después de cenar, Dalí, Federico y el que esto escribe entramos en un cabaret de la Plaza del Teatro que, si mal no recuerdo, se llamaba **Mónaco**. Después de una animada conversación, en el curso de la cual Dalí disertó sobre la necesidad de adaptar la música clásica al jazz, Lorca se levantó de su silla y se despidió de nosotros con estas palabras:
> —Me voy. Quiero acostarme pronto. Mañana quiero ir al Oficio solemne de la Catedral. ¡Qué aroma de pompa antigua!—agregó, poniendo los ojos en blanco y con una suave sonrisa vagando por sus labios finos.
> —Me interesa más esta aceituna—cortó, raudo, Dalí, señalando una sobre la mesa con el dedo índice.[3]

En cuanto a la correspondencia, los documentos todavía existentes (o de cuya existencia sabemos actualmente) son inevitablemente parciales. El tomo *Salvador Dalí escribe a Federico García Lorca* recoge treinta y seis cartas, fragmentos de cartas o tarjetas postales firmadas por Dalí o por Dalí en compañía de amigos o con miembros de su familia.[4] Se fechan entre 1925 y 1936. A este corpus habría que añadir una tarjeta postal más (de 1927), que está repro-

---

1   Gasch, *Expansió de l'art català al món*, p. 145. La carta es del 21 de noviembre de 1927: Fanés, *Salvador Dalí*, p. 22, nota 7 (p. 218).

2   *Salvador Dalí escribe a Federico García Lorca*, p. 58.

3   Gasch, "Mi Federico García Lorca," p. 11.

4   Además se incluyen en el volumen cuatro *collages* hechos por Dalí y enviados a Lorca ("El casamiento de Buster Keaton," "Libro de las varices," "Nacimiento del niño Jesús. Homenaje a Fra Angélico," "*Collage* de los zapatos"), una carta de

ducida y transcrita en un libro por Martínez Nadal.[5] El interés filológico de estos textos es muy variable, ya que corren la gama desde brevísimos saludos telegramáticos hasta cartas densas de cuatro o seis páginas cubiertas con la típica letra daliniana. Desgraciadamente, la mayor parte de la otra "mitad" de este intercambio epistolar parece haberse perdido. Cuando Christopher Maurer y yo compilamos el *Epistolario completo* lorquiano, sólo pudimos localizar siete cartas, fragmentos de cartas o tarjetas dirigidas por Lorca a Dalí, fechadas entre 1927 y 1930. El número reducido de documentos sugiere que deben de haber desaparecido varias docenas de otras misivas de esta misma índole.

Uno de los máximos ejemplos de colaboración artística sería el proyecto inacabado del libro de *Los putrefactos*, con dibujos de Dalí e introducción de Lorca, proyecto que se plasmó durante la primera estancia de Lorca en Cataluña, durante la Semana Santa de 1925.[6] Importantes también son los decorados y trajes que Dalí diseñó para el estreno de *Mariana Pineda*, de Lorca, en Barcelona (24 junio 1927). Y se podrían mencionar, además, los orígenes del "Manifest Groc," que empezaron a componer juntos durante el verano de 1927,[7] un diseño para un "Ex-Libis" [*sic*], enviado por Dalí a Lorca, o la insignia o viñeta para la revista *gallo* (*Salvador Dalí escribe*, pp. 18, 75).

Las conversaciones indirectas, a través de textos publicados y obras pictóricas, son, como era de esperar, más variopintas. La serie arranca con la "Oda a Salvador Dalí," publicada en la *Revista de Occidente* en abril de 1926. El próximo año Dalí dedica su texto "Sant Sebastià" (*L'Amic de les Arts*, 31 julio 1927) "A F. García Lorca."[8] Dos meses más tarde reseñó la exposición de dibujos de Lorca en las Galerías Dalmau (Barcelona).[9] Lorca respondió, implícitamente, a "Sant Sebastià" con el primero de sus poemas en prosa, "Santa Lucía y San Lázaro," que apareció en la *Revista de Occidente* en noviembre de 1927.[10]

Lidia Noguer a Dalí (X), una tarjeta de Ana María Dalí a Lorca (XXVI), y una carta de Salvador Dalí i Cusí a Lorca (XXXVII).

5   *Federico García Lorca. Mi penúltimo libro...*, pp. 218-219.

6   El tema ha sido estudiado en profundidad por Santos Torroella, por lo que renunciamos a dar más detalles aquí.

7   *Epistolario completo*, p. 492. Luego Lorca se desentendería del proyecto, y le reemplazarían Gasch y Lluís Montanyà.

8   Traducido al castellano, se reimprimió en el primer número de *gallo*, la revista granadina fundada y dirigida por Lorca.

9   "Federico García Lorca: exposió de dibuixos colorits (Galeries Dalmau)."

10   Aunque está dedicado a Sebastià Gasch, evidentemente se dirige, en gran medida, a Dalí.

Alrededor de este momento (septiembre 1927-febrero 1928), Lorca recibió de Dalí, en múltiples envíos, un haz de poemas y poemas en prosa, a los cuales reaccionó componiendo los otros textos que forman el libro proyectado de *Poemas en prosa*. Luego, en su conferencia "Sketch de la nueva pintura," dictada en Granada el 27 de octubre de 1928, Lorca proyectó unas diapositivas de cuadros de Dalí como "ejemplos de sobrerrealistas" (*Conferencias*, II, p. 47).

En cuanto a materia pictórica, tendrían que citarse varios retratos de Dalí dibujados por Lorca, por ejemplo *Retrato de Dalí* (no. 82), *Slavdor Adíl* (no. 83), y [*Retrato de Salvador Dalí*] (no. 116), que figuró en la exposición de Lorca en Dalmau.[11] Por parte de Dalí, existen pocos dibujos explícitamente identificados como retratos de Lorca—*Federico García Lorca en el Café de Oriente* y *El poeta en la platja d'Empúries vist per Salvador Dalí* son dos de ellos[12]—, pero Rafael Santos Torroella ha argumentado que la cabeza de Lorca se incorpora iconográficamente, y de manera más o menos obvia, en muchos lienzos y dibujos de Dalí correspondientes a este período.[13]

Ahora bien, todas estas conversaciones—convivencias, debates, relaciones, colaboraciones, influencias, lecturas, reacciones, etc.—constituyen el amplio contexto para un corto texto, poco conocido, que quisiera comentar aquí con más detenimiento. Pero antes de abordarlo, tenemos que hacer breve referencia a ciertas obras lorquianas, no relacionadas directamente con Dalí, pero que también desembocan en el texto en cuestión.

En 1925 Lorca compuso la mayoría de los textos que denominaba "diálogos," con vistas a recogerlos en un volumen con el mismo título, proyecto que, desgraciadamente, nunca se llevó a cabo. Entre éstos se hallan dos diálogos inconclusos, ambos sin título y por esto bautizados, por su contenido, "[Diálogo con Luis Buñuel y Augusto Centeno]" y "[Diálogo de la Residencia de Estudiantes]." Ambos reflejan la vida cotidiana en la Residencia de Estudiantes a mediados de los años veinte. La acotación inicial del primero—

---

11   Los números de identificación remiten siempre al *Libro de los dibujos de Federico García Lorca*, de Mario Hernández.

12   El primero es supuestamente de 1924, aunque podría ser muy posterior; el segundo apareció en *L'Amic de les Arts*, año II, no. 15 (30 junio 1927), p. 45, con "Reyerta de gitanos" de Lorca.

13   Por ejemplo, *Naturaleza muerta al claro de luna malva*; *Naturaleza muerta. (Invitación al sueño)*; *Pez y balcón. (Naturaleza muerta al claro de luna)*; *Homenaje a Erik Satie*; *Cabeza amiba*; *Autorretrato desdoblado en tres*; *Arlequín*; "Autorretrato" (*L'Amic de les Arts*, 31 enero 1927); "La playa" (*Verso y prosa*, abril 1927); *Cenicitas*; y *La miel es más dulce que la sangre*. Contra Santos Torroella sostiene Fanés una posición distinta en su artículo de 2000.

"(Habitación blanca con los muebles de pino. Por la ventana se ven largas nubes dormidas. Los personajes están tomando té.)"—contiene varios detalles elocuentes, entre ellos la sencillez rústica de los cuartos de la Residencia y la costumbre—el rito—común entre los residentes que Lorca llamó "la desesperación del té." El segundo diálogo está escrito en papel con el membrete de la Residencia. Buñuel y Augusto Centeno fueron residentes, y también es posible identificar a casi todos los que intervienen, o que se mencionan, en el segundo.[14]

Ahora bien, la relación de estos dos textos con la "realidad" no es fácil de precisar. Los diálogos que los constituyen no son, evidentemente, transcripciones de palabras pronunciadas por sus personajes, sino parlamentos ficticios creados por Lorca. Por otro lado, al leerlos, uno tiene la fuerte sensación de que las ideas, opiniones, actitudes, bromas, etc. que se atribuyen a los personajes reflejan, en gran medida, la realidad, y que los estudiantes reales detrás de los personajes se representan en los diálogos tal como eran o, quizás mejor dicho, tal como los otros residentes, y Lorca, los veían.

El texto que nos ocupa aquí es también un diálogo, y es también inconcluso. Se trata de "Corazón bleu y coeur azul," una prosa suelta recogida en apéndice a mi edición de los *Poemas en prosa* lorquianos (pp. 91-92). Aquí hay sólo dos interlocutores: "Yo," luego identificado como "Poeta," y "Mi amigo," luego "A," pero precisamente como en el "[Diálogo con Luis Buñuel y Augusto Centeno]," cada uno de los personajes sostiene una posición distinta, rasgo que vincula todos estos textos, aunque a gran distancia, con los diálogos platónicos. El título extraño parecería relacionar el diálogo con uno de los poemas en prosa, "Coeur azul. Corazón bleu" (pp. 89-90), pero aparte de la presencia de dos personajes, en este caso un "yo" masculino y una mujer "amiga mía," es difícil percibir muchas conexiones entre ellos. En nuestro texto una posible hipótesis es que el juego cruzado de sinónimos en castellano y francés significara que ambos interlocutores participan en calidades similares, aunque uno se ve más afiliado a España y el otro a Francia.

Al empezar la lectura de "Corazón bleu y coeur azul," descubrimos rápidamente que lo que presenta es una discusión sobre temas estéticos, con dos posiciones claramente diferenciadas, y que mientras "Yo"/"Poeta" puede identificarse fácilmente con el mismo Lorca, tampoco es difícil ver en el "amigo," por las ideas que emite, a Salvador Dalí. De esta manera, Lorca se convierte aquí, por decirlo así, en ventrílocuo de su amigo. Aunque el manuscrito no está fechado, parece reflejar conversaciones, reconstruidas en el

---

14   Véase el Anexo 3 del libro de Sáenz de la Calzada.

recuerdo, que habrían tenido lugar durante el verano de 1927, en la segunda de las visitas de Lorca a Cataluña, por lo que cabe situar su composición en la segunda mitad de 1927 o, a más tardar, en 1928.

El texto comienza *in medias res*: la discusión acerca de las imágenes—y tal vez, más particularmente las metáforas—ya está en camino. El tema básico es la conexión que existe entre las cosas, o bien la ausencia de tal conexión. "Yo"—es decir, Lorca—defiende su posición: para él las imágenes son todavía válidas, pero no le interesan las metáforas manidas y trilladas, y por eso evita las asociaciones fáciles y busca más bien los vínculos enrarecidos. Expresa tal actitud con un lenguaje en sí figurativo: "Cuando subo y bajo las escaleras no me acuerdo del ascensor. Del ascensor me acuerdo en el desierto o en la mesa del café." Para crear una buena imagen hay que emprender una búsqueda o una caza, y sólo gracias al esfuerzo puede finalmente captarse "el hilo quebradizo que una a todas las cosas con cada cosa y a cada cosa con todas las demás."

Aquí, por un lado, Lorca parece recordar la teoría que servía de fundamento al concepto poético en la Edad de Oro. Si todo el universo es creación de Dios, si existe la gran cadena del ser, entonces con suficiente agudeza el poeta podrá descubrir los insospechados puntos en común que comparten dos cosas dispares. Por otro lado, la noción de un "hilo quebradizo" también remite a un teórico mucho más reciente: Vicente Huidobro, quien aseveraba que el poeta "tiende hilos eléctricos entre las palabras," que "ve los lazos sutiles que se tienden las cosas entre sí," y que "es aquel que sorprende la relación oculta que existe entre las cosas más lejanas, los ocultos hilos que las unen."[15]

La posición de "Mi amigo"—Dalí—es mucho más radical. Él rechaza contundentemente la mera idea de las conexiones existentes entre las cosas, y con esto quiere liberarse de toda la práctica metafórica, aun en sus evoluciones más avanzadas o matizadas. Más bien le interesan las cosas en sí mismas, apreciadas por su valor consustancial, su ser literal y nada más: "las mismas cosas aisladas." Poniendo completamente al revés las ideas convencionales sobre lo que es poético y lo que no lo es, llama "antipoétic[a]" "la relación lógica entre dos objetos de la clase que sean"; por esto, quiere romper "las amarras," puesto que es sólo cuando las cosas circulan libremente por el mundo que adquieren "la verdadera poesía." Los poetas convencionales, argumenta, siempre quieren ver otra cosa en el objeto que tienen a mano, pero tal deseo les impide percibir el hecho que los objetos en sí mismos disponen de "una extrema belleza y de una vida propia tan intensa como la tuya."

---

15   *Poética y estética creacionistas*, pp. 126, 127, 148-149.

En el diálogo parece que el personaje "poeta" no llega a comprender completamente la esencia tan radical de la propuesta de su "amigo." Efectivamente, aquél sigue elogiando la capacidad transformadora—es decir, metafórica—de la poesía, y por consiguiente el "amigo" empieza a enfadarse. Le interrumpe y afirma de nuevo que las cosas pueden existir en y por sí mismas, acompañadas por otras cosas pero no en combinaciones figurativas con ellas: "[el] zapato [...] puede ir con una aceituna o con una nariz, por el mar del Sur, en medio de una simple emoción de brisa." Sin embargo, para el terco poeta tal formulación le parece muy cercana a una imagen o, como la llama, "un hecho poético más."

En su última intervención el "amigo" procura explicarse otra vez. La palabra "poético" es problemática porque él quiere redefinirla como algo que el poeta no entiende: no como un efecto de la metáfora, de la literatura, sino como el efecto, en sí, de cualquier objeto observado con suficiente detenimiento. Los "hechos poéticos," aunque puedan parecer modernos, son realmente anticuados y pertenecen, exclusivamente, al mundo de los libros, barrera o límite que el "amigo" quiere traspasar. Por esto propone una "visión" de varias cosas muy dispares que *no* tienen nada figurativo en común entre sí: "Yo he visto un burro con cabeza de ruiseñor y una gran ola como tres leones de agua, detenida por el pavor que le causaba un granito de sal."

Desgraciadamente, el diálogo queda truncado aquí. Pero no es difícil ver en él a Lorca luchando intelectualmente con dos estéticas incompatibles: la suya, basada en el "hecho poético," y la de Dalí, basada en lo que podríamos llamar una nueva literalidad. El texto refleja, pues, el choque de sus posiciones respectivas alrededor de 1927-28; demuestra que Lorca, a diferencia del personaje del "poeta," entendía perfectamente las ideas de su amigo, pero simultáneamente sugiere la razón por la que no pudo seguirle en el camino hacia el surrealismo.

Una vez superada la fase de las imágenes gongorinas, el "hecho poético" fue el concepto central de la teoría poética de Lorca durante los años en cuestión. La descripción más detallada que ofrece del "hecho poético"—en términos simplificados, una especie de imagen atmosférica o afectiva y difícil de explicar—se halla en las distintas versiones de su conferencia "Imaginación, inspiración, evasión" (*Conferencias*, vol. II), aunque volvió a referirse a él en varias otras ocasiones entre 1928 y 1935.[16] Irónicamente, es probable que Lorca hubiera derivado el nombre del concepto de precisamente la persona contra quien ahora lo esgrime—Salvador Dalí—. En una cita de Le Corbu-

---

16   Para más detalles, véase mi artículo "Lorca at the Crossroads."

sier-Saugnier que sirve de epígrafe a un artículo de Dalí, aparece la frase francesa "fait poétique," y en dos otros artículos suyos se halla la frase catalana "fet poètic."[17]

En cuanto a la "nueva literalidad" de Dalí, la podemos detectar en artículos y poemas suyos, y varias de sus cartas a Lorca. En la carta XX (principios de marzo, 1927), por ejemplo, aboga por la "ironía=desnudez, *ver claro*, ver límpidamente, descubrir la desnudez de la naturaleza" (*Salvador Dalí escribe*, p. 48); en la carta XXV (principios de junio, 1927), informa que "hoy lo objetivo poéticamente es para mí lo que me gusta más, y sólo en lo objetivo veo el estremecimiento de lo Etéreo" (p. 59); en "Els meus quadros del Saló de Tardor" (31 octubre 1927) asegura que "saber mirar un objecte, un animal, d'una manera espiritual, és veure'l en la seva màxima realitat objectiva" (*L'alliberament dels dits*, p. 40); en la carta XXXIII (principios de diciembre, 1927), escribe que "estoy hallando cosas que me dejan una profundísima emoción y procuro pintarlas honestamente, o sea, exactamente" (p. 80); mientras que en la carta XXXVI (principios de septiembre, 1928), insiste en "la importancia del dato estrictamente objetivo obtenido anti-artísticamente por un riguroso método analítico" (p. 92).

En "Nous límits de la pintura [I]" (29 febrero 1928) se refiere a "l'autonomia poètica de les coses i de les paraules" (*L'alliberament dels dits*, p. 62), y en la carta XXXVI (principios de septiembre, 1928) desarrolla su tesis de que "en realidad, no hay ninguna relación entre dos danzantes y un panal de abejas, a menos que sea la relación que hay entre Saturno y la pequeña cuca que duerme en la crisálida, o a menos de que en realidad no exista *ninguna diferencia* entre la pareja que danza y un panal de abejas" (pp. 89-90). Por esto, concluye, "hay que dejar las cositas *libres* de las ideas convencionales a que la inteligencia las ha querido someter. Entonces estas cositas monas ellas solas obran de acuerdo con su real y *consustancial* manera de ser" (p. 91).

Finalmente, también encontramos aquí menciones de algunas de las "cosas" y los "objetos" que figuran en "Corazón bleu y coeur azul." En "Nous límits de la pintura [I]" (29 febrero 1928), por ejemplo, Dalí afirma que "per a nosaltres, el lloc d'un nas, lluny d'ésser necessàriament en un rostre, ens sembla més adequat trobar-lo en una barana de canapè; cap inconvenient, tampoc, que el mateix nas s'aguanti dalt d'un petit fum" (*L'alliberament dels dits*, pp. 61-62). Pero sin duda el texto daliniano más cercano al diálogo escrito por

---

17   "Poesia de l'útil standarditzat" (31 marzo 1928); "La fotografia, pura creació de l'esperit" (30 septiembre 1927); "Els meus quadros del Saló de Tardor" (31 octubre 1927); *L'alliberament dels dits*, pp. 95, 33 y 41.

Lorca es su poema en prosa "Pez perseguido por una uva."[18] Aquí encontramos las siguientes frases que guardan un parentesco con palabras o frases específicas del diálogo lorquiano: "El pez en cuestión había sido pequeña sal"; "mi amiga mirando bizco y arrugando la naricita como una pequeña bestia"; "El camino era una flauta con 8 agujeros y en cada agujero había un pequeñito burro podrido"; "Sobre una piedra una aceituna está quieta"; "aquel turbador burro podrido con la cabeza de ruiseñor"; y "La aceituna quieta lleva una pequeña falda" (*Salvador Dalí escribe*, pp. 76-79).

"Corazón bleu y coeur azul" es, pues, un documento más que ilumina la trayectoria de las relaciones entre pintor y poeta durante 1927-28. Lo que pasa durante estos meses puede cifrarse en dos cartas de Dalí a Lorca. En el número XXV (principios de junio, 1927) se disculpa por ciertos comentarios que debe de haber hecho acerca del libro *Canciones*, de Lorca, recién publicado, y aunque defiende una estética de la modernidad, al mismo tiempo se apresura a asegurarle con respecto a "mi *verdadero entusiasmo* por tus canciones deliciosas" (p. 58). Esto puede compararse con la carta XXXVI (principios de septiembre, 1928), donde le comunica su reacción a la próxima colección de Lorca, el *Romancero gitano*, y ahora, quince meses más tarde, puede expresar sin ambages su desagrado ante la mayor parte del libro: "Tú te mueves dentro de las nociones aceptadas y anti-poéticas" (p. 90). Si Lorca le causó a Dalí una gran impresión cuando se conocieron, creemos que durante este período de su relación—de sus conversaciones—, el pintor influía más fuertemente en el poeta que *viceversa*. "Corazón bleu y coeur azul" expresa ambas posiciones con bastante fidelidad. El diálogo nos muestra a Lorca reflexionando sobre sus diferencias estéticas, y nos permite vislumbrar la lucha interna que éste sostuvo hacia finales de los años veinte, entre la tentación del método daliniano, un camino que conducía hacia el surrealismo, y sus propias convicciones literarias, con un afán de modernizarse pero sin renunciar completamente a la intencionalidad artística.

---

18   El original mecanografiado reproducido en *Salvador Dalí escribe* (pp. 76-79) no corresponde en absoluto a las características del "poema" que Dalí dice que está mandando adjunto a su carta XXXII (noviembre 1927). No obstante, el envío de "Pez perseguido" probablemente se efectuó en fechas próximas, ya que en su carta XXX (octubre/noviembre 1927), anuncia a Lorca que "pronto recibirás casi un libro de *poemas* míos" (p. 71). Éste acusó recibo de "Pez perseguido" (entre "tus últimas cosas") en una carta que verosímilmente sería de noviembre o principios de diciembre de 1927 (*Epistolario completo*, pp. 532-533).

Obras citadas

Anderson, Andrew A. "Lorca at the Crossroads: 'Imaginación, inspiración, evasión' and the 'novísimas estéticas.'" *Anales de la Literatura Española Contemporánea* (Boulder, Colorado), XVI, nos. 1-2 (1991), 149-173.

Dalí, Salvador. "Sant Sebastià." *L'Amic de les Arts* (Sitges), año II, no. 16 (31 julio 1927), 52-54.

——. "Federico García Lorca: exposició de dibuixos colorits (Galeries Dalmau)." *La Nova Revista* (Barcelona), III, no. 9 (septiembre 1927), 84-85.

——. "Els meus quadros del Saló de Tardor." Hoja suelta en *L'Amic de les Arts* (Sitges), año II, no. 19 (31 octubre 1927), s.p.

——. "San Sebastián." *gallo* (Granada), no. 1 (febrero 1928), 9-12.

——. "Nous límits de la pintura [I]." *L'Amic de les Arts* (Sitges), año III, no. 22 (29 febrero 1928), 167-169.

——. *Salvador Dalí escribe a Federico García Lorca [1925-1936]*. Ed. Rafael Santos Torroella, número doble especial de *Poesía* (Madrid), nos. 27-28 (1987).

——. *L'alliberament dels dits. Obra catalana completa*. Ed. Félix Fanès (Barcelona: Quaderns Crema, 1995).

Fanés, Fèlix. *Salvador Dalí. La construcción de la imagen 1925-1930* (s.l.: Electa, 1999).

——. "Dalí, García Lorca i la pintura." En *Federico García Lorca i Catalunya*, ed. Antonio Monegal y José María Micó (Barcelona: Institut Universitari de Cultura, Universitat Pompeu Fabra / Àrea de Cultura, Diputació de Barcelona, 2000), pp. 117-121.

García Lorca, Federico. "Oda a Salvador Dalí." *Revista de Occidente* (Madrid), año IV, vol. XII, no. 34 (abril 1926), 52-58.

——. "Santa Lucía y San Lázaro." *Revista de Occidente*, año V, vol. XVIII, no. 53 (noviembre 1927), 145-155.

——. *Conferencias*. Ed. Christopher Maurer, 2 vols. (Madrid: Alianza, 1984).

——. *Epistolario completo*. Ed. Andrew A. Anderson y Christopher Maurer (Madrid: Cátedra, 1997).

——. *Diálogos*. Ed. Andrew A. Anderson (Granada: Comares / Fundación Federico García Lorca, 1998).

——. *Poemas en prosa*. Ed. Andrew A. Anderson (Granada: Comares, 2000).

Gasch, Sebastià. "Mi Federico García Lorca." En Federico García Lorca, *Cartas a sus amigos* (Barcelona: Cobalto, 1950), pp. 7-14.

———. *Expansió de l'art català al món* (Barcelona: s.e., 1953).

Hernández, Mario. *Libro de los dibujos de Federico García Lorca* (Madrid: Tabapress / Fundación Federico García Lorca, 1990).

Huidobro, Vicente. *Poética y estética creacionistas.* Ed. Vicente Quirarte (México D.F.: U.N.A.M., 1994).

Martínez Nadal, Rafael. *Federico García Lorca. Mi penúltimo libro sobre el hombre y el poeta* (Madrid: Casariego, 1992).

Sáenz de la Calzada, Margarita. *La Residencia de Estudiantes. 1910-1936* (Madrid: Consejo Superior de Investigaciones Científicas, 1986).

Santos Torroella, Rafael. *La miel es más dulce que la sangre. Las épocas lorquiana y freudiana de Salvador Dalí* (Barcelona: Seix Barral, 1984).

———. *"Los putrefactos" de Dalí y Lorca. Historia y antología de un libro que no pudo ser* (Madrid: Consejo Superior de Investigaciones Científicas / Asociación Amigos de la Residencia de Estudiantes, 1995).

4

García Lorca's *Poemas en prosa* and *Poeta en Nueva York:* Dalí, Gasch, Surrealism, and the Avant-Garde

I N SPAIN IN THE latter half of the 1920s, the French Surrealist movement was commonly seen as another iteration of the avant-garde impulse among a throng of other "isms," and one that had arrived rather late on the scene (Bergamín; Masoliver). Furthermore, although it undoubtedly offered certain exciting innovations and paths to be explored, there was no vacuum that Surrealism in particular served to fill, for there had been a continuous tradition of avant-garde writing in Spain from 1919 onwards (earlier in Catalonia), embodied first in the Ultra movement (1919-24) and later (1925-8) in a number of largely independent authors.[1]

Conventional literary history situates the ten poets most commonly thought of as belonging to the so-called "Generation of 1927" at the center of poetic production in Spain in the 1920s and 1930s, and over the decades there has been a marked tendency to single out four of them—Alberti, Aleixandre, Cernuda, and García Lorca—as the paragons of "Spanish Surrealism." And of course, since Lorca is the best-known of all, it is his collection *Poeta en Nueva York* that has sometimes been held up as the "cumbre del surrealismo español" (Marco, 1). This categorization is what I wish to test and question in what follows. The whole issue of the relationship of Lorca's poetical works with Surrealism needs to be addressed anew, stripped of the many accumulated layers of hasty labelling, received wisdom, and unthink-

---

1   Among them Luís Amado Blanco, César M. Arconada, Rogelio Buendía, Pedro Garfias, Juan Gutiérrez Gili, José María Hinojosa, Juan Larrea, Fernando María de Milícua, and Juan Vidal Martínez. Information on all these figures can be found in Bonet's *Diccionario de las vanguardias en España*.

ing repetition. Such a project can be approached in two possible ways, from the historical and biographical angle, and from an ahistorical and intrinsic perspective, and I propose to utilize both—that is, the contextual and the textual—in what I hope will be a complementary fashion.

Lorca would likely have browsed the articles about Surrealism and translations of Surrealist works appearing in such Spanish magazines as *Revista de Occidente, Alfar, Litoral*, and *La Gaceta Literaria*, and it was no doubt a topic that arose from time to time in the café *tertulias* that he attended.[2] However, biographical evidence suggests that he would have learnt most about the movement and discussed it most intensely within the framework of his friendships and correspondence with Salvador Dalí and the Catalan art critic Sebastià Gasch.

Lorca met Dalí at the beginning of 1923, and their relationship evolved and deepened over the subsequent years. The period of interest here is 1927-8, when Dalí was gradually moving closer to Surrealism, and when Lorca spent an extended period of time in Catalonia over spring-summer 1927. The two never saw entirely eye-to-eye, but Lorca took very much to heart Dalí's commentaries and criticisms of his poetry,[3] and he was motivated to explore a more avant-garde aesthetic by Dalí's encouragement and by his example in both paintings and diverse writings. Their discussions are transparently reflected in a little-known, undated dialogue fragment that Lorca entitled "Corazon bleu y coeur azul" (*PP*, 91-2). Here "Yo" (i.e. Lorca) still defends metaphor and the image: "veo el hilo quebradizo que una a todas las cosas con cada cosa y a cada cosa con todas las demás," whereas "Mi amigo" (Dalí) favors quite simply "las mismas cosas aisladas" that produce "la verdadera poesía" *(PP*, 91). The significant impact of Dalí's ideas and artistic practice can be gauged above all in Lorca's two 1928 lectures, "Imaginación, inspira-

---

2   An early and representative example: in November 1925 he wrote to his brother Francisco, then in Bordeaux, and asked his impression of "los chicos surrealistas" (*EC*, 308). Parenthetical references in this essay will use the following abbreviations: *EC* for *Epistolario completo*; "IIE" for "Imaginación, inspiración, evasión," in *Conferencias*, II, 13-31; *PNY* for *Poet en Nueva York*; and *PP* for *Poemas en prosa*; in each case followed by page number(s).

3   Compare Dalí's lukewarm response to *Canciones* (1927), in his letter XXV (Dalí, *Salvador Dalí escribe*, 58-9), with his dismantling of *Romancero gitano* (1928), in letter XXXVI (88-94).

ción, evasión" ("IIE") and "Sketch de la pintura moderna," and in his prose
poems of 1927-8 (*Poemas en prosa*), to be discussed below.[4]

Lorca met Gasch in the course of the same 1927 stay in Catalonia, and
they corresponded at some length over the remainder of that and the following year. Although Lorca mentions his new writing projects in these letters,
perhaps the primary topic of discussion are the drawings that he was producing, many of which he sent to Gasch. Among the numerous articles that
Gasch published over this period were a review of Lorca's exhibition of drawings at the famous Dalmau gallery in Barcelona (held in late June 1927), and
a subsequent piece entitled "Lorca dibujante." Gasch was a fervent but not
indiscriminate apologist of modern art. Firmly believing that modern artists
needed to combine inspiration in subject matter with a degree of formal or
compositional care, he lambasted those painters who tended to either pole
and provided only one of these two essential elements. The latter stages of
synthetic Cubism and total abstraction were for him two egregious examples
of empty formalism, while on the other hand Surrealism was the worst of-
fender in purveying nothing but the outpourings of uncontrolled instinct
or inspiration. Exempted from this condemnation were, among others, Picasso and Miró, who, despite their connection with Surrealism, nonetheless
achieved in Gasch's opinion the fusion or equilibrium that he sought.[5]

During these same years Lorca found himself at an important but difficult juncture in his own writing. In autumn 1927 he was finishing up the last
of the poems for *Romancero gitano* (*EC*, 521), which was published the following summer, in December he repeated his lecture "La imagen poética de
don Luis de Góngora" at the Residencia de Estudiantes, and later that same
month he recited poems from the *Romancero* in Seville. By early spring 1928,
though, he had embarked in earnest on his planned book of *Odas* (*EC*, 550,
576, 579, 582, 587), a project that he described as being the "polo opuesto al
Romancero y creo que de más agudeza lírica" (*EC*, 590).[6]

Despite the fresh direction marked by the *Odas*, the time was plainly
ripe for a more radical break. Since the summer of 1926, Dalí had been elabo-

---

4   I study Dalí's influence on Lorca in more detail in my article "Lorca at the
Crossroads," and see Hernández. "Sketch" appears in *Conferencias*, II, 33-49.

5   I summarize here a considerably more detailed account of Gasch's ideas on
modern art that can be found in my essay "Sebastià Gasch y Federico García Lorca:
influencias recíprocas y la construcción de una estética vanguardista."

6   As was the case with several other projects, the *Odas* were never published,
despite a report in 1934 that the book was ready for the press. A partial reconstruction is possible based on extant manuscripts.

rating a personal aesthetic based on the iconographic representation of the martyrdom of Saint Sebastian, a figure who embodied for the painter what he called "la Santa Objetividad."[7] This culminated in his Catalan text "Sant Sebastià," a unique cross between an aesthetic manifesto and a prose poem, which appeared in print at the end of July 1927, dedicated to Lorca, just a few days after he had left Catalonia. Saint Sebastian would, therefore, have doubtless been one of their topics of discussion, and upon receiving the issue of *L'Amic de les Arts* in Granada Lorca responded effusively in letters to Dalí, his sister Ana María, and Gasch, calling it "una prosa nueva llena de relaciones insospechables y sutilísimos *puntos de vista*" and "uno de los más intensos poemas que pueden leerse" (*EC*, 511-12; 506; 508).

But this was not all. On 25 August 1927 Lorca informed Gasch that:

> En prosa hago ahora un ensayo en el que estoy interesadísimo. Me propongo dos temas literarios, los desarrollo y luego los analizo. Y el resultado es un poema. Trato de unir mi instinto con el virtuosismo que posea. (*EC*, 513-14)[8]

Almost certainly what he is describing here is "Santa Lucía y San Lázaro," the first of the *Poemas en prosa* and the only one written in 1927. As McMullan has demonstrated, the piece includes a multitude of details that testify to an intimate acquaintance with the geography of Barcelona. But above all the indebtedness to Dalí is manifold: the text is a hybrid, a narrative cum prose poem cum aesthetic meditation, and each of the two aesthetic positions delineated is centered on the figure of a saint. And when "Santa Lucía" appeared in the *Revista de Occidente* in November, dedicated to Gasch, he reported to Lorca Dalí's generally warm and positive response (Gibson, I, 527).

There is no evidence to suggest that Lorca returned to the prose poem genre until August 1928. But during the intervening eleven months Dalí was busy sending him a series of writings, and publishing some of them, which again would serve as a model and catalyst for Lorca's later compositions. Conflating poetic prose, prose poems, and free verse, we can hypothetically reconstruct this corpus as follows: "una prosa extraña, con grandes éxitos, pero *desorbitada*"; "Poema de las cositas"; "casi un libro de *poemas* míos"; "mi

---

7   Dalí, *Salvador Dalí escribe*, 42; see also 44, 46, 48, 59. For a detailed commentary on the concept, see Hernández and Monegal, "Las palabras y las cosas, según Salvador Dalí."

8   "Instinct" and "virtuosity" correspond, of course, to the two basic elements required by Gasch.

'poema' con fotos para *gallo*"; "Poema [Pelos de debajo del brazo]"; "Pez per-seguido por una uva"; "tus últimas cosas [...] tus poemas"; "Dues proses: 'La meva amiga i la platja.' 'Nadal a Brussel.les (Conte antic)'"; "unos ensayos poéticos que son un encanto"; and "Poema [A la Lydia de Cadaqués]," of which six texts are extant and several more are presumed lost.[9]

Meanwhile, as already noted, from early February till late September 1928 Lorca was working primarily on his *Odas*. But in the course of this lat-ter month he started to mention a shift of emphasis: "Yo trabajo con gran amor en varias cosas de géneros muy distintos. Hago poemas de todas clases. [...] Mi poesía tiende ahora otro vuelo más agudo todavía. Me parece que un vuelo personal" (*EC*, 585). The new initiative referred to here is precisely that of the *Poemas en prosa*, and as the *Odas* were brought to a close, their period of composition overlapped briefly with what lay ahead: "Después de construir mis *Odas*, en las que tengo tanta ilusión, cierro este ciclo de poesía para hacer otra cosa" (*EC*, 587).[10]

Besides the sense of the cycle of odes coming to a close, another reason for striking out in a new direction was surely Lorca's extended meditation on that onslaught of intensely avant-garde texts sent to him by Dalí over the im-mediately preceding months.[11] Lorca's first response seems to be evidenced in the composition of "Degollación del Bautista" in August 1928, the date that appeared at the foot of the text upon its publication in 1930. And then, very soon afterwards, Lorca received one of the last letters of substance written to him by Dalí, which spelt out his withering critique of *Romancero gitano*

---

9   References for the complete list are, respectively: (1) September 1927: *EC*, 521, unidentified/lost; (2) October 1927: Dalí, *Salvador Dalí escribe*, 68, later pub-lished in Catalan as "Poema de les cosetes" (August 1928); (3) October/November 1927: Dalí, *Salvador Dalí escribe*, 71, unidentified; (4) November 1927: Dalí, *Sal-vador Dalí escribe*, 74, lost; (5) c. November 1927: Dalí, *Salvador Dalí escribe*, 75, text preserved, letter lost; (6) c. November 1927: Dalí, *Salvador Dalí escribe*, 76-9, text preserved, letter lost, later published in Catalan as "Peix perseguit per un raïm" (September 1928); (7) November 1927: *EC*, 532-3, among them "Pez perseguido por una uva"; (8) published in Catalan (November 1927); (9) January 1928: *EC*, 543, un-identified; (10) published February 1928.

10   "Santa Lucía y San Lazaro," stylistically somewhat different from the rest of the *Poemas en prosa*, constitutes the exception to this chronological rule. Similarly, Lorca would take up again the fourth and last part of "Oda al Santísimo Sacramento del Altar" in September 1929, when he was in New York.

11   Obviously, they also continued to correspond, and there are nine surviving letters from Dalí (XXVII-XXXV), which date from the intervening eleven months (September 1927-July 1928): Dalí, *Salvador Dalí escribe*, 64-84.

and proposed a very different aesthetic, one already well down the road that led from "Sant Sebastià" and "la Santa Objetividad" to Surrealism. The letter in question likely arrived in Granada at the very beginning of September.[12] The precise dates are significant because the first draft of another prose poem, "Nadadora sumergida," is dated 4 September, and was therefore probably composed in the immediate aftermath of its receipt.[13] Furthermore, like "Santa Lucía," "Nadadora" can be read, in part, as an aesthetic statement, and certain passages in the text assert the need for a radical break with the past.

The other three published prose poems followed in short order.[14] "Suicidio en Alejandría" must have been written either immediately before or after "Nadadora," as Lorca sent the pair to Gasch for publication in *L'Amic de les Arts*, where they appeared in the number dated 31 [*sic*] September 1928.[15] That autumn he must also have composed "Amantes asesinados por una perdiz," as it, along with "Degollación del Bautista," were sent to Juan Guerrero Ruiz for the issue of *Verso y Prosa* slated to appear in December 1928/January 1929 but which, in the event, was never published (*EC*, 599-600). Likewise, "Degollación de los Inocentes" was set down before the end of the year, as it came out in *La Gaceta Literaria* in January 1929. With the exception of "Santa Lucía," then, the *Poemas en prosa* fall into a narrow temporal band with dates of composition between August and, at latest, December 1928. It is entirely plausible that Lorca would have considered himself well on the way towards producing a whole sequence of prose poems, a genre much in vogue in the 1920s, but the only direct reference that we have to such a collection comes

---

12   Letter XXXVI: Dalí, *Salvador Dalí escribe*, 88-94. Santos Torroella dates its composition to the beginning of September, but it was most probably sent at the end of August (*EC*, 584-5, n502). The content overlaps considerably with Dalí's article "Realidad y sobrerrealidad."

13   A more detailed account of the chronology appears in my "Lorca at the Crossroads," 150-1. On the heels of the appearance of the news item in the Spanish press (30 August), on 1 September 1928 Lorca had also composed the "Meditaciones a la muerte de la madre de Chariot" (*PP*, 93-100), a prose piece with many connections to the prose poems.

14   Two further compositions were never finished: a nearly complete text entitled "Coeur azul. Corazón bleu" (not to be confused with the Lorca-Dalí dialogue), and a brief fragment "Mi amor en el baño" (*PP*, 89-90; 103).

15   In an August 1928 letter to Gasch, Lorca announced "unos dibujos y un poema inédito" that he was going to send to the magazine (*EC*, 579), which could have been "Suicidio." Lorca then sent two drawings, followed later by "sus poemas correspondientes," i.e. "Nadadora" and "Suicidio" (*EC*, 585, 588); all four works appeared on the same page in *L'Amic*.

years later: in 1936 when asked by an interviewer what books he had ready to be published, Lorca replied, with some hyperbole: "cinco [...] *Tierra y luna, Diván del Tamarit, Odas, Poemas en prosa,* y *Suites*."[16]

As regards *Poeta en Nueva York,* the details regarding its textual history are well documented and need only be briefly rehearsed. There was a gap of at least seven months between the composition of the last of the *Poemas en prosa* and the first of the poems included in *Poeta en Nueva York,* during which time Lorca, uncharacteristically, wrote virtually nothing. All, or almost all, of the poems belonging to this collection were set down between August 1929 and June 1930; thereafter the book and its texts underwent a complex process of repeated revisions over the subsequent six years. Lorca dropped off a semi-finished typescript at the *Cruz y Raya* offices of Jose Bergamín in late June 1936, clearly with the intent to bring out the volume with that magazine's publishing house (Ediciones del Árbol) the following autumn. In the event, of course, *Poeta en Nueva York* appeared in New York and Mexico City, in two different "first editions," in the spring of 1940.[17]

* * *

BEFORE CONSIDERING *Poemas en prosa* and *Poeta en Nueva York,* we need to familiarize ourselves with the specific critical vocabulary that Lorca used during this period. In particular, he articulated the radical break mentioned above around a shift from a poetry based on "imaginación," which uses "lógica humana" to construct "metáforas" with elements drawn from "la realidad," to one now based on "inspiración," which deploys "una lógica poética" to create "hechos poéticos" that in turn enable the poem to rise to "una realidad distinta" existing on "un último plano de pureza y sencillez" ("IIE," *passim*). This parallels a development in modern painting where, in a reaction against Purism and Constructivism, there had arisen a "un modo espiritualista en el cual las imágenes ya no son dadas por la inteligencia, sino por [el] inconsciente, por la pura inspiración directa" ("Sketch de la moderna pintura," *Conferencias,* II, 38). Here Lorca was following Dalí at every turn: in rejecting

---

16   This is the source of the title for the putative collection. The interview was published posthumously by Otero Seco.

17   After many years of uncertainty and controversy, the whereabouts of this typescript (which also included a few printed clippings and some autographs), once thought lost or destroyed, have now been ascertained. While at the time of writing this "original" is still in private hands and unpublished, the edition of *Poeta en Nueva York* from which I cite (ed. Christopher Maurer, New York: The Noonday Press, 1998), has been revised in the light of a photocopy of said document.

the decipherable, riddle-like metaphor, in setting inspiration against imagination, in calling the building blocks of the new poetry "hechos poéticos," and in referring to a "modo espiritualista."[18] However, in championing the concept of the mysterious and irreducible "hecho poético" Lorca stopped short of Dalí's emphasis on the literalness of things in and of themselves (the distinction that was nicely made in "Corazon bleu y coeur azul").

From "Corazon bleu" (1927?) to "Imaginación, inspiración, evasión" (1928-30), to his commentary-recitals of *Poeta en Nueva York* (1932-5) and *Romancero gitano* (1935-6), Lorca unwaveringly reiterated his adhesion to the "hecho poético," but it is not a concept easily defined, as he usually described it with language that was itself poetic. Basically, the "hecho poético" seems to be a kind of image that affects or moves us without recourse to a metaphorical link to reality, and which therefore is resistant to traditional forms of interpretation and requires a certain kind of receptiveness on the part of the reader. All these characteristics suggest a close similarity with T.S. Eliot's notion of the "objective correlative."

Finally, Lorca called the act of breaking free from reason and the plane of reality and entering into this new and mysterious world an "evasión." He saw at least two ways of achieving this, via the paths of dream and the subconscious offered by Surrealism, and via the path of the "hecho poético" ("IIE," *Conferencias*, II, 18, 20-1, 25-6). He himself favored the latter alternative, for while giving dream and the subconscious their due, he characterized the path as "muy pura, poco diáfana," and although they might catch on in Northern Europe, he felt that in Spain they would not, since "los latinos queremos perfiles y misterio visible. Forma y sensualidades" (*Conferencias*, II, 21).

Yet again Lorca had borrowed this concept of escape and its relationship to Surrealism from Dalí. While the term starts off in the latter's letters meaning little more than an avant-garde rejection of convention, it evolves into a

---

18   On the riddle, see letter XXX, Dalí, *Salvador Dalí escribe*, 71, and "Realidad y sobrerrealidad." On imagination versus what Dalí calls Lorca's "l'instint afrodisíac," see Dalí, "Federico García Lorca: exposició de dibuixos colorits." For imagination versus "la pura inspiració," see Dalí, "Les arts. Joan Miró." References to "teoria espiritualista," "pintura espiritualista," etc. abound in Dalí's article on Lorca's exhibition, just cited. As for the "hecho poético," Dalí writes of "Sant Sebastià" that "net de simbolismes, era un fet en la seva única i senzilla presència," he places a quotation from Le Corbusier concerning the "fait poétique" as an epigraph to an article published March 1928, and the Catalan phrase "fet poètic" appears in two articles that he published in September and October 1927.

radical shift of *gestalt,* enabling the viewer to see the world anew, free of all received ideas and prejudices:

> Precisamente estoy convencido que el esfuerzo hoy en poesía sólo tiene sentido en la evasión de las ideas que nuestra inteligencia ha ido forjando artificialmente hasta dotar a éstas de su exacto sentido real. (XXXVI, *Salvador Dalí escribe,* 89)[19]

As of August 1928, then, Dalí went on to define his current position in this way:

> El surrealismo es *uno* de los medios de Evasión.
> Es *esa* evasión lo importante.
> Yo voy teniendo mis maneras al margen del surrealism, pero esto es algo vivo. (XXXVI, *Salvador Dalí escribe,* 94)

Just as Dalí prioritizes the escape, points to Surrealism as one of the means, and defines his own position alongside, but not inside, Surrealism, so Lorca does exactly the same, and declares his allegiance to the "hecho poético" over dream/the unconscious. But where Dalí would soon advance to a full espousal of Surrealism,[20] Lorca went no further, for he shared with Gasch (and perhaps influenced by him) certain nagging doubts and suspicions.

All this enables us to appreciate exactly Lorca's statements as to what he was aiming at in the *Poemas en prosa*. In the month before he delivered the "Imaginación, inspiración, evasión" lecture, he wrote to Jorge Zalamea:

> Ahora hago una poesía de *abrirse las venas,* una poesía *evadida* ya de la realidad con una emoción donde se refleja todo mi amor por las cosas y mi guasa por las cosas. (*EC,* 587)

and shortly afterwards the oft-quoted passage to Gasch:

---

19   The prior references can be found in letters XXVIII and XXXII (Dalí, *Salvador Dalí escribe,* 67, 74). In letter XXXVI (late August 1928), Dalí exemplifies the *gestalt* shift with how we might perceive a rider on horseback, and in his article on Joan Miró (June 1928), with a similar example involving a canopied cart pulled by a horse; both are repeated in "Realidad y sobrerrealidad."

20   By October, in "Realidad y sobrerrealidad," Dalí was praising on equal terms "todo el arte directo, producido bajo una intensa presión de lo desconocido y de los instintos" (i.e. Surrealism) and "todo el antiarte."

Ahí te mando los dos poemas. [...] Responden a mi nueva manera *espiritualista*, emoción pura descarnada, desligada del control lógico, pero, ¡ojo!, ¡ojo!, con una tremenda *lógica poética*. No es surrealismo, ¡ojo!, la *conciencia* más clara los ilumina.

Son los primeros que he hecho. Naturalmente, están en prosa porque el verso es una ligadura que no resisten. Pero en ellos sí notaras, desde luego, la ternura de mi actual corazón. (*EC*, 588-9)

These poems, then, have been composed without logical control (i.e. the human logic of imagination) and rather with the poetic logic of inspiration, and have hence managed to escape from reality and correspond to his new "manera *espiritualista*."[21] Whether rightly or wrongly, in 1928 Lorca, together with Gasch, still closely associated Surrealism with psychic automatism, and so, while Lorca thought he was doing something quite similar or analogous, it was *not* in his opinion Surrealism, as he remained conscious, while the Surrealists immersed themselves in dreams or the unconscious. The difference between North and South Europe, between the hazy and the limpid, is, *mutatis mutandis,* the same contrast made here between Surrealism (i.e. automatism) and consciousness combined with poetic logic. However, even though it was relatively easy for Lorca to draw the theoretical distinction, unsuspecting readers might have been forgiven for mistaking the texts as examples of Surrealism, given the proximity of the styles and the results.

* * *

ALL OF Lorca's early books of poetry (from *Libro de poemas* through to *Romancero gitano)* clearly operate under the aegis of what might broadly be called a symbolist / postsymbolist / modernist aesthetic, and the first true exploration of the spirit of the avant-garde occurred with the innovative and genre-bending *Diálogos* of 1925. His second incursion came with the *Poemas en prosa,* not coincidentally another hybrid form, and upon reading these pieces, one is most immediately and forcefully struck by their radically illogical quality, both on a micro and macro scale: everywhere there are lexical mismatches, narrative *non sequiturs,* disconcerting juxtapositions, unmotivated actions, and so forth.

---

21   The usual translation of the adjective into English as "spiritualist" is misleading, because of its distinctive connotations. We need to remember that in Spanish *espíritu* can mean mind as well as spirit; the Real Academia gives a range of meanings, among them "Ser inmaterial y dotado de razón," "Alma racional," "Vivacidad, ingenio."

But before exploring further the implications of this style of writing, three other shared characteristics should be noted: (1) pastiche, which here involves the incorporation or more indirect suggestion of various set styles, evoked and combined with a parodic or other subversive intent; (2) a kind of allegory, where the "surface" texture of what masquerades as narrative covers and at the same time gestures to a very different kind of content, not story-telling at all but rather an aesthetic meditation; and (3) a dead-pan tone of recounting extraordinary, incoherent, and often horrific events.

Thus "Santa Lucía" offers a disconcerting mixture of travelogue, hagiography, and biblical tale; "Nadadora" a combination of love story, society column, newspaper *fait divers*, and police report; "Suicidio" another over-wrought love story; "Amantes" love story again, together with mystery novel and autobiographical confession; while "Degollación del Bautista" and "Degollación de los Inocentes" transform the biblical accounts they are based on, the first again adding elements of hagiography and sports page.

As regards the second characteristic, definitive statements are more difficult, as it is not always easy to gauge to what extent the text in question is itself *enacting* the kind of aesthetic upon which it also appears to offer a veiled meditation. The subterfuge is most obvious in "Santa Lucía," with its debts to Dalí's "Sant Sebastià" and that text's barely hidden programmatic nature. Lucy is associated with eyes and sight, surfaces and exteriors, and hence comes to embody an aesthetic stance very similar to Dalí's "Santa Objetividad." Lazarus, on the other hand, is connected with ears and hearing, as well as with death and resurrection, and so comes to represent the opposite to Lucy, interiors, depths, and their subjective exploration. There is no clear expression of preference for one over the other, nor is it clear if the text is propounding a fusion of the two or some kind of equipoise; certainly the style of the writing suggests an intermediate position. Just as in the "manifest" story-line, the subtext of "Nadadora" involves a farewell, not to lovers or friends, but rather to an old world and to outmoded cultural values and artistic approaches: the speaker asserts that after his last embrace with the countess, "dejé la literatura vieja que yo había cultivado con gran éxito. / Es preciso romperlo todo para que los dogmas se purifiquen y las normas tengan nuevo temblor" (*PP*, 68).

With respect to the seemingly emotionless tone, in that letter from late August 1928, Dalí had also written:

¿Feo – bonito? Palabras que han dejado de tener todo sentido. Horror, eso es otra cosa, eso es lo que nos proporciona, lejos de toda *estética*, el conocimiento de la realidad, ya que el lirismo sólo es posible dentro de las nociones más o menos aproximativas que nuestra inteligencia puede percibir de la realidad. (XXXVI, *Salvador Dalí escribe*, 91-2)

and in a slightly earlier missive, the following:

Ningún animal más capacitado para la *crueldad* y antipatía que la palomita.
Ningun animal en cambio más capacitado para la ternura que el *hipopotamito*. (XXXIV, *Salvador Dalí escribe*, 83)

Combining both sets of ideas, in his lecture "Imaginación, inspiración, evasión" Lorca insisted that:

El poema evadido de la realidad imaginativa se sustrae a los dictados de feo y bello como se entiende ahora y entra en una asombrosa realidad poética, a veces llena de ternura y a veces de la crueldad más penetrante. (*Conferencias*, II, 18)

and in a speech as late as May 1929 he still referred to:

el duelo a muerte que sostengo [...] con la poesía.
[...] con la poesía, para construir, pese a ella que se defiende como una virgen, el poema despierto y verdadero donde la belleza y el horror y lo inefable y lo repugnante vivan y se entrechoquen en medio de la más candente alegría. (*Obras completas*, III, 414-15)

The *Poemas en prosa* are the first compositions in which Lorca strives to make good that escape, and in them he also seeks to transcend the traditional categories of aesthetics, eliminate sentimentalism, adopt objectivity, and reach that "asombrosa realidad poética" where tenderness and cruelty coexist and where such apparent extreme opposites might even interact or combine. Reflecting on Dalí's important painting *La miel es más dulce que la sangre* (1927), Lorca had asserted that "la mujer seccionada es el poema más bello que se puede hacer de la sangre" (*EC*, 499), and now he proceeded to put these opinions into practice.

"Santa Lucía" lingers over Lucy's martyrdom, in "Nadadora" the speaker has a scalpel stuck through his throat, and the Countess of X is found with a fork impaled in the nape of her neck, "Suicidio" opens with a severed head and ends with honeymooners' double suicide, "Amantes" similarly suggests lovers' double suicide, despite the alternative cause of death implied by the title, while the gore ramps up, predictably enough, in the two "Degollaciones" (*PP*, 58-9, 67, 68, 70, 71, 73, 75). A howling, blood-thirsty crowd attends the ceremony of the beheading of John, and the narrator exclaims: "Hay que levantar fábricas de cuchillos. Para que el horror mueva su bosque intravenoso" (*PP*, 79). The enthusiastic witness of the second text treats the slaughter of the children as pure poetry, calling it an "¡Alegrísima degollación!" and concluding that "Si meditamos y somos llenos de piedad verdadera daremos la degollación como una de las grandes obras de misericordia" (*PP*, 82).

Lorca's conception of that "asombrosa realidad poética" is certainly reminiscent of the sur-reality of Surrealism, but is it the same? Riffaterre writes that:

> Because logical discourse, teleological narrative, normal temporality, and descriptive conformity to an accepted idea of reality are rationalized by the reader as proof of the author's conscious control over his text, departures from these are therefore interpreted as the elimination of this control by subconscious impulses. This is precisely what creates the appearance of automatism (regardless of whether this appearance is obtained naturally or by artifice). I shall call it the *automatism effect*. (Riffaterre, 223-4)

In his analysis of two passages from André Breton's *Poisson soluble* (1924), he demonstrates how each of the two prose poem-like sections chosen follows a model ("typical folktale," "common sexual fantasy," 224), and the "predictability" produced by the prior familiarity of the reader with the model "can only underscore the discrepancies that create the automatism effect" (224). Although Riffaterre does not refer explicitly to pastiche, what he describes is surely similar to one of the primary effects of the *Poemas en prosa*, which likewise offer tantalizing glimpses of comfortingly recognizable genres in the interstices between the wholesale "departure from logic, temporality, and referentiality" (223). While the laws of syntax are rigorously maintained, incompatibilities or nonsense occur, again as Riffaterre indicates, on both the macro and micro levels: sometimes sentences, logical in themselves, do not "follow" one from the other, sometimes the lexical components within a sentence do not "fit," and often the combination of both. Thus: "Era preferible no haber hablado con él. En las islas Azores. Casi no puedo llorar. Yo puse dos telegramas," or "¿Será posible que del pico de esa paloma cruelísima que tiene corazón de elefante salga la palidez lunar de aquel transatlántico que se aleja?" (*PP*, 76, 73).

On the other hand, Lorca has not been able to banish completely all traces of his powerful image-creating ability, and hence it is on occasions possible to make perfect sense of what at first sight looks arbitrary. One instance will have to suffice. In "Nadadora" the speaker observes that "la orquesta lejana luchaba de manera dramática con las hormigas volantes" (*PP*, 67). A disturbingly strange and unnatural combat is given a very different twist if we conceive of the flying ants as an extravagant metaphor for the semiquavers on the musicians' scores that, given the speed of the music, the orchestra was struggling to play.

Beguiled but not one hundred percent won over by Dalí, with the *Poemas en prosa* Lorca sought to achieve a new departure in his poetic writing, one that paralleled the compositional technique that he was using for his drawings from the same period. But Lorca was also heavily influenced by Gasch, for whom, as for the great majority of Spaniards in the 1920s, Surrealism was virtually synonymous with automatic writing, and so he worked out the theory of the "hecho poético" which achieved much that was distinctly fresh and challenging without falling into the potential traps of dream or the subconscious. But whether the *practice* of the "hecho poético" produced perceptibly different works is a lot less clear. Riffaterre's opinion, of course, is that the question is irrelevant, for the "automatism effect" is purely text-based:

> Thus it really does not matter whether automatic texts are genuine or not; their literariness does not reside in their recording of subconscious thought. Their literariness stems from their function as a mimesis of that subconscious. (238)

Notwithstanding, a few of Lorca's contemporaries and friends did offer their judgements on the matter. Unfortunately, we only have Dalí's reaction to "Santa Lucía" and not the other prose poems from 1928. He wrote to Gasch:

> Supongo que habrás leído el maravilloso escrito de Lorca, que te dedica. [...]
>   Lorca parece ir coincidiendo conmigo—¡oh paradoja!—en muchos puntos, el tal escrito es muy elocuente [...]

Lorca, sin embargo, pasa por un momento intelectual, que creo durará poco (aunque por su aspecto los señores putrefactos creerán que se trata de un escrito superrealista)... (Gibson, I, 527)

In a letter to Juan Guerrero, Vicente Aleixandre predicted that commentators would link his *Pasión de la tierra* with Surrealism, but he asserted that his prose poems "que parecen en libertad, siguen un rigor implacable, el de la lógica poética, que no es el externo de la realidad aparente. Creo que hay un hilo firme que pincha las palabras y las engrana."[22] Aleixandre continued that: "En España esta prosa está inédita. Mejor dicho hace un mes he visto de Lorca una cosa en *La Gaceta [Literaria]* que viene del superrealismo: 'La degollación de los inocentes.' Vamos por caminos diferentes" (Morelli, 21).

Luis Buñuel's response to the same text, in a letter to José Bello, is quite different:

Comprenderás la distancia que nos separa a ti, Dalí y yo de todos nuestros amigos poetas. Son dos mundos antagónicos, el polo de la tierra y el sur de Marte, y que todos sin excepción se hallan en el cráter de la putrefacción más apestante. Federico *quiere* hacer cosas surrealistas pero falsas, hechas con la inteligencia, QUE ES INCAPAZ DE HALLAR LO QUE HALLA EL INSTINTO. Ejemplo de su maldad el último fragmento publicado en la *Gaceta [Literaria]*. Es tan artístico como su "Oda al Santísimo Sacramento," oda fétida y que pondrá erecto el débil miembro de Falla y de tantos otros artistas. A pesar de todo dentro de lo irremediablemente tradicional Federico es de lo mejor, si no lo mejor, que existe. (Sánchez Vidal, 198)

It is surely not coincidental that two of Spain's most thorough-going Surrealists—Dalí and Buñuel (cf. Masoliver and Hernandez, 312)—should concur in finding Lorca's avant-garde writing essentially cerebral ("intellectual," "intelligence"), and hence in contravention of the fundamental principle of Surrealism. In his essay on "The Intentional Fallacy" Wimsatt argued that "the design or intention of the author is neither available nor desirable as a standard for judging the success of a work of literary art" (3), and so Riffaterre is arguably doubly right in insisting on an "automatism effect" that exists in the textual realm and, hence, in excluding *a priori* any inquiries— whose results would, of course, be quite impossible to verify—regarding the

---

22   Morelli, 21. While the first phrase seems to refer to Futurism's "words in freedom," his appeal to "lógica poética" is identical to Lorca's in his 1928 lecture.

actual process of composition.[23] Nonetheless, it is tempting to trust the acute sensibilities of such accomplished practitioners as Dalí and Buñuel; like the expert antiquarian who intuitively senses the difference between a skillful reproduction and the real thing, perhaps they too could tell that Lorca's heart was not quite in it, that the automatic-seeming writing was indeed predominantly cerebral in nature.

* * *

POEMAS EN PROSA as a collection was left unfinished and unpublished. In early editions of the Aguilar *Obras completas*, the texts were grouped together under the erroneous label of "Narraciones" and not even recognized as prose poems. Their first publication as a separate edition in book form occurred in 2000. *Poeta en Nueva York*, although posthumous, followed a very different course. The second English translation, made by Ben Belitt and published by Grove Press in 1955, was "discovered" by a whole new generation of writers and critics, most of them non-Spanish speaking, a literary phenomenon that then gradually seeped back into Spain and contributed significantly to the emerging against-the-grain reading of Lorca as a modernist and antifolkloric writer: it was *Poeta en Nueva York* versus *Romancero gitano,* with the former increasingly triumphant.

But as the *Poemas en prosa* were essentially invisible, they were not recognized or acknowledged as the most profoundly avant-garde and most nearly Surrealist poetry that Lorca ever produced, nor could readers realize that *Poeta en Nueva York* was a step back from the most audacious innovations, and a further stage in the ongoing process of poetic evolution that would lead in the 1930s to *Diván del Tamarit* and *Llanto por Ignacio Sánchez Mejías* (Martínez Nadal, 106; García-Posada, "Lorca y el surrealismo," 171). At the same time, it is hard to escape the impression of the *Poemas en prosa* as exercises, as attempts on Lorca's part deliberately to write his way into the new aesthetic, and, because of the imperative of cool objectivity, it is very clear that the writer behind the texts is not emotionally engaged in their content.

Things are very different in *Poeta en Nueva York*. Where the *Poemas en prosa* foregrounded dislocation, indifference, cruelty, and irony, in the next collection we find Lorca's visceral reaction to the city and the reappearance of certain enduring personal preoccupations that lie squarely within the Romantic-Expressionist-Existential tradition. Stylistically, he stays generally

---

23   Such considerations lead us to the question of whether Surrealism is to be viewed as a literary style or an ethics and/or metaphysics. If the latter, then by definition only those espousing Surrealism could possibly write truly Surrealist works.

faithful to his concept of the "hecho poético," and in the 1932 commentary-recital he warned his audience that:

> esta clase de poemas que voy a leer [...], por estar llenos de hechos poéticos dentro exclusivamente de una lógica lírica y trabados tupidamente sobre el sentimiento humano y la arquitectura del poema, no son aptos para ser comprendidos rápidamente sin la ayuda cordial del duende. (*Obras completas*, III, 348)

However, Lorca is not now aiming to transcend the ugly/beautiful dichotomy and not interested in horror for its own sake, and the metaphor-spinning and often highly symbolic poet, which he had tried to suppress in the *Poemas en prosa,* is allowed to return to the scene (García-Posada, *Lorca: interpretación,* 89).

In point of fact, the poetic discourse in *Poeta en Nueva York* is very varied and mixed, and few critics, other than Derek Harris, have attempted to analyze, categorize, and generalize about it, preferring rather to concentrate on thematic material or explicate individual poems.[24] For the purposes of my analysis, I shall establish four working categories of discourse that can be found in the collection: direct, non-imagistic language, which is actually relatively rare, and at least three levels of imagistic language, each of which I shall seek to differentiate both by its internal functioning and by the degree of difficulty involved in interpreting it. These latter may be described as: (1) straightforward, readily understandable metaphors and symbols, whose modes of operation are already familiar; (2) difficult but nevertheless ultimately decipherable images; and (3) enigmatic, hermetic images.[25]

By direct, non-imagistic language, I mean this kind of phrase: "No es el vómito de los húsares sobre los pechos de la prostituta, / ni el vómito del gato que se tragó una rana por descuido" (*PNY*, 48). Similarly, type (1) imagery can easily be demonstrated. In the lines "No importa que cada minuto / un niño nuevo agite sus ramitos de venas" (*PNY*, 60), the dendritic pattern of the newborn's circulatory system is likened to that of a tree (with the further reverberations of tree trunk-human torso [trunk] and of bloodline/family [genealogical] tree).

---

24   Harris, *Federico García Lorca,* 15; Harris, "La elaboración textual"; Harris, "'Tierra y luna' de Federico García Lorca."

25   I offer more extended analyses of all these types in my article "*Et in Arcadia Ego:* Thematic Divergence and Convergence in Lorca's 'Poema doble del lago Edén.'"

Type (2) takes several forms. One frequently occurring means of producing this kind of imagistic writing is through radical ellipsis and the resulting compression.[26] Thus the line "el árbol de muñones que no canta" (*PNY*, 4) will produce on first reading a disconcerting and troubling impact, but on further reflection it can be "unpacked" and understood quite logically. The "stumps" are not those of felled trees, but rather of amputated limbs, and so here we have a tree that has been severely pollarded; furthermore, if it has no branches (limbs), no birds can perch in it, and hence no singing will emanate from it (Harris, *Federico García Lorca*, 26). The image works in two ways: emotively, as immediately suggestive of nature mutilated and unjoyous, and intellectually, as we tease out and comprehend its precise terms.[27]

Another way of producing type (2) imagery is through the linkage of dramatically distinct symbolic elements that may have an imprecise but emotional impact on the literal level and which can also be "worked out" intellectually on the symbolic level (but note that in this case there is no ellipsis). Thus "mariposa ahogada en el tintero" (*PNY*, 4) immediately elicits feelings of sorrow and distress and of something gone terribly wrong. As we venture further into the image we tease out the various connotations of butterfly: small, delicate, fragile, beautiful, colorful, elusive, and so on, as well as a possible allusion to Psyche, the personification of the soul. Likewise, the inkwell seems to suggest the writer and his craft, in addition to the idea of a miniature well-shaft containing a staining black liquid. When these two symbolic elements are linked by the notion of drowning, various complementary interpretations are generated: in the city the natural is destroyed, the poet can no longer write of the beautiful, colorful, fragile, etc., and perhaps the speaker also feels soulless.

Trompe l'œil images (again to be found in the earliest of Lorca's writings) normally involve an embedded metaphor, and with a minor shift of perception one can grasp, for instance, that the strange scene of "la nieve que ondula / blancos perros tendidos" (*PNY*, 70) actually refers to shifting snowdrifts. One other rather different technique that also creates a certain sense of mystery is direct transliteration. Hence "esos perros marinos se persiguen" (*PNY*,

---

26   Harris, "A la caza"; Derek Harris, *Metal Butterflies and Poisonous Lights*, 89.

27   As with "type (1)" imagery, this technique is again not greatly different from that which Lorca used earlier in his career. Compare two lines from *Canciones* (1927): "Ojos de toro te miraban. / Tu rosario llovía" (from "La soltera en misa"). Here the ellipsis involves first a church painting of St. Lucy with her eyes on a tray, and then the metaphor of beads like raindrops, which are also reminiscent of tears.

78) is not an obscure reference to a rare type of dog or fish, but rather to seasoned sailors—"sea dogs." Likewise "las heladas montañas del oso" (*PNY*, 26) may not be a recondite reference to the topography of the Arctic Circle but rather to Bear Mountain, situated north of New York City and on the way to Newburgh (where Lorca spent a few days).

Lastly, there is a good measure of truly perplexing, enigmatic, or hermetic imagery (type (3)). Sometimes it is possible to assign a broadly negative or positive connotation to it, and sometimes it leaves the reader thoroughly disoriented (García-Posada, *Lorca: interpretación*, 330). Thus the opening of "El rey de Harlem," where the protagonist takes on crocodiles and monkeys with nothing but a spoon, has received extraordinarily divergent interpretations, and no "definitive" reading seems possible. When Lorca writes: "Era el momento de las cosas secas: de la espiga en el ojo y el gato laminado" (*PNY*, 40), the images in the second line are likely taken as negative, but in an unfocused way. The first has a vaguely biblical feel, perhaps combining the usually positive connotations of wheat with the mote in the eye. Animals are frequently under attack in these poems (crushed, flattened, etc.), but why, one wonders, specifically this rather technical verb here?

An important feature to notice is that all these images, whether type (1), (2), or (3), are always cast within grammatically correct sentence patterns. Consequently, when trying—most often in vain—to discover meaning in type (3) images, we encounter disparate and apparently nonsensical lexical elements presented in formally acceptable syntactic structures, and it is here that *Poeta en Nueva York* comes closest to Riffaterre's "automatism effect." An example: "Un traje abandonado pesa tanto en los hombros / que muchas veces el cielo los agrupa en ásperas manadas" *(PNY, 66)*.

Furthermore, sometimes it appears that the incongruous concatenation of words has been determined by a process of acoustic generation (alliteration, etc.) (Harris, "La elaboración textual"; "'Tierra y luna'"); for instance: "las puertas de pedernal donde se pudren nublos y postres" (*PNY*, 48). However, the greatest number of these cases is actually found in discarded manuscript variants, and here, if the links are initially created by some kind of free association, then the results, and the different iterations of the line as it is progressively revised, do seem subsequently to be judged by a conscious, artistic, guiding mind, and then rejected, accepted, or modified as the poet moves on (Harris, "La elaboración textual, 312, 314; "'Tierra y luna," 34).[28]

---

28   Many of the autograph first drafts of poems from *Poeta en Nueva York* are reproduced in facsimile in García Lorca, *Manuscritos neoyorquinos*. We should

If we agree with Marshall McLuhan that the medium *is* the message, then two rather different arguments could be made. The radical disjunction that the poet-persona feels in these urban surroundings, the overwhelming swirl of negative sensations and the tenuous grasp on a sense of self are *rendered* in the discourse itself, as he clings to the architecture of grammar as the only support or structure in a disconcerting, incongruous, dissolving, and hostile world, an experience that the reader then relives at second hand as he or she tries to make sense of the text—in other words, this is again Expressionism rather than Surrealism (Harris, *Metal Butterflies*, 85-7). Conversely, it is interesting to note that chaotic enumeration is not prevalent here, nor do we find the actual breakdown of syntax, equally or even more extreme poetic techniques, which might suggest that the poet-persona had actually succumbed, falling over the precipice into the abyss.

To sum up, I would argue that all type (2) and (3) imagery falls within the scope of Lorca's "hecho poético." These are not hard-and-fast categories, as one always reads this poetry waiting, as it were, for the kind of minor epiphany that will illuminate what had up to that moment been an utterly hermetic phrase.[29] Emotively, a great deal of both type (2) and (3) imagery functions in exactly the same way as Eliot described the "objective correlative" (Harris, *Federico García Lorca*, 12), but unlike the true "objective correlative" some of it can also be teased out intellectually and assigned a fairly clear and unambiguous meaning or value (Harris, *Metal Butterflies*, 86). In part, this is because there is such a strong symbolic current underpinning all the writing in *Poeta en Nueva York*, with elements deriving from mythology, Christianity, Nature, as well as Lorca's own personal "imaginative world." These symbolic elements, though often polyvalent, are not arbitrary or indeterminate. Finally, because all of these kinds of poetic discourse are mixed together in different measures and patterns throughout the poems, an individual text can seem to go in and out of focus (sometimes repeatedly) as the reader progresses through its lines and stanzas, which can appear by turns transparent and opaque. Likewise, some poems are considerably more approachable than others.

The collection covers a number of themes, both philosophical and social in nature. The uniting thread, if there be one, is that of pain and suffering (Havard, 112). The adult human is shut off from the innocence of childhood,

---

remember also that discarded manuscript variants were never intended for public consumption.

29   See, for instance, Rodríguez Herrera's interpretation of some perplexing lines previously commented on by Harris.

he or she struggles unsuccessfully to achieve authenticity or any kind of satisfying human relationship, and is subject to the twin constants of passing time and mortality. The city is a place of inhuman buildings, relentless commerce, runaway consumption, and polluting industry, of avarice, superficiality, rootlessness, alienation, and (hypocritical) organized religion; poverty and exploitation are all around. On occasions Lorca adopts an apocalyptic tone in looking forward, though in vague terms, to a day when all this will somehow be swept away and replaced by a natural, integrated new order.

These are not themes or attitudes that we most characteristically associate with French Surrealism; Lorca is primarily concerned with the real world, with the here and now and the human condition. There is no interest in the state of *surréalité* described in the First and Second Manifestoes nor in setting words free and celebrating this new radical freedom (Harris, *Metal Butterflies*, 114). There is no truly metaphysical exploration here, as the philosophical dimension points directly to Existential concerns, nor did Lorca warm to Dalí's "paranoia-critical method," the gestation phase of which he was able to observe first-hand. Where one does discover a possible overlap with Surrealism is in the desire to cast off bourgeois prejudices and inhibitions; Lorca, like Cernuda, must have imagined a world in which it would be easier to live openly as a homosexual (though the Surrealists themselves were hardly very liberal on this particular issue), and a world with greater social justice, though it should again be remembered that one did not have to be a Surrealist to think like this.

Ironically, by the time that he reached Cuba and then on his return from the New World (1930), Lorca started asserting with regard to *Poeta en Nueva York* what he had vehemently denied concerning the *Poemas en prosa*, namely that the compositions were indeed Surrealist. We have at least two testimonies to this effect:

> Cuando yo llegué a La Habana y fui a buscarlo a su hotel, un simpático hotel de aire colonial, me lo encontré envuelto en su famoso albornoz amarillo, recostado en la cama, en medio de doce o catorce muchachos que le escuchaban boquiabiertos.
> —¿Pero qué es eso, Federico? ¿Qué diablos estás recitando?
> —Son mis poemas de Nueva York y son surrealistas. (Salazar, 30)

> Contaba la memoria oral de sus compañeros de generación que cuando Lorca volvió a España leía el manuscrito de *Poeta en Nueva York*

a los amigos y que—entusiasmado él mismo—preguntaba de vez en cuando: "¿Verdad que es surrealista?" (Blanco Aguinaga, 115)

I believe that we need to take Lorca's judgement with a grain of salt, and that he was influenced by extra-literary factors. In the "Imaginación, inspiración, evasión" lecture, fearing that he was lagging behind the latest trends, he had tried to present difficult but eminently "solvable" metaphors from *Romancero gitano* as if they were true "hechos poéticos," and he would stick to this view in the late commentary-recital of that collection (1935-6: *Obras completas*, III, 343) (cf. García-Posada, "Lorca y el surrealismo," *passim*). These reported comments on *Poeta en Nueva York* are very much, I believe, in the same vein. With one stroke—the publication of *Sobre los ángeles* in June 1929—Alberti had positioned himself at the very forefront of Spanish poetic production, and contemporary critics were calling *Sobre los ángeles* Surrealist, nowadays a debatable judgement. In the summer of 1929, upon his arrival in New York, Lorca was not slow to rise to the challenge of regaining his position on the cutting edge (García-Posada, "Lorca y el surrealismo," 172).

The poems of *Poeta en Nueva York* certainly share some surface similarities with Surrealist works, but the modern critic needs to go beyond Lorca's wishful thinking. If the imagery in the collection is predominantly of the types analyzed above, and if similarly the major themes are as they have been described, then we must entertain very severe reservations regarding the stretching of the Surrealist label to cover a literary work so many of whose facets do not fall squarely within the purview of Surrealism proper (Monegal, "La 'poesía nueva' de 1929," 57-8). There is a clear need in criticism of Spanish poetry of the 1920s and 1930s to distinguish between modernist writing (broadly continuing a symbolist line) and avant-garde writing, and again between avant-garde writing and specifically Surrealist writing. As a case in point, *Poeta en Nueva York* can be found to be solidly avant-garde but very little Surrealist, in intent, theme, or poetic discourse.

Works Cited

Anderson, Andrew A. "Lorca at the Crossroads: 'Imaginación, inspiración, evasión' and the 'novísimas estéticas,'" *Anales de la Literatura Española Contemporánea*, XVI, nos. 1-2 (1991), 149-73.

————. "*Et in Arcadia Ego:* Thematic Divergence and Convergence in Lorca's 'Poema doble del lago Edén,'" *Bulletin of Hispanic Studies* (Glasgow), LXXIV, no. 4 (1997), 409-29.

————. "Sebastià Gasch y Federico García Lorca: influencias recíprocas y la construcción de una estética vanguardista," in *Federico García Lorca i Catalunya,* ed. Antonio Monegal and José María Micó (Barcelona: Universitat Pompeu Fabra-Institut Universitari de Cultura / Diputació de Barcelona-Àrea de Cultura, 2000), pp. 93-110.

Bergamín, José. "Literatura y brújula," *La Gaceta Literaria,* III, no. 51 (1 February 1929), 1, 5.

Blanco Aguinaga, Carlos. *Sobre el modernismo, desde la periferia* (Granada: Comares, 1998).

Bonet, Juan Manuel. *Diccionario de las vanguardias en España (1907-1936)* (Madrid: Alianza, 1995).

Dalí, Salvador. "Sant Sebastià," *L'Amic de les Arts,* II, no. 16 (31 July 1927), 52-54.

————. "Federico García Lorca: exposició de dibuixos colorits (Galeries Dalmau)," *La Nova Revista,* III, no. 9 (September 1927), 84-85.

————. "Les arts. Joan Miró," *L'Amic de les Arts,* III, no. 26 (30 June 1928), 202.

————. "Realidad y sobrerrealidad," *La Gaceta Literaria,* II, no. 44 (15 October 1928), 7.

————. *Salvador Dalí escribe a Federico García Lorca (1925-1936),* ed. Rafael Santos Torroella, special double number of *Poesía,* nos. 27-28 (Winter-Spring 1987).

García Lorca, Federico, *Conferencias,* ed. Christopher Maurer, 2 vols. (Madrid: Alianza, 1984).

————. *Obras completas,* vol. III: *Prosa. Dibujos,* ed. Arturo del Hoyo, 22nd ed. (Madrid: Aguilar, 1986).

————. *Manuscritos neoyorquinos. "Poeta en Nueva York" y otras hojas y poemas,* ed. Mario Hernández (Madrid: Tabapress/Fundación Federico García Lorca, 1990).

————. *Epistolario completo,* ed. Andrew A. Anderson & Christopher Maurer (Madrid: Cátedra, 1997).

————. *Poet en Nueva York,* ed. Christopher Maurer, trans. Greg Simon & Steven F. White, revised ed. (New York: The Noonday Press, 1998).

————. *Poemas en prosa,* ed. Andrew A. Anderson (Granada: Comares, 2000).

García-Posada, Miguel. *Lorca: interpretación de "Poeta en Nueva York"* (Madrid: Akal, 1981).

———. "Lorca y el surrealismo: una relación conflictiva," *Barcarola*, nos. 54-55 (December 1997), 159-174.

Gibson, Ian. *Federico García Lorca*, vol. I: *De Fuente Vaqueros a Nueva York, 1898-1929* (Barcelona: Grijalbo, 1985).

Harris, Derek. "A la caza de la imagen surrealista en Lorca," *Ínsula*, XXXII, nos. 368-369 (July-August 1977), 19.

———. *Federico García Lorca: "Poeta en Nueva York"* (London: Tamesis [Grant & Cutler], 1978).

———. "La elaboración textual de *Poeta en Nueva York*: el salto mortal," *Revista Canadiense de Estudios Hispánicos*, XVIII, no. 2 (1984), 309-315.

———. "'Tierra y luna' de Federico García Lorca: un ejemplo de neorromanticismo surrealista," *Donaire*, no. 5 (October 1995), 33-39.

———. *Metal Butterflies and Poisonous Lights: The Language of Surrealism in Lorca, Alberti, Cernuda and Aleixandre* (Anstruther: La Sirena, 1998).

Havard, Robert. *The Crucified Mind: Rafael Alberti and the Surrealist Ethos in Spain* (London: Tamesis, 2001).

Hernández, Mario. "García Lorca y Salvador Dalí: del ruiseñor lírico a los burros podridos (poética y epistolario)," in *L'"imposible/posible" di Federico García Lorca,* ed. Laura Dolfi (Naples: Scientifiche Italiane, 1989), pp. 267-319.

Marco, Joaquín. "Muerte o resurrección del surrealismo español (I)," *Ínsula*, XXVII, no. 316 (1973), 1, 10.

Martínez Nadal, Rafael. *"El público." Amor y muerte en la obra de Federico García Lorca*, 3rd ed. (Madrid: Hiperión, 1988).

Masoliver, Juan Ramón. "Possibilitats i hipocresia del surrealisme d'Espanya," *Butlletí de l'Agrupament Escolar de l'Acadèmia i Laboratori de Ciències Mèdiques de Catalunya*, nos. 7-9 (July-September 1930), 198-206.

McMullan, Terence. "Federico García Lorca's 'Santa Lucía y San Lázaro' and the Aesthetics of Transition," *Bulletin of Hispanic Studies*, LXVII, no. 1 (1990), 1-20.

Monegal, Antonio. "La 'poesía nueva' de 1929: entre el álgebra de las metáforas y la revolución surrealista," *Anales de la Literatura Española Contemporánea*, XVI, nos. 1-2 (1991), 55-72.

———. "Las palabras y las cosas, según Salvador Dalí," in *El aeroplano y la estrella*, ed. Joan Ramon Resina (Amsterdam / Atlanta: Rodopi, 1997), pp. 151-76.

Morelli, Gabriele. "La escritura surrealista de Vicente Aleixandre: nuevos datos y algunas reflexiones," *Ínsula*, LI, no. 592 (April 1996), 20-22.

Otero Seco, Antonio, "Una conversación inédita con Federico García Lorca," *Mundo Gráfico*, XXVII, no. 1321 (24 February 1937), n.p.

Riffaterre, Michael. "Semantic Incompatibilities in Automatic Writing," in *About French Poetry from Dada to "Tel Quel." Text and Theory*, ed. Mary Ann Caws (Detroit: Wayne State UP, 1974), pp. 223-41.

Rodríguez Herrera, José Luis. "La coherencia de la imaginería surrealista en *Poeta en Nueva York*," *Philologica Canariensia*, no. 1 (1995), 363-80.

Salazar, Adolfo. "In memoriam. Federico en La Habana," *Carteles*, XXXI, no. 4 (23 January 1938), 30-31.

Sánchez Vidal, Agustín. *Buñuel, Lorca, Dalí* (Barcelona: Planeta, 1988).

Wimsatt, W.K., Jr. *The Verbal Icon* (London: Methuen, 1970).

5

Paysage d'âme and Objective Correlative: Tradition and Innovation in Cernuda, Alberti, and García Lorca

T HE NOTION OF THE *paysage d'âme* or *paisaje del alma* seems to have slipped into the standard corpus of literary-critical terminology through the back door. After consulting a variety of studies that employ the concept, I find that none of them testifies to its origin or evolution, somehow implying that both the history and definition of the term are sufficiently well known not to require further elucidation. This widespread phenomenon is exemplified by Hönnighausen's *The Symbolist Tradition in English Literature*, where the author includes a brief section entitled "The Landscape of the Soul" but offers no documentary background to the phrase, which is also used on several other occasions throughout the book (169-71 and *passim*). In this Hönnighausen is joined by a host of other critics, before and after him, who proceed in like fashion. My purpose, therefore, is to present a survey of the ancestry of both technique and label, and then to test the historical boundaries of the procedure in Spanish poetry, in three examples drawn from the late 1920s.

The presence of nature and, more specifically, landscape in poetry goes back to ancient times, but what is understood specifically as the *paysage d'âme* is much more recent, emerging in the mid-nineteenth century. Broadly speaking, landscape poetry involves a number of constitutive features, the most basic being the presence in the text of a subject and an object, the former a human figure or speaking voice, the latter the natural scene, and some sort of relationship between the two. Variation in the kind of connection and interaction between subject and object is the primary factor in giving poems their distinguishing characteristics, flavor, and style. The range of vocabulary used to designate this link is wide: sympathy, affinity, harmony, resonance, interplay, reciprocation, parallel, correspondence, correlation, analogy, allegory, equivalence, consonance, congruence, mirror.[1] The diversity of this terminology points to other important considerations, such as the degree of separation or compenetration between subject and object, the priority of subject over object or vice versa, and the nature of the dynamic or dialectic between subject and object as it is presented in the composition (De Man, 195-96).

Besides the specific details of the relationship, other variables include whether the landscape is perceived as "real" (described in some particularity and geographically localized) or imaginary (a scene that often tends towards generality or rhetorical convention, such as the *locus amoenus*); the implicit attitude of the writer towards the interconnectedness of mankind and nature (whether this is a deep-seated conviction or an expedient used mainly as a structural component); whether the description of landscape serves primarily as some kind of vehicle for philosophical speculation, assertion, or moralizing, or as the embodiment of mood or sentiment; and finally the length of the text (long, discursive elaboration versus concentration and brevity).

Different moments in the development of landscape poetry have tended to exhibit different combinations of cluster-points on these various scales or axes, thereby producing a characteristic set of qualities. To anticipate the gist of my conclusions below, for the *paysage d'âme* it can be said that the object is very much at the service of the subject yet, somewhat paradoxically, in the text the subject may be barely perceptible or totally invisible. Emphasis falls on often complex emotions and states of mind; the landscape is more imaginary than real; the technique is deployed for literary (or psychological) reasons, rather than philosophical or religious ones; and the compositions tend towards shortness and pithiness.

The prehistory of the *paysage d'âme* can be observed in English and French verse from the eighteenth and early nineteenth centuries.[2] Spanish lyric offers a rather different case, less rich in nature and landscape until the mid- and late nineteenth century (Gil y Carrasco, Bécquer, Rosalía de Cas-

---

1   In Abrams's *The Correspondent Breeze* the analyses offered are typically very incisive, but even he fudges the issue: the term "intervolvement" (77) is a neologism that could be added to the list given here.

2   Parallels could be identified in other European literatures, most notably German, but these lie beyond the scope of the present essay.

tro, and Machado).[3] In the English Romantic period, an important antecedent is to be found in a newly evolved form that Abrams baptizes the "Greater
Romantic Lyric" (*The Correspondent Breeze*, 77). With the emergence of this
type of poem, the dynamic or dialectic between subject and object changed,
since the landscape "is both the occasion of reminiscence and the source of
the metaphors by which reminiscence is described," and "the best Romantic
meditations on a landscape [...] all manifest a transaction between subject
and object in which the thought incorporates and makes explicit what was
already implicit in the outer scene."[4]

In the 1830s John Stuart Mill outlined a model of poetic composition
that anticipated what would essentially become, later in the century, the full-
blown *paysage d'âme* technique (Abrams, *The Mirror and the Lamp*, 25). As
Mill observed:

> Poetry is feeling [...] bodying itself forth in symbols which are the near-
> est possible representations of the feeling in the exact shape in which it
> exists in the poet's mind.

> The objects in an imaginary landscape cannot be said, like the words of
> a poem or the notes of a melody, to be the actual utterance of a feeling;
> but there must be some feeling with which they harmonize, and which
> they have a tendency to raise up in the spectator's mind.[5]

And in a review of Tennyson's first two books of poetry, from 1830 and 1833,
Mill wrote:

> Of all the capacities of a poet, that [...] in which he most excels, is that of
> scene-painting, in the higher sense of the term: [...] the power of *creating*
> scenery, in keeping with some state of human feeling; so fitted to it as

---

3   Unamuno comments precisely on this apparently widespread lack of feeling for nature in the first section ("El sentimiento de la naturaleza") of *Paisajes*, 10-13.
So too does Azorín with regard to the Spanish Romantic poets, in "El paisaje en los
versos," 7.

4   Wimsatt, 109; Abrams, *The Correspondent Breeze*, 102. Cf. also Hartman,
391-92.

5   "What is Poetry?" (January 1833), collected in *Essays on Poetry*, 12 and 20.
See also "The Two Kinds of Poetry" (October 1833), in *Essays on Poetry*.

to be the embodied symbol of it, and to summon up the state of feeling itself, with a force not to be surpassed by anything but reality.[6]

The poem by Tennyson that came closest to fulfilling Mill's ideas was "Mariana," from *Poems, Chiefly Lyrical* (1830), and modern critics have been similarly impressed. McLuhan claims that "'Mariana' is there to prove that the most sophisticated symbolist poetry could be written fifty years before the Symbolists" (138-39; cf. 144, 161.). Donoghue usefully nuances this bold assertion: for him, Tennyson "is the first point at which the Symbolist ways become audible in English poetry," and he does indeed "establish a landscape which corresponds so intimately to a 'state of mind' that it becomes that state, for the life of the poem" (106, 97). However, there is a crucial difference from what would later become mainstream Symbolist practice:

> Tennyson puts Mariana into the landscape, but he does not hand over her feeling to the landscape. He tells her feeling directly, by making her tell it in her own words [...] True, most of the feeling is given by the landscape, in the sense that the feeling is contained "in principle" in the details of the scene [...] The effect of Mariana's words is merely to bring out what is already implicit in the scene. But still: Mariana and the landscape are not one and the same, subject and object are distinct. (99)

After Tennyson, English poetry continued to revisit the interconnectedness of the landscape and the self, but not in particularly striking ways (Roper, 8).

In French literature it is also possible to chart a course from Rousseau to Bernardin de Saint-Pierre, Chateaubriand, Lamartine, Nerval, and Hugo, among others. However, it appears that for the half century or more after Rousseau's ground-breaking *Rêveries du promeneur solitaire* (published posthumously in 1782) there was relatively little further innovation. According to Sabin: "The history of French Romantic poetry suggests that the withdrawal to feeling elaborated by Rousseau had only limited value as a thematic and rhetorical source for lyric poetry, at least until Baudelaire added to it a more complex idea of artistic truth" (100).[7] Baudelaire, then, is credited by many

---

6   "Tennyson's Poems" (July 1835), collected in *Essays on Poetry*, 48.

7   This observation might serve to explain why much of the other criticism that I have consulted is largely inattentive to the issue of evolving practice over time: see Béguin; Collot; De Man, 174-82, 200-05; and Moreau, 20-21.

with taking the next, crucial step, which Tennyson could or would not take, and creating the fully fledged psychological landscape in poetic form.[8]

Baudelaire's work demonstrates, for the first time, the complete set of features briefly enumerated above. The balance between subject and object has shifted significantly, and perhaps definitively, towards the former.[9] In conjunction with this change, from Baudelaire onward the emphasis falls more heavily on feeling or mood rather than intellection. Likewise, Tennyson and then Baudelaire begin again to move away from the real-life specificity of the landscape, and the scene is increasingly an imagined one in the later Symbolists. As far as his belief system is concerned, Baudelaire certainly does not share the pantheistic vision of a Wordsworth or a Coleridge. Through all this, the structural model of the poem based on the description of a landscape survives, though inevitably modified, and in particular discursiveness decreases on the way towards the greater concentration and impressionism of the later Symbolists.[10]

Baudelaire, therefore, establishes the paradigm for the *paysage d'âme*, which critics have also referred to as the *paysage intérieur, paysage introspectif,* or psychological landscape.[11] While the building-blocks are still elements

---

8   Donoghue, 104; Hargrove, 27; McLuhan, 153-54. Obviously, the other major innovation associated with Baudelaire is the introduction of city scenes as part of a broader conception of "landscape."

9   Sabin observes that "Baudelaire makes a new kind of symbol out of natural things. He creates a symbol that has spiritual meaning, yet without attributing spirit to nature itself, for the symbol originates altogether in the human mind and it postulates only the spirit of the human observer" (214); this she labels the "self-reflecting symbol" (214, 215). De Man finds that "the relationship with nature has been superseded by an intersubjective, interpersonal relationship [...] the priority has passed from the outside world entirely within the subject" (196). Here he is referring to Coleridge and Wordsworth, but it seems to me that the shift is not fully realized until Baudelaire.

10   On the durability of the model see Abrams, *The Correspondent Breeze*, 78. Regarding the move away from the discursive, Donoghue notes "the withdrawal of comment and reflection" (103) and points out that "the poets were not engaged by the task of 'saying things.' They were concerned with states of mind [...]. The problem of language was to find a verbal equivalent to those states of mind" (96). In this, he is essentially echoing the much earlier French critic Jean Dornis, who stated: "Il ne s'agit plus pour lui [le poète] d'exprimer les idées, mais, imprégné d'elles, de provoquer chez le lecteur, des impressions, des états d'âme qui le conduiront aux confins de l'invisible" (106).

11   Donoghue, 96; McLuhan, 144; Moreau, 17.

drawn from nature, and while they are usually combined into a scene that *could* exist in the real world, increasingly the dominant organizing principle is not mimesis but rather the emotion, mood, or state of mind to be expressed. As Donoghue indicates:

> if any image required for the feeling was not there before your eyes, you could put it in. The great advantage of the landscape technique was that you could adjust the images and arrange the relationships between them in such a way that the "scene" would stand for the feeling just as vigorously as it stood for a certain landscape in Nature. The picture refers "in" as well as "out." (Donoghue, 96)[12]

A good example would be Baudelaire's evocation of dawn in Paris and, through it, of a whole complex of feelings, in "Le Crépuscule du matin" from the "Tableaux parisiens" section of *Les Fleurs du mal* (1857), a poem that Benjamin described as "the sobbing of an awakening person reproduced through the material of a city."[13] Verlaine, Rimbaud, Mallarmé, and Laforgue all borrow much from Baudelaire and further develop the procedure in a variety of directions (Raymond, 3-40). Above and beyond the evident differences between these poets, Donoghue is surely right in seeing that "as this technique developed into the later phases of Symbolism, the human figures were secreted more and more deeply in the landscape," and likewise that "the state of mind is more and more deeply secreted in the landscape, the 'scene'" (99, 103). Finally, from Rimbaud and the late Mallarmé into the early twentieth century, the naturalistic coherence of the imaginary landscape begins to break down, leading to "landscape by means of discontinuity" and "the apposition of widely diverse objects," since "the interior landscape [...] moves naturally towards the principle of multiple perspectives" (McLuhan, 144, 155). As early as Rimbaud's *Illuminations*, probably written between 1873 and 1875 though not published until 1886, Perloff finds an "*anti-paysage*" where "images [...] refuse to cohere in a consistent referential scheme" (45).

While there have been many analyses of the poetic technique of psychological landscape, quite where the precise term *paysage d'âme* comes from is today still far from clear, as the history and evolution of the critical taxonomy

---

12   *Mutatis mutandis*, this is what Dornis is describing when he says that Mallarmé's goal was to achieve in a poem "un parfait ensemble, comme la transfiguration artistique d'un état d'âme complet" (107). See also Abrams, *The Mirror and the Lamp*, 24-25; McLuhan, 144, 154-55; Roper, 78.

13   Baudelaire, 116; Benjamin, 83.

are difficult to trace and not a little contradictory. In researching this essay, I have not encountered any documented study comparable, say, to what Calinescu has to offer for the term "avant-garde" as it came to be applied to literature. However, online databases are increasingly helpful in this regard, and somewhere close to the headwaters of the tradition would seem to stand the Swiss writer Henri-Frédéric Amiel (1821-1881), who kept a massive *Journal intime* from 1839 until 1881. His *Fragments d'un journal intime* was first published posthumously, in two volumes, in 1882 and 1884. In an entry dated to Sunday, 31 October 1852, Amiel wrote: "Un paysage quelconque est un état de l'âme, et qui lit dans tous deux est émerveillé de retrouver la similitude dans chaque détail" (*Fragments d'un journal intime*, I, 55-56).[14] However, this phrase did not appear in print until late 1882, among the first *Fragments* to be made public.

Meanwhile, Paul Verlaine (1844–1896) was at work on the poems that would be collected together as his second book of verse, *Fêtes galantes* (1869). The opening poem of the collection, "Clair de lune," was first published two years earlier, as "Fêtes galantes." The first line of this composition put forth the memorable statement that "Votre âme est un paysage choisi" (Verlaine, *Œuvres poétiques*, 83). Although it comes fifteen years later than Amiel's journal entry, Verlaine's poem is also fifteen years earlier than the publication of that entry. Since direct transmission seems extremely unlikely—Amiel and Verlaine certainly did not move in the same circles—one is forced to conjecture either a parallel history, with each writer formulating his own version of the notion independently, or else a common source for both which has yet to be identified.[15] For the moment, then, definitive resolution of the matter remains elusive.

Once Amiel's proposition had been published, it was soon repeated and commented upon, its acceptance and popularity in some instances no

14   There is a modern critical edition of the text: Amiel, *Journal intime*. There the first half of the sentence is printed in italics, and a slightly different wording appears in the second half: "*Un paysage quelconque est un état de l'âme*, et qui sait lire dans tous deux est émerveillé de retrouver la similitude dans chaque détail" (295).

15   Currently, one candidate would be Maurice de Guérin, whose writings are collected in *Journal, lettres et poèmes*. On 20 January 1834 he had observed that "Rien ne peut figurer plus fidèlement cet état de l'âme, que le soir qui tombe en ce moment" (69); the journal was first published in 1861. In 1835-36 Stendhal had written *Vie d'Henri Brulard*, but the manuscript of his autobiographical novel was not published until much later, in 1890. There he noted that "les paysages étaient comme un archet qui jouait sur mon âme" (15).

doubt reinforced by the notable resonance with Verlaine's famous line. In 1885 Bourget quotes the dictum approvingly though incorrectly: "Quelle admirable entente de la mysticité de la nature que celle qui lui a permis de dire: 'Tout paysage est un état de l'âme'" (285-86). Three years later Ferdinand Brunetière offers another erroneous variation on the phrase: "'Un paysage est un état de l'âme': on se rappelle ce mot d'Amiel; c'est le seul que l'on ait sauvé du naufrage de son *Journal intime*" (217). By 1891 André Gide could write quite naturally to Paul Valéry that: "chacune de ces lettres serait quelque subtil paysage d'âme, plein de frissonnantes demi-teintes et de délicates analogies s'éveillant comme des échos aux vibrations des harmoniques" (43). Two years later, Valéry wrote back to Gide concerning certain aspects of the latter's manuscript of the *Voyage d'Urien*: "il ne faut pas trop y stagner... pas plus que dans les jeux assez tristes du 'paysage d'âme'" (179).

In 1892 the minor Symbolist poet Camille Maryx published a sonnet memorable only for its title, "Paysage d'âme," the term being used, apparently, without any archness or other cloaked intent. The scene of sunset over a "vaste forêt" is entirely conventional, and in the second quatrain the effect of the glow of the setting sun is compared to the light in the eyes of the female addressee. The parallel and, indeed, the correspondence between the woman and the wood at dusk are developed through the tercets; Maryx adapts another famous phrase from Verlaine to describe the wind blowing through the trees "comme de longs sanglots," and the poem closes with the silence of night as an expression of "ton cœur taciturne." Finally, by 1901 Pellissier was able to offer a survey of typical Symbolist practice over the last quarter-century: "En face d'un paysage, [...] le Symboliste, découvrant sous les apparences sensibles ce qu'elles recèlent de latent, traduira la 'correspondance' de ce paysage avec son âme, car l'âme des choses, à vrai dire, c'est l'âme même du poète" (639).

I have not been able to establish exactly when the translated term *paisaje del alma* entered Spanish literary or critical discourse. The earliest documented explicit connection made between "paisaje" and "estado de alma" appears in Pardo Bazán's *La quimera* (1903–05), where Minia states: "El paisaje, en mí, determina el estado de alma" (156). However, it is very likely that this had become a widely known notion in the twenty years between the publication of Amiel's journal and of Pardo Bazán's novel.[16] The first occurrence of

---

16   Azorín cites Amiel obliquely in his newspaper review of Machado's *Campos de Castilla*, "El paisaje en la versos" (1912), collected as "El paisaje en la poesía." In the historical CORDE text-base maintained by the Real Academia Española, the association of "paisaje" with "estado de alma" is found with greater frequency from the late teens into the 1920s.

the precise wording that I have found appears in the title of a prose vignette that Unamuno published in a newspaper in early 1918, entitled "Paisajes del alma," but the natural manner in which he employs it again suggests that the phrase was already in common parlance by that date.[17] What is most plausible, therefore, is that the term *paisaje del alma* entered Spanish usage via turn-of-the-century exposure to Amiel, the French Symbolists, principally Verlaine, and the French theorists of Symbolism.[18] While absolute certainty about the exact phrase may be elusive, there is no doubt that the technique is firmly established in Manuel Machado's *Alma* (1900), Jiménez's early collections *Almas de violeta* (1900), *Ninfeas* (1900), and *Rimas* (1902), and in the first edition of Antonio Machado's *Soledades* (1903). Unamuno's descriptive prose pieces published simply as *Paisajes* (1902) should also be noticed.

The *paisaje del alma* technique, as it appears in Spanish poetry at the turn of the nineteenth to twentieth centuries, was largely in accord with the practice of its immediate French antecedents: the absolute priority of the subject, plausible but probably imaginary landscape (that sometimes tended to cliché in the repetition of certain constitutive elements), use of the technique as a compositional device, the predominance of mood and states of mind, and considerable concision. Poem XXXII, "[Las ascuas de un crepúsculo morado]," from Antonio Machado's *Soledades* (127), exemplifies all of these points. Here the self-effacing observer limits himself to recording a series of features in the overall scene. These lie on three geographical planes: the sunset on the horizon, in middle distance the silhouetted cypress grove, and closest to him the park and its avenues, at the crossroads of which sits the silent fountain surmounted by a stone statue of Cupid. Although never stated explicitly, as demanded by the genre, it is nonetheless manifestly clear, from the opening smoldering embers onwards, that each and every noun, adjective, and verb carries a variety of extended meanings whose ultimate impact and import are determined by, and coalesce in, the scene as a whole, which in turn serves as the embodiment of a particular and highly nuanced state of mind. This demonstrates how a successful poem employing the *paisaje del alma* is always much more than the sum of its parts: the degree of prominence of each natural element in the whole, and their disposition

---

17   The text is collected in *Paisajes del alma*, a posthumous compilation first published in 1944. There are no entries at all for "paisaje del alma" in CORDE. In a search of the Biblioteca Nacional's digitized newspapers and magazines, the first occurrence found is from 1923, in the magazine *España*.

18   See Aguirre; Ferreres; Gayton; and Ribbans.

and juxtaposition, allow for a complex and subtle modulation that goes far beyond the possibilities of plain expository language.[19]

The Symbolist period in France, and the *modernista* period in Spain, represent the maturity and culmination of the *paysage d'âme* technique. But what happened next? Of course, the answer varies with respect to different countries. In Britain, where the Victorians gave way to the Modernists, the procedure seems to have continued, if further adapted and developed, as will be seen below. Abrams still finds "variations on [...] the greater Romantic lyric" and Perloff "symbolist landscapes" in the work of Wallace Stevens and W.H. Auden.[20] In France, the successive waves of Cubist poetry, Dada, and Surrealism would have been largely hostile to the practice, but not so another concurrent tradition represented by Claudel and Valéry. As for Spain, the question has rarely been posed. After Machado and Jiménez and the long line of late *modernistas*, and as new, often more abrasive, poetic styles and strategies came into the ascendancy, did the *paisaje del alma* fall into complete disuse and disappear, or did it continue, suitably modified and adapted into different, associated forms?

It is here that the notion of the objective correlative must be introduced, and in order to explore its precise connection with the *paysage d'âme* it will be helpful to consider a perspective coming from a perhaps unexpected source: Christine Brooke-Rose's *A Grammar of Metaphor*. The kind of metaphor that she dubs "Simple Replacement" is one of the most straightforward: the figurative term is substituted for the literal term (9), which does not appear, and so the reader is obliged to make an effort in order to recuperate the literal component. Regardless of whether the Simple Replacement is largely self-evident or more difficult in nature (33, 46), two further observations can be made. One obvious way in which the reader recognizes metaphorical usage is that the proposition where it occurs is often not literally acceptable or possible, or at the least is very unlikely: the lady would experience considerable discomfort with real roses actually embedded in her cheeks (40). Secondly, given that the literal component is absent, context becomes all-important in deciphering the metaphor correctly: the same figurative terms appearing in different contexts can serve as "replacements" for widely different ideas (28).

What Brooke-Rose describes as a "modern development" of the Simple Replacement typology, which has been "particularly noticeable after the

---

19   As McLuhan writes, "the arrangement of the landscape is the formula of the emotion and can be repeatedly adjusted until the formula and the effect are in precise accord" (154-55).

20   Abrams, *The Correspondent Breeze*, 78; Perloff, 22, 27.

advent of Symbolism," involves the production of a "kind of double meaning" (29) wherein there is a "pleasant ambiguity, that the replacing word also makes literal sense in the sentence" (40); that is to say, "part of the charm [...] lies precisely in the fact that the noun not only can 'replace' more than one unstated idea, but in the fact that it can also be taken quite literally" (29).[21] Quoting a couple of lines from Yeats: "A living man is blind and drinks his drop. | What matters if *the ditches* are impure?," she remarks that

> *The ditches* "replaces" almost anything we care to think up, such as knowledge, life, love, religion, art, but it can also be taken as real ditches. The poet imagines a scene and describes it literally, so that, strictly speaking, in the sense of words changing other words, there is no metaphor, no creative use of language. (29)

The metaphorical link here is becoming very weak, so that the figurative term "ditches" starts to impose itself more in its own right—that is, literally—rather than gesturing to other hidden ideas for which it stands. Brooke-Rose continues:

> Eliot describes a Waste Land, with the dead tree, the cricket, the red rock and its shadow, all symbols which we have learnt to recognise, but the words are simply put down as if he were describing a real landscape. This is usually called "imagery" in criticism, and the technique has been described as that of the "objective correlative."[22] It is the logical development of the Simple Replacement metaphor, stretched as far as it will go. It also means that whatever the poet mentions may or may not have all sorts of symbolic meanings read into it. (29-30)

And this leads her to conclude:

---

21   Compare this with what T.S. Eliot has to say about Baudelaire: "Baudelaire" (1930), in *Selected Essays*: "It is not merely in the use of imagery of common life, not merely in the use of imagery of the sordid life of a great metropolis, but in the elevation of such imagery to the *first intensity*—presenting it as it is, and yet making it represent something much more than itself—that Baudelaire has created a mode of release and expression for other men" (425-26).

22   Brooke-Rose rightly complains that "the use of the term 'image' to cover metaphor as well as literal symbol or description is confusing but frequent in modern criticism" (34).

To my mind, the kind of literal but symbolic noun found in Yeats and Eliot is not metaphor at all, since no other definite though unstated object is being changed into something else: the poet simply mentions something and various connotations arise in our minds, as they might if we ourselves saw the same thing in fact; or he makes them arise in our minds by mentioning it in a context of other objects. Hence the importance of juxtaposition in modern poetry. But the thing mentioned is literal, it belongs to the *scenery* of the poem. (35, emphasis added)[23]

These last two quotations shift from metaphor to symbol or the symbolic: metaphors, in this critic's view, are brought into being by constructions of language (16, 24), and do not need to have been conceived of ever before; indeed, they are typically more successful for being fresh. On the other hand, symbols are usually grounded in cultural tradition, and newly minted symbols may be difficult or impossible to decipher, while the less precise notion of the "symbolic" seems effectively synonymous with connotation (288).

Furthermore, more often than not metaphors do not occur in single, isolated instances, and Brooke-Rose observes, in particular, that "most Simple Replacement metaphors are in fact used in prolonged metaphor [...] rather than entirely alone" (66). While such extended passages are found in all historical periods, "what modern poets have done, especially Eliot and sometimes Yeats and Thomas, is to use the same technique with words which are far less obviously figurative" (67). This fits neatly enough with Eliot's own "foundational" definition of the "objective correlative":

The only way of expressing emotion in the form of art is by finding an "objective correlative"; in other words, a set of objects, a situation, a chain of events which shall be the formula of that *particular* emotion; such that when the external facts, which must terminate in sensory experience, are given, the emotion is immediately evoked.[24]

Brooke-Rose's "prolonged metaphor" is echoed by Eliot's "set" or "chain." Evidently, then, the objective correlative evolves directly and organically out of the *paysage d'âme.*

---

23   Cf. also Brooke-Rose, 67, 91-92.

24   "Hamlet and his Problems" (1919), collected the next year in *The Sacred Wood*, 100. Abrams rightly calls attention to the similarity between Mill's formulations, quoted above, and Eliot's (*The Mirror and the Lamp*, 25).

The continuity of technique through this transition can be witnessed in much of the early production of the Imagist movement, where many poems still seem extraordinarily indebted to Symbolism.[25] Indeed, taken quite literally, the phrase "objective correlative" captures with reasonable accuracy how the described scene in a *paysage d'âme* operates.[26] However, the specific technique of the "objective correlative" as exemplified in works such as *The Waste Land* (1922) differs from the *paysage d'âme* in at least one key way. The requirement—or at least, the recommendation—that the landscape depicted in the *paysage d'âme* be imaginable as existing in the real world is now eliminated, giving way to potentially fragmented, unreal, or fantastic visions that could never be encountered in everyday reality.[27] Thus the internal coherence on the denotative level of the *paysage d'âme* disappears, and the component elements of the new kind of scene can often present a challenge to integration even on the connotative level; indeed, much of their effect may depend precisely on the impression of disparity and disassociation. McLuhan dwells on precisely this feature:

> This landscape by means of discontinuity [...] effected the apposition of widely diverse objects [...] in psychological landscape the juxtaposition of various things and experiences becomes a precise musical means of orchestrating that which could never be rendered by systematic discourse. (144)

and elsewhere he suggests that

> the interior landscape [...] moves naturally towards the principle of multiple perspectives [...]. This is "cubist perspective" which renders, at once, a diversity of views with the spectator always in the centre of the picture, whereas in picturesque art the spectator is always outside. (155)[28]

---

25   A representative example would be Richard Aldington's "Au vieux jardin," included in the *Des Imagistes* anthology prepared by Ezra Pound in 1914: see Jones, ed., *Imagist Poetry*, 53. Cf. Abrams, *The Correspondent Breeze*, 118.

26   McLuhan uses the term insistently with just such a generic meaning (138, 144, 152-53, 155); cf. also Donoghue, 96, and Aguirre, 148.

27   In her analysis of further passages from Yeats and Dylan Thomas, Brooke-Rose states: "In both these examples the metaphor is really a literal object in an imagined scene, though the scene is fantastic" (41).

28   Contrasting Shelley's treatment of landscape with that of Blake and Eliot, Roper employs precisely the same painterly term (78).

The applicability of the concept of the objective correlative to Spanish poetry of the late 1920s and early 1930s has not gone completely unnoticed. It was Luis Cernuda himself who drew attention to just such a technique in relation to certain of his poems in *Un río, un amor*, written in 1929 and published in 1936:

> Quería yo hallar en poesía el "equivalente correlativo" para lo que experimentaba, por ejemplo, al ver a una criatura hermosa [...] o al oír un aire de *jazz*. Ambas experiencias, de la vista y del oído, se clavaban en mí dolorosamente a fuerza de intensidad, y ya comenzaba a entrever que una manera de satisfacerlas, exorcizándolas, sería la de darles expresión.[29]

In this collection there are a number of poems that hint at something of the technique that I am seeking, but "Destierro" is probably the strongest contender.[30] There are the vestiges of a cityscape here—doors, pavements, the sleeping inhabitants, a distant light in a window, and in conjunction with this a clearly defined temporal frame—night then giving way to dawn. The observed, masculine figure walks the deserted, unlit streets, solitary, cold, excluded, insomniac, and ill-starred. These elements certainly put one in mind of the urban *paisaje del alma*. A specific scene is described, but at the same time much of the poem can easily and effectively be read as evoking powerful feelings of alienation and abandonment.[31] For instance, the past participles connected with the doors and the pavements, the quite literal "cerradas," and rather more metaphorical "apagadas," contribute to the physical description and simultaneously constitute a clear invitation to treat the two phrases as distinctly symbolic or connotative. Likewise, the transition from night to dawn is read as holding out momentarily the promise of respite or solace, but immediately the subject is dogged by "sombra" with, in context, a more emotional than literal significance.

---

29   Cernuda, "Historial de un libro (*La realidad y el deseo*) (1958)," 632.

30   Cernuda, *Un río, un amor. Los placeres prohibidos*, 55. Other possible candidates are "Remordimiento en traje de noche," "Cuerpo en pena," "Como el viento," "No intentemos el amor nunca," "Linterna roja," and "Razón de las lágrimas." For a brief but incisive commentary on these poems, see Harris, 162-64.

31   The poem was written on 2 May 1929, while Cernuda was living in Toulouse, but the exile of the title does not have to be read in national terms and can equally refer to a kind of inner exile or exclusion, not from a country but from the community of humankind.

However, this is evidently not a classic *paisaje del alma*, for several different reasons. The text is punctuated, and hence interrupted, by broad, sweeping statements ("Fatiga de estar vivo, de estar muerto, | Con frío en vez de sangre"), and by a kind of hallucinatory anthropomorphism ("Sobre un río de olvido, va la canción antigua"; "Una luz lejos piensa"; "Con frío que sonríe insinuando"). The presence of both these features disrupts the descriptive coherence and concreteness of the urban landscape and at the same time requires the reader to incorporate them into an overall interpretation. And in doing so, they also function as textual flags or indicators, somewhat different from those typically found in Symbolist practice, that there are indeed further, perhaps more abstract, resonances to be found in the nocturnal scene as it is described.[32]

With regard to the function of the objective correlative in Rafael Alberti's *Sobre los ángeles* (1929), Debicki has already made a convincing case:

> El libro entero puede considerarse una gran escena dramática que sirve de "correlativo objetivo" a la visión del poeta. [...] Dentro de esta escena general, diversos ángeles y otros elementos sirven de "correlativos objetivos" estáticos que nos hacen sentir significados y problemas particulares. Combinando así las dos versiones de su procedimiento clave, logra Alberti comunicarnos precisamente sus significados. (292)

I would simply want to push this statement one notch further. While it may indeed be possible to consider the entire book as "a great dramatic scene," whole individual poems within it surely also constitute dramatic scenes, some of which might equally, or better, be conceived of as *paisajes del alma* reinvented in avant-garde terms, and then in turn populated with small-scale objective correlatives.

In "Los ángeles muertos" the overwhelming first impression is of a rubbish dump (Alberti, 154-55). The accumulation of "cañerías olvidadas," "basuras," "charcos," "sortija rota," "escombros," "ladrillo," "muebles desvencijados," "polvo," "casco perdido de una botella," "suela extraviada," and "navaja de afeitar," to cite only the most significant, conjures up the visual scene, just as the successive naming of the items in the text turns the poem, in parallel,

---

32   The most common Symbolist indicators would be, in the first place, the omnipresent, tacit, and diffuse suggestion of implied symbolic meaning in a description of nature and, secondly, those occasions when the speaking subject interjects and more or less explicitly draws a specific parallel between the scene and his "état d'âme."

into a kind of verbal dumping-ground. In his commentary Debicki refers precisely to an "amontonamiento" of modern objects, without realizing just how apt his word choice is: the objects are piled up on the heap just as the nouns pile up in the poem (300).

As with Cernuda's "puertas bien cerradas" and "aceras apagadas," Alberti puts the past participle to especially good use. Things are broken, worn out, lost, thrown away, mislaid, abandoned, and forgotten about, creating a ubiquitous impression of worthlessness, pointlessness, exhaustion, decay, and destruction. This is reinforced by an allied, though slightly less obvious, emphasis on having fallen: the star, the brick, the chimney-stacks, the leaves. Rarely does the text turn to the sky, and when it does, there is always a negative sense associated. The puddles are unable to reflect a cloud and the star is trampled under foot. Lack, void, and death assert themselves in the second half of the poem, with kindling consumed *without* fire, sunken absences, cold, and dust, while the razor blade, apt for acts of violence, finally picks up the oxymoronic angels of the title.[33]

In his lecture "Imaginación, inspiración, evasión" (1928, 1930), and in recital commentaries (1932, 1935) of *Poeta en Nueva York* and *Romancero gitano*, García Lorca referred repeatedly to an effect that he called an "hecho poético." While the metaphor, according to Lorca, is the controlled product of the imagination, it is inspiration that is responsible for this more mysterious trope:

> el "hecho poético" que la inspiración descubre, "hecho" con vida propia, leyes inéditas y que [...] rompe con todo control lógico. Poesía en sí misma llena de un orden y una armonía exclusivamente poéticos. Las últimas generaciones de poetas se preocupan de reducir la poesía a la creación del hecho poético y seguir las normas que este mismo impone, sin escuchar la voz del razonamiento lógico ni el equilibrio de la imaginación.[34]

"Hechos poéticos," then, are phrases or images that function by their own rules, resist logical explanation, and yet are nonetheless ultimately expressive. As he noted in a presentation of *Poeta en Nueva York*, "esta clase de poemas que voy a leer [...], por estar llenos de hechos poéticos dentro exclusivamente

---

33   Another poem from *Sobre los ángeles* with a similar technique is "Invitación al arpa" (144-45), though here the physical description is of the interior of a nineteenth-century house.

34   *Conferencias*, II, 17, and cf. *"Romancero gitano,"* 341.

de una lógica lírica [...], no son aptos para ser comprendidos rápidamente sin la ayuda cordial del duende" ("Un poeta en Nueva York," 348). Despite the different nomenclature and the more "poetic" flavor of the rhetoric, it is clear that what Lorca is referring to is something that comes very close to the objective correlative.

Elsewhere I have argued for the recognition of the impact of the aesthetic ideas of Sebastià Gasch on García Lorca, especially during the period 1927-28, years which cover Lorca's second visit to Cataluña and, immediately thereafter, the most intense phase of their correspondence.[35] Some of Lorca's drawings were exhibited in Barcelona in 1927, and of them Gasch observed that they offered "la traducción de un estado de alma por medio de ritmos de líneas y colores." What is more:

> Los dibujos de Lorca no imitan al natural. [...] El arte no debe cometer la insensatez de querer imitar lo inimitable. Lo esencial para el artista son las resonancias de su mundo interior al chocar con el mundo exterior.
>
> El verdadero artista, con elementos extraídos de la realidad, construye su mundo interior, que alimenta la fantasía. Un mundo interior que guarda almacenados recuerdos de la realidad que se instalan en él, no agrupados según una lógica objetiva, sino según una lógica subjetiva que es la única que interesa al artista. Y estos paisajes interiores son los que plasma el artista en sus obras. Son los que plasma Lorca en sus dibujos eminentemente anímicos, esencialmente poéticos...[36]

This is Wordsworth's "emotion recollected in tranquillity" or Bécquer's "cuando siento no escribo," but with a greater value given both to the subjectivity of experience and to the subjectivity of poetic expression, all of which gives rise to these "interior landscapes" that the artist then exteriorizes and crystallizes in his works. Lorca seems to be remembering Gasch's phrase when he writes in his lecture "Imaginación, inspiración, evasión" that "el poeta está [...] a solas con su paisaje interior" (*Conferencias*, II, 16, 30). And, furthermore, Gasch's conceptualization comes very close, I believe, to Lorca's poetic practice in *Poeta en Nueva York* (written 1929-30, published 1940).

---

35   Anderson, "Sebastià Gasch y Federico García Lorca."

36   Compare also Gasch's similar comments in his letter to Lorca from the middle of January 1928: "Yo [. . .] creo en las resonancias de [las] cosas en nuestro interior, creo en el choque del mundo exterior y de nuestro mundo interior, creo que el lirismo estriba, como dijo un poeta francés en el choque de una sensibilidad sólida al contacto con la realidad," quoted in Rodrigo, 177.

As with *Un río, un amor* and *Sobre los ángeles*, then, some of the New York poems can be read as avant-garde *paisajes del alma*, filled with "hechos poéticos." The most thoroughgoing example is "La aurora."[37] As was the case with Alberti, there are a number of features mentioned that constitute the building-blocks of the physical scene: New York, "palomas," "aguas podridas," "escaleras," "aristas," "cadenas," "barrios." And as with Cernuda, this scene is also peopled, by "abandonados niños" and, in particular, by the workers leaving home for the new work-day: "los primeros que salen."

The first four lines contain two "hechos poéticos": "cuatro columnas de cieno" and "un huracán de negras palomas | que chapotean las aguas podridas." The imprecision of the first of these is part of its strength: although the columns could be seen metaphorically as factory chimneys, as the smoke and soot belching from them, or as the dirt-stained neoclassical portico on a Wall Street building, it is ultimately the emotional impact of the phrase, centered on "cieno," that is important. The second is more intelligible, yet no less expressive: doves, birds of peace, of Venus, should be white, not black, the flock is turned into a figurative hurricane, and their living conditions are repugnant, as they splash around in these fetid puddles. The next four lines focus attention on the sharp-cornered apartment buildings swathed by external fire escapes, with much of the effect coming from the verb "gime" and the contrast between the rectilinear geometry of the architecture and the soft curves and beauty found in nature.

The archetypal connotations of dawn are actualized in lines 9-12, and overlaid on the notion of the Eucharist: ironically, the inhabitants of New York do *not* receive renewal, a new life, a new birth on awaking every morning. The city, as already defined, blocks out that possibility. Given this environment, and the stress on commercialism and materialism found there, the next "hecho poético" can readily be understood: coins, representative of capitalism and greed, organize themselves like swarms of wasps or killer bees (reminiscent of the "hurricane of black doves"), and attack the abandoned children. This fantastic image can be teased out to some extent when it is remembered that a passer-by might toss a few small coins into a begging child's cap or tin, possibly the visual point of departure for the wasps, and also that it may well have been economic conditions that led to the situation of the children.

---

37   García Lorca, *Poeta en Nueva York*, 209. There are several other poems that are informed, to a lesser extent, by a similar technique, such as "Vuelta de paseo," "Nacimiento de Cristo," "Vaca," and "Crucifixión."

After they awake, the workers start to leave their apartment houses, but they know, in their bones, that, contrary to traditional associations, the dawning of a new day in New York does not bring with it anything positive: here in the city there is and will be no idyllic paradise or salvation, no innocent love (the "she loves me, she loves me not" plucking of a flower's petals). Rather, they must go and perform their thankless, workaday tasks, governed by the rules of the metropolis and Wall Street. Finally, in the last four lines, the very essence of dawn—light—is negated. Here it is shackled, literally and figuratively, by the port and industry; technology and machinery, alienating, rootless, inhuman, govern the day. Negation is coupled with absence, in the repetition "sin arte, sin fruto, sin raíces." The poem closes with a final panorama of the boroughs, rather like a cinematographic aerial shot. Unrefreshed by their night of restless, fitful sleep, or sleeplessness, caused by the alienating environment in which they must needs exist, the inhabitants stagger along, half-awake, like survivors emerging from a wreck. Although the wreck itself may have been violent and bloody, the mention of blood gestures also to more conventional Symbolist and *modernista* descriptions not of sunrise but of sunset. If sunset can be rendered, conventionally, as the drowning of the sun on the western horizon, then dawn in New York is invested with the negative connotations of dusk. Dawn here is not elevation but sinking, not light but spilt blood.

Once again the poem functions literally and symbolically, giving a vision of New York City life and at the same time using the particularities of that vision to stimulate in the reader a complex set of emotional responses. Lorca's dawn scene of Manhattan invites comparison with Baudelaire's dawn scene of Paris, though I am not suggesting any direct, textual connection. In "La aurora" the picture is still imaginable, but it is fragmented, with abrupt and unexpected transitions and the commingling of more abstract elements with the concrete description, creating precisely what I conceive of as the avant-garde *paisaje del alma*.

Cernuda, Alberti, and Lorca all read Bécquer, Darío, Machado, and Jiménez and had varying exposure to the French tradition, and hence would have been thoroughly conversant with the *paysage d'âme* technique. The fact that this characteristically Symbolist strategy lives on into their avant-garde phase says something important, I believe, about their allegiances, influences, and poetic practice at this time. Marjorie Perloff writes that

> what we loosely call "Modernism" in Anglo-American poetry is really made up of two separate though often interwoven strands: the Symbol-

ist mode that Lowell inherited from Eliot and Baudelaire and, beyond them, from the great Romantic poets, and the "anti-Symbolist" mode of indeterminacy or "undecidability," of literalness and free play, whose first real exemplar was the Rimbaud of the *Illuminations*. (vii)

She goes on to develop this idea by considering *The Waste Land*, which, she finds, "has, despite its temporal and spatial dislocations and its collage form, a perfectly coherent symbolic structure" (13). Consequently:

> However difficult it may be to decode this complex poem, the relation-ship of the word to its referents, of signifier to signified, remains essen-tially intact. It is [...] the undermining of precisely this relationship that characterizes the poetry of Rimbaud and his heirs. (17-18)

There can be few critics who would call the Eliot of *The Waste Land* avant-garde, and surely none who would characterize him as Surrealist. The pre-ferred term here, as just seen, is Modernist, in contradistinction to the more radical "mode of indeterminacy or 'undecidability.'" This in turn suggests that we need to approach with caution and perhaps reassess the most fre-quent categorizing labels that have been applied to Spanish poetry from the end of the 1920s by Cernuda, Alberti, Lorca, and others, where, as has been demonstrated, the objective correlative is a dominant feature and the *paisaje del alma* lingers on in a transformed yet still recognizable form.

Works Cited

Abrams, M.H. *The Mirror and the Lamp: Romantic Theory and the Critical Tradition*, 2nd ed. (Oxford: Oxford UP, 1971).

———. *The Correspondent Breeze: Essays on English Romanticism*, foreword by Jack Stillinger (New York: Norton, 1984).

Aguirre, J.M. *Antonio Machado, poeta simbolista*, 2nd ed. (Madrid: Taurus, 1982).

Alberti, Rafael. *Sobre los ángeles. Yo era un tonto y lo que he visto me ha hecho dos tontos*, ed. C. Brian Morris (Madrid: Cátedra, 1981).

Amiel, Henri-Frédéric. *Fragments d'un journal intime*, ed. Edmond Scherer, 2 vols.: I (Paris: Sandoz et Thuillier; Geneva: Librairie Desrogis; Neuchâtel: Librairie J. Sandoz, 1883 [*sic*: late 1882]); II (Paris: P. Robert; Geneva, Bâle; Lyon: H. Georg, 1884).

————. *Journal intime*, ed. Bernard Gagnebin and others, 12 vols. (Lausanne: L'Âge d'Homme, 1976-1994), II, ed. Bernard Gagnebin and others (1978).

Anderson, Andrew A. "Sebastià Gasch y Federico García Lorca: influencias recíprocas y la construcción de una estética vanguardista," in *Federico García Lorca i Catalunya*, ed. Antonio Monegal and José María Micó (Barcelona: Institut Universitari de Cultura, Universitat Pompeu Fabra/ Àrea de Cultura, Diputació de Barcelona, 2000), pp. 93-110.

Azorín, "El paisaje en los versos," *ABC*, 2 August 1912, pp. 6-7.

————, "El paisaje en la poesía," in *Clásicos y modernos* (Madrid: Rafael Caro Raggio, 1919), pp. 99-105.

Baudelaire, Charles. *Les Fleurs du mal*, ed. Antoine Adam (Paris: Garnier, 1961).

Béguin, Albert. *L'Âme romantique et le rêve: essai sur le romantisme allemand et la poésie française* (Paris: Corti, 1967).

Benjamin, Walter. *Charles Baudelaire: A Lyric Poet in the Era of High Capitalism*, trans. by Harry Zohn (London: NLB, 1973).

Bourget, Paul. *Nouveaux essais de psychologie contemporaine* (Paris: Alphonse Lemerre, 1885).

Brooke-Rose, Christine. *A Grammar of Metaphor* (London: Secker & Warburg, 1958).

Brunetière, Ferdinand. "Symbolistes et décadents," *Revue des Deux Mondes*, XC, no. 1 (1 November 1888), 213-26.

Calinescu, Matei. *Five Faces of Modernity: Modernism. Avant-Garde. Decadence. Kitsch. Postmodernism* (Durham, NC: Duke UP, 1987).

Cernuda, Luis. *Un río, un amor. Los placeres prohibidos*, ed. Derek Harris (Madrid: Cátedra, 1999).

————. "Historial de un libro (*La realidad y el deseo*) (1958)," in *Obra completa*, II: *Prosa I*, ed. Derek Harris and Luis Maristany, 2nd ed. (Madrid: Siruela, 2002), pp. 625-61.

Collot, Michel. "Paysage et subjectivité," in *Modernité et romantisme*, ed. Isabelle Bour and others (Paris: Champion, 2001), pp. 235-50.

De Man, Paul. *Blindness and Insight: Essays in the Rhetoric of Contemporary Criticism*, intro. by Wlad Godzich, rev. 2nd ed. (Minneapolis: U of Minnesota P, 1983).

Debicki, Andrew P. "El 'correlativo objetivo' en la poesía de Rafael Alberti," in Debicki, *Estudios sobre poesía española contemporánea: la generación de 1924-1925*, 2nd ed. (Madrid: Gredos, 1981), pp. 265-304.

Donoghue, Denis. *The Ordinary Universe: Soundings in Modern Literature* (London: Faber & Faber, 1968).

Dornis, Jean. *La Sensibilité dans la poésie française contemporaine (1885-1912)* (Paris: Arthème Fayard, [1912]).

Eliot, T.S. "Baudelaire," in *Selected Essays*, 3rd enlarged ed. (London: Faber & Faber, 1972), pp. 419-30.

————. "Hamlet and his Problems," in *The Sacred Wood: Essays on Poetry and Criticism* (repr. London: Methuen, 1974), pp. 95-103.

Ferreres, Rafael. *Verlaine y los modernistas españoles* (Madrid: Gredos, 1975).

García Lorca, Federico. "Imaginación, inspiración, evasión," in *Conferencias*, ed. Christopher Maurer, 2 vols. (Madrid: Alianza, 1984), II, pp. 9-31.

————. "*Romancero gitano*," in *Obras completas*, III: *Prosa. Dibujos*, ed. Arturo del Hoyo, 22nd ed. (Madrid: Aguilar, 1986), pp. 339-46.

————. "Un poeta en Nueva York," in *Obras completas*, III: *Prosa. Dibujos*, ed. Arturo del Hoyo, 22nd ed. (Madrid: Aguilar, 1986), pp. 347-58.

————. *Poeta en Nueva York*, ed. Andrew A. Anderson (Barcelona: Galaxia Gutenberg, 2013).

Gasch, Sebastián. "Lorca dibujante," *La Gaceta Literaria*, II, no. 30 (15 March 1928), 4.

Gayton, Gillian. *Manuel Machado y los poetas simbolistas franceses* (Valencia: Bello, 1975).

Gide, André, and Paul Valéry. *Correspondance 1890-1942*, ed. Robert Mallet (Paris: Gallimard, 1955).

Guérin, Maurice de. *Journal, lettres et poèmes*, ed. G. S. Trébutien, prologue by M. Sainte-Beuve, 2nd ed. (Paris: Didier, 1862).

Harris, Derek. *Metal Butterflies and Poisonous Lights: The Language of Surrealism in Lorca, Alberti, Cernuda and Aleixandre* (Anstruther: La Sirena, 1998).

Hartman, Geoffrey H. "Wordsworth, Inscriptions, and Romantic Nature Poetry," in *From Sensibility to Romanticism: Essays Presented to Frederick A. Pottle*, ed. Frederick W. Hilles and Harold Bloom (New York: Oxford UP, 1965), pp. 389-413.

Hargrove, Nancy Duvall. *Landscape as Symbol in the Poetry of T.S. Eliot* (Jackson: UP of Mississippi, 1978).

Hönnighausen, Lothar. *The Symbolist Tradition in English Literature: A Study of Pre-Raphaelitism and "Fin de Siècle"* (Cambridge: Cambridge UP, 1988).

Jones, Peter, ed. *Imagist Poetry* (Harmondsworth: Penguin, 1972).

Machado, Antonio. *Soledades. Galerías. Otros poemas*, ed. Geoffrey Ribbans (Madrid: Cátedra, 1983).

Maryx, Camille. "Paysage d'âme," *Mercure de France*, VI, no. 34 (October 1892), 161.

McLuhan, Marshall. *The Interior Landscape: The Literary Criticism of Marshall McLuhan 1943-1962*, ed. Eugene McNamara (New York: McGraw-Hill, 1969).

Mill, John Stuart. *Essays on Poetry*, ed. F. Parvin Sharpless (Columbia: U of South Carolina P, 1976).

Moreau, Pierre. *Âmes et thèmes romantiques* (Paris: Corti, 1965).

Pardo Bazán, Emilia. *La quimera*, ed. Marina Mayoral (Madrid: Cátedra, 1991).

Pellissier, Georges. "L'Évolution de la poésie dans ce dernier quart de siècle," *La Revue et Revue des revues*, XXXVI, no. 6 (15 March 1901), 638-49.

Perloff, Marjorie. *The Poetics of Indeterminacy: Rimbaud to Cage* (Princeton: Princeton UP, 1981).

Raymond, Marcel. *From Baudelaire to Surrealism* (New York: Wittenborn, Schultz, 1950).

Ribbans, Geoffrey. "La influencia de Verlaine en Antonio Machado," in *Niebla y soledad: aspectos de Unamuno y Machado* (Madrid: Gredos, 1971), pp. 255-87.

Rodrigo, Antonina. *García Lorca, el amigo de Cataluña* (Barcelona: EDHASA, 1984).

Roper, Alan. *Arnold's Poetic Landscapes* (Baltimore: Johns Hopkins UP, 1969).

Sabin, Margery. *English Romanticism and the French Tradition* (Cambridge, MA: Harvard UP, 1976).

Stendhal, *Vie d'Henri Brulard*, ed. Henri Martineau (Paris: Garnier, 1953).

Unamuno, Miguel de. *Paisajes* (Salamanca: Est. Tip. Calón, 1902).

———. "Paisajes del alma," *El Sol*, 6 January 1918, p. 5.

———. *Paisajes del alma*, ed. M. García Blanco (Madrid: Alianza, 1997).

Verlaine, Paul. "Fêtes galantes," *La Gazette rimée*, no. 1 (20 February 1867), 11.

———. *Œuvres poétiques*, ed. Jacques Robichez (Paris: Garnier, 1969).

Wimsatt, W. K., Jr. *The Verbal Icon: Studies in the Meaning of Poetry* (London: Methuen, 1970).

6
Imagery and How it Works in Lorca's *Poeta en Nueva York*: The Case of "1910 (Intermedio)"

"IMAGE" AND "IMAGERY" MUST be two of the most used and abused terms in modern literary criticism of poetry, but nevertheless I intend to use them in what follows, for reasons that will be explained below. My goals here are several: to provide a brief overview of the range of meanings attached to "image" and "imagery"; to offer a detailed stylistic analysis of one poem from *Poeta en Nueva York*, "1910 (Intermedio)," in an effort to illustrate certain kinds of imagery that are present both here and in other poems in the collection; and finally to locate my findings within the much broader and still unresolved debate over Lorca's possible stylistic affiliation with Surrealism.

We can trace some of the confusion regarding the literary-critical usages of "image" all the way back to Aristotle. In his *Rhetoric* he employs the Greek word *eikôn* (likeness, image) to denote a simile and *metaphora* for metaphor, and states that the only difference between the two is the presence or absence of a linking word (like, as, etc.) (*Rhetoric*, 3.4.1-4). Greek *eikôn* is translated in Latin as *imago*, the former giving us English "icon" and the latter "image," both words in their more basic senses closely linked with the ocular/pictorial.[1] Thus the notion of the image as both some sort of visually perceived representation *and* a rhetorical trope is enshrined from ancient times.[2]

---

1   In Latin rhetorics, subtle distinctions were made between *imago* and *similitudo*: for an exhaustive exploration of this topic, see McGavin, chapter 1.

2   In his essay on "'Figura,'" Auerbach traces a parallel history of the evolution of the meaning of that term from plastic form to rhetorical figure, and closes with useful comments on Quintilian's distinction between figure and trope (11-28).

Very little has been written on the history of the use of these terms in Spanish literary criticism. Gracián, in the middle of the seventeenth century, employs the word "imagen" in interesting ways in his discussion of "De la agudeza por semejanza." He opens with the broad statement that "la semejanza es origen de una inmensidad conceptuosa," a claim that he justifies by pointing out that "de ella [la semejanza] manan los símiles conceptuosos y disímiles, metáforas, alegorías, metamorfosis, apodos y otras innumerables diferencias de sutileza" (Gracián, I, 114). He then elaborates on how this kind of trope is constructed:

> En este modo de conceptuar caréase el sujeto, no ya con sus adyacentes proprios, sino con un término extraño, como imagen, que le exprime su ser o le representa sus propriedades, efectos, causas, contingencias y demás adjuntos, no todos, sino algunos, o los más principales. (Gracián, I, 114)

The "concepto por semejanza," then, involves the "sujeto" (I. A. Richards's "tenor") being set beside a "término extraño" ("vehicle"), which he glosses as "imagen," suggesting that its meaning for him can extend well beyond the exclusively optical. A few pages later, he nuances this initial description, tempering "extraño" with "conforme," but again using "imagen" in a fairly open sense: "Siempre ha de ser conforme el término de la asimilación, porque como se escoge para imagen, se requiere en él la propiedad" (Gracián, I, 121). The database of the Hemeroteca Digital (Biblioteca Nacional, Madrid) offers instances of the use of the phrase "imagen poética" from 1793 onwards, but "imaginería poética" only from 1927.[3] In his 1957 discussion of Gómez de la Serna's *greguerías*, the distinction that Cernuda draws between metaphor and image is both unhelpful and clearly flawed, perhaps reflecting the ongoing lack of a tradition of critical inquiry into this topic (Cernuda, 129-30).

More detailed historical research has been carried out in the field of English literature and criticism. Frazer demonstrates that for Renaissance writers, images were essentially visual, while rhetorical tropes were commonly known as "figures" (Frazer, 149-50). After 1660, a major change in taste exiled the metaphor from both creative writing and criticism. Then, in the eighteenth century, as poetry became highly descriptive, images (in the pictorial sense) came to be mentioned with increasing frequency, and so in the latter half of the century the term "image" was gradually extended to encompass

---

3   In CORDE (Real Academia Española), the attestations for "imagen poética" are much later, and there are none for "imaginería poética."

figurative language, filling the gap left by "metaphor" (Frazer, 150-59). For his part, Furbank (27-30) takes issue with Frazer's chronology: he suggests that the shift really occurred somewhat later, and attributes the cause mainly to Coleridge and his theory of the imagination.[4]

More than one subsequent commentator has pointed out that, in the influential twentieth-century work by C. Day Lewis *The Poetic Image*, the author fails to make a clear distinction and at moments employs the term in both its acceptations.[5] In fact, modern-day manuals of literary-critical terminology and introductory works of criticism rarely coincide in their definitions of "image."[6] Some limit it to simile and metaphor; others would extend it to other rhetorical tropes. For some, simile and metaphor are virtually identical and for others much more distinct; for more than one scholar a true metaphor is created when only the figurative term appears, and if both appear (the tenor *and* the vehicle), then it is an image; on the other hand, Ullmann argues that "there are many metaphors and comparisons which cannot be regarded as images. [.. .] [T]here can be no question of an image unless the resemblance it expresses has a concrete and sensuous quality" (178). The collective notion of "imagery" can range over a wide terrain, and sometimes critics apply it not just to the ensemble of figurative language to be found in a poem or a collection but expand it to encompass that which is broadly symbolic (Mitchell, 24-25).[7] My own perspective on the issue is slightly different: while simile, metaphor, metonymy, synecdoche, personification, etc. should be used with precision and in accordance with the most commonly held definitions, I believe that the concepts of "image" and "imagery" still have a role to play, as umbrella terms for distinctive types of figurative language that have no classical label and which in most cases only originated in the later nineteenth or twentieth centuries.

The 1910s and 20s saw the publication of many programmatic statements on the topic. For Marinetti, writing in 1912, images are "the very lifeblood of

---

4   Evidently, the etymology of "imagination" links directly to Latin *imaginari* and *imago*.

5   In Lewis's book, see, for example, p. 18.

6   Furbank offers the most comprehensive critique of this situation; see also Mitchell, 19-31, and Ziolkowski, 6-9.

7   I would contend that most symbols originate and inhere in culture, while personal symbols can also be created by writers, most typically through textual repetition (see Wheelwright, 92- 110, and Ullmann, 193). The components of individual linguistic metaphors that are neither inscribed in culture nor subsequently repeated in a literary work cannot rise to the level of the symbolic.

poetry" and hence "poetry should be an uninterrupted flow of new images" (120); they are the product of intuition, which captures analogies, analogy being "the deep love that binds together things that are remote, seemingly diverse or inimical" (121, 120). To achieve the revolution in poetic language that he sought, it was necessary to eliminate the connector words of comparisons and similes and "better yet, to merge the object directly into the image which it evokes, foreshortening the image to a single essential word" (120). This is the goal that Marinetti called "wireless imagination," achieved "when we dare to suppress all the first terms of our analogies in order to render nothing other than an uninterrupted sequence of second terms" (123).

In 1913, Ezra Pound defined an image as presenting "an intellectual and emotional complex in an instant of time" and argued that it was this particular effect "which gives that sense of sudden liberation" ("A Few Don'ts," 200). The following year, he wrote of the "'one image poem'" that "is a form of super-position, that is to say, it is one idea set on top of another. [...] [O]ne is trying to record the precise instant when a thing outward and objective transforms itself, or darts into a thing inward and subjective"; as an example he cites his poem "In a Station of the Metro" ("Vorticism," 467). Using the analogy of equations in analytic geometry, which "cause form to come into being," he explains that "by the 'image' I mean such an equation [...] about *sea, cliffs, night*, having something to do with mood" ("Vorticism," 469). Pound's concept of the "image" comes fairly close to how his friend T. S. Eliot articulated the "objective correlative" in 1919, which is clearly a kind of image yet does not fall into any of the classical categories:

> The only way of expressing emotion in the form of art is by finding an "objective correlative"; in other words, a set of objects, a situation, a chain of events which shall be the formula of that *particular* emotion; such that when the external facts, which must terminate in sensory experience, are given, the emotion is immediately evoked. ("Hamlet and his Problems," 941)

In the same year, Eliot also wrote of "various feelings, inhering for the writer in particular words or phrases or images, [which] may be added to compose the final result [the poem]" ("Tradition and the Individual Talent–II," 72).[8]

---

8   Eliot develops here on a proposition found in T.E. Hulme's "Lecture on Modern Poetry" of 1908/9, where Hulme is still really describing the *paysage d'âme* technique rather than the objective correlative: "We are [...] concerned [...] that some vague mood shall be communicated [...]. Say the poet is moved by a certain

For Pierre Reverdy, in 1918, the "image" was not a comparison but rather the juxtaposition of two more or less distant elements; it depended on the two having some remote but at the same time "true" or "appropriate" connection, and it failed if there were no link at all or if the two were direct opposites. However, Reverdy's definition begs the question inasmuch as he does not tell us in what such "rapports [...] justes" might consist. André Breton's "Manifeste du surréalisme" (1924) offered a decidedly revisionist reading of Reverdy's pronouncements. While Breton accepts the basic notion of the "rapprochement de deux réalités plus ou moins éloignées" (Reverdy, n.p.) he rejects the idea that they are brought together voluntarily, that is to say consciously, with any degree of premeditation ("une création pure de l'esprit": Reverdy, n.p.). Thus Breton echoes Reverdy in asserting that the quality of the image obtained depends on the degree of difference between the two components involved, with a slight dissimilarity producing only a humdrum comparison. But for him it is the somehow *fortuitous* bringing-together of two disparate terms that we should aim for, as it is from this event that springs the "spark," the sought-after "lumière de l'image" (51). Furthermore, he does not believe that it falls within the power of human beings deliberately to arrange the conjunction of two realities that start out being so far apart, and hence he is obliged to conclude that "ils sont les produits simultanés de l'activité que j'appelle surréaliste" (51). Needless to say, Breton's choice of the word "fortuit" alludes directly back to Lautréamont's *Les Chants de Maldoror* (1869), where a series of similes attempting to capture something of the teenager Mervyn's beauty culminates in the famous line: "surtout, comme la rencontre fortuite sur une table de dissection d'une machine à coudre et d'un parapluie!" (Ducasse, 290), a proposition that anticipates Breton's Surrealist theories much more directly than do any of Reverdy's.

The critic Philip Wheelwright coined the term *diaphor* for a type of metaphor that seems to have somewhat more in common with Reverdy's image than with Breton's, since he defines it as characterized by "the creation of new meaning by juxtaposition and synthesis" (72). He also distinguishes *diaphor* from *epiphor*, the latter being "the outreach and extension of meaning through comparison" (72). According to Wheelwright, pure diaphor is next to impossible to achieve in writing—Gertrude Stein appears to come

---

landscape, he selects from that certain images which, put into juxtaposition in separate lines, serve to suggest and to evoke the state he feels" (264-66). On the evolution of one technique into the other, see Brooke-Rose, 29-35; McLuhan, 135-55; and Anderson, "*Paysage d'âme* and Objective Correlative," 170-77.

closest,[9] for "as soon as the [diaphoric] contrast is viewed in a larger context, an element of epiphor peers forth," as in a reading of the two lines of Pound's "In a Station of the Metro" (80). Nonetheless, the diaphoric aspect is important for "the sheer presentation of diverse particulars in a newly designed arrangement" (81). The degree of actual or perceived haphazardness in the juxtaposition is variable:

> In some instances, a diaphoric synthesis is held together and as it were symbolized by a presiding image. Such an image may be chosen arbitrarily, by the poet's private sense of some hidden or potential congruence, or it may have some already recognizable relevance. (83)

Indeed, Wheelwright concludes that "usually the most interesting and effective cases of metaphor are those in which there is in some manner or other a combination of epiphoric and diaphoric factors" (86).

Although Lorca titles his 1926 lecture "La imagen poética de don Luis de Góngora," it is unequivocally clear that what he is exclusively interested in here is metaphor, and that he is using the two terms interchangeably. According to the most straightforward definition that he offers in his text, "la metáfora une dos mundos antagónicos por medio de un salto ecuestre que da la imaginación," and he praises Góngora in particular because this poet "armoniza y hace plásticos de una manera violenta en ocasiones los mundos más distintos" ("La imagen poética," I, 101-02).[10] Elaborating figuratively on these statements, Lorca asserts that his idea of a "good" metaphor involves it being both challenging yet ultimately intelligible (and, hence, able to be appreciated): "El núcleo se abre como una flor que nos sorprende por lo desconocida, pero en el radio de luz que lo rodea hallamos el nombre de la flor y aspiramos la calidad de su perfume" (I, 101).

Two and a half years later, Lorca offered a strikingly different viewpoint in his lecture "Imaginación, inspiración, evasión." Góngora as a model is replaced by San Juan de la Cruz, imagination (the motive force behind metaphor) is superseded by inspiration, and now instead of metaphor Lorca is interested in what he calls the "hecho poético" (II, 14-17, 20, 21, 26). Imagination, he tells us, is limited by reality, reason, and "nuestra lógica humana," and so the poet needs to strive to free himself in order that he might work

---

9   Note that, with the exception of Mallarmé, Wheelwright limits his examples to English language literature.

10   Further references to the *Conferencias* volumes are given in the text as volume and page number.

in the sphere of inspiration, which moves in "las ascuas sin lógica ni sentido" and operates according to "una lógica poética" (II, 14-17). To achieve that liberation and hence escape (the "evasión" of his title), "se necesita saber rechazar con vehemencia toda tentación de ser comprendido" (II, 20). Finally, what inspiration "discovers" or "invents" is the "hecho poético," evidently a kind of image significantly different from metaphor (II, 17, 20). His description of the "hecho poético" is more lyrical than precise, but we can intuit something of its nature when he states that it affords the reader access to "emoción poética," that "las últimas generaciones de poetas se preocupan de reducir la poesía a la creación del hecho poético [...], sin escuchar la voz del razonamiento lógico," and that "Juan Larrea y su discípulo Gerardo Diego construyen poemas a base de hechos poéticos encadenados" (II, 15, 17, 25, 26).

Lorca also wrote about the "hecho poético" in the unfinished prose dialogue "Corazón bleu y cœur azul," which must date from 1927 or 1928. He again couches his goal in lyrical terms: "unir un término vulgar y lejano con la pequeña paloma que late entre mis dedos," and he reaffirms his quest for "el hilo quebradizo que una todas las cosas con cada cosa y a cada cosa con todas las demás" (91). Indeed, thanks to his prowess as a poet, he claims that "yo puedo convertir el zapato en un barquito" (92). Later, in New York, in conversation with Columbia University students on this very topic, he gave as an example this simile: "My love is like a pair of old shoes!" (Crow, 7), which is further picked up in the opening line of "Luna y panorama de los insectos": "Mi corazón tendría la forma de un zapato" (*Poeta en Nueva York*, 243). He returned to the "hecho poético" in revisions of the "Imaginación, inspiración, evasión" lecture delivered in 1929 and 1930, in the recital texts of *Poeta en Nueva York* (1932), and of *Romancero gitano* (1935).[11] In Madrid in 1932 Lorca described the poems in *Poeta en Nueva York* as:

> llenos de hechos poéticos dentro exclusivamente de una lógica lírica y trabados tupidamente sobre el sentimiento humano y la arquitectura del poema, [y] no son aptos para ser comprendidos rápidamente sin la ayuda cordial del duende. (*Manuscritos neoyorquinos*, 250)

Several critics have already explored and elucidated a number of the sources—among them Le Corbusier, Jean Epstein, Guillermo de Torre, José Ortega y Gasset, Vicente Huidobro, and Salvador Dalí—from which Lorca

---

11   *Manuscritos neoyorquinos*, 245-66; *Romancero gitano*, 149-59.

derived his notion of the "hecho poético."[12] However, it is worth quoting some passages from Epstein's *La Póesie d'aujourd'hui* (1921), where he takes as his main subject for analysis recent French Cubist poetry (by Reverdy and his group). In language that closely anticipates Lorca's lecture, this critic asserts that "la logique rationnelle se trouve bannie de la littérature" (103) and, as might be expected, the result is "l'illogisme des lettres modernes" (95). He states further that "pour s'évader de la logique, il fallait donc s'évader de la grammaire. C'était une fuite difficile" (97). In modern poetry, then, there is a predominance of "la pensée-association" (over what he calls "la pensée-phrase"), which manifests itself thus:

> La logique rationnelle et grammaticale n'a plus rien à voir ici. L'enchaînement des idées, si on peut appeler cela des idées, se fait selon des associations partielles et absolument illogiques [...]; les idées s'y enchaînent par association, par contiguïté de souvenirs, d'images, de sons et de couleurs [...]; la pensée-association ne souffre pas de logique. (101-02)

Still, it is hard for Epstein to conceive that there is no underlying organizing principle at work, and so he posits that "la pensée-association connaît un ordre assurément très compliqué mais tout de même compréhensible" (108). And this "other logic," he conjectures, may have more than one point of contact with dream logic, though they are far from identical (109).

It is also enlightening, I believe, to set Lorca's statements alongside T.S. Eliot's thoughts on Saint-John Perse's *Anabasis*, this time purely as an analogy rather than a possible source (the "Preface" to the translation dates from 1930):

> any obscurity of the poem, on first readings, is due to the suppression of "links in the chain," of explanatory and connecting matter, and not to incoherence, or to the love of cryptogram. The justification of such abbreviation of method is that the sequence of images coincides and concentrates into one intense impression of barbaric civilization. The reader has to allow the images to fall into his memory successively without questioning the reasonableness of each at the moment; so that, at the end, a total effect is produced.

---

12   Hernández; Anderson, "Lorca at the Crossroads"; Urrutia; García; and Maurer.

Such selection of a sequence of images and ideas has nothing chaotic about it. *There is a logic of the imagination as well as a logic of concepts.* (10; my italics)

Now, there is a wealth of commentary dedicated to *Poeta en Nueva York*, and numerous critics have proposed different perspectives on Lorca's imagistic practice. Flys argues that there is a major shift in Lorca's writing after *Romancero gitano*: the dominance of the metaphor gives way rapidly to that of the symbol, and in *Poeta en Nueva York*, he claims, true metaphors are extremely rare (47, 68-69). Correa finds an ordering of the poetic material into positive and negative symbols, sometimes counterposed and at other times combined, and typically the former are undermined or nullified by the latter (166). Harris's thinking on the subject evolves through a series of writings from the 1970s to the 1990s. He stresses the variety of procedures that produce "una intensificación emocional," ranging from the use of symbols and traditional techniques (paradox, personification, transferred epithet) to expressionism (incoherence, violence, surprising juxtapositions, compression/condensation) and surrealism (the arbitrary and incongruous, subversion of semantics and logic, metamorphosis) ("Introducción: *Poeta en Nueva York*," 24-29). He also studies the evolution of the revisions that Lorca made on the original manuscripts, evidence that can be fascinating but which is, ultimately, inconclusive with respect to what Lorca was thinking or what his intentions were ("La elaboración textual"). In the book chapter of 1998, Harris detects in the poems a distinct predominance of expressionism over surrealism (*Metal Butterflies*, 83-122).

Predmore acknowledges that "many passages in many poems are abstruse in the extreme" and concentrates on the presence of a "highly personal symbolic system" wherein a number of deliberately ambiguous symbols proliferate (x). He echoes Correa in identifying the "joining in one semantic unit of two or more words of antithetical value" (12).[13] García-Posada emends the opinions offered by Flys and Correa, proposing instead the very strong presence of a personal symbolic system *combined* with the frequent use of metaphoric imagery, some of which, at first sight, may not appear to consist of true—or obvious—metaphors, because of their considerable complexity (*Lorca: Interpretación*, 89-108, 108-94). For my part, I underline the similarity of Eliot's "objective correlative" with Lorca's "hecho poético," and seek to understand the latter as a non-metaphoric image whose internal structure

---

13   See more broadly the chapter on "The Rhetoric of Ambiguity," 11-32.

and level of complexity may vary considerably ("García Lorca's *Poemas en prosa*," 177-80).

Flys judges *Poeta en Nueva York* as "en algunos momentos desigual" (43), while Harris points out that "la gama de los procedimientos imaginísticos en *Poeta en Nueva York* es muy extensa" ("Introducción," 29); I concur, adding that "because all of these kinds of poetic discourse are mixed together in different measures and patterns throughout the poems, an individual text can seem to go in and out of focus (sometimes repeatedly) as the reader progresses through its lines and stanzas, which can appear by turns transparent and opaque" ("García Lorca's *Poemas en prosa*, 180-81). Indeed, there is a considerable diversity of images here, in terms both of how they work and how approachable they are for the reader. Consequently, one of the most disconcerting features of the collection is the wide stylistic variability of the text, both within individual poems and from one poem to the next.

Such a state of affairs obviously presents an obstacle to any attempt at broad generalization concerning imagery in *Poeta en Nueva York*. At the same time, it tends to favor a closer approach to individual poems, so that we can at least determine, more or less specifically, what is going on in a given composition. Clearly, there is no one "representative" poem to be found here, no one poem whose analysis would allow the critic to exhaust the gamut of Lorca's stylistic practice. For the purposes of this article, then, I have chosen to focus on "1910 (Intermedio)," because there is a reasonable degree of consensus regarding what the poem is about (hence, the issue of basic thematic interpretation becomes secondary),[14] and because in its relative brevity it still offers a considerable range of examples of imagistic technique.

The original first-draft manuscript of "1910 (Intermedio)" has survived and shows a good deal of revision, both in the immediate act of composition and subsequently; the place and date are given as New York and August 1929 (García Lorca, *Manuscritos neoyorquinos*, 40-43). There is a typed fair copy that must have been prepared from a later manuscript version (one that is, as far as is known, not extant), and that typed copy has a few further revisions made on it in Lorca's hand and another's (Anderson, "Introducción," 84-85, 93).

Within the collection, "1910 (Intermedio)" is the second poem in section I, "Poemas de la Soledad en Columbia University."[15] In light of the date of composition, the year in the title represents for the speaker a moment in

---

14   C. Marcilly's close commentary (13-21) offers an insightful interpretation.

15   García Lorca, *Poeta en Nueva York*, 166; all quotations of the text are drawn from this edition.

the relatively distant past. The subtitle is ambiguous: given that the majority of poems are concerned with the speaker's vision of New York and his experiences there, the text, focusing as it does on the past, may constitute a brief intermission from the impressions of the big city. Similarly, it may offer a temporary break (though ultimately no real respite) for the speaker, who, for a short while, turns his attention away from the present and back to the past. Alternatively, "(Intermedio)" may be read in conjunction with "1910" as a gloss on what that specific year meant for the speaker, the "interlude" of childhood before puberty and adulthood.[16]

The opening lines can be read literally and figuratively. "Aquellos ojos míos" establishes that these eyes *are* and simultaneously *are not* the speaker's: they correspond to a younger version of himself, and he is, and is not, that same person, a fact emphasized by the distancing demonstrative adjective and the verbal formulation that necessitates the use of the third-person plural (preterite), rather than the first-person singular. The eyes stand synecdochically for the person in the past, and beyond this what is implied is the child's distinctive perspective that only notices certain things (and then processes them in a certain way). Likewise, line 2—"no vieron enterrar a los muertos"—can simply mean that the speaker, when young, did not attend graveside ceremonies, but it can be extended to suggest that burials did not impinge on his consciousness, or even, more broadly still, that he was somehow unaware of the fact of death.[17]

Lines 3-4 join line 2 in parallelistic fashion, enumerating other things that the child did not fix his attention on or of which he was somehow ignorant. Line 3—"la feria de ceniza del que llora por la madrugada"—may be related to line 2, in that both ashes and weeping are associated with death and funeral services, and it presents the first challenge to the reader, from the point of view of both syntax and interpretation. On initial acquaintance, its structure suggests familiar metaphoric forms, either the genitive link type (e.g. "tambor del llano") or the simple replacement type in a descriptive geni-

---

16   Most critics offer a biographical reading, calculating Lorca's age as twelve (though he often claimed 1899 as his birthdate, and even on occasions 1900). The family moved from the Vega to Granada when Lorca was eleven, and his sister Isabel García Lorca finds various reminiscences in the text both of Fuente Vaqueros and of the Acera del Darro: *Recuerdos míos*, 29-30. Such biographism is completely unhelpful for a stylistic analysis of the poem.

17   The fallacy of biographism is again demonstrated by an autobiographical prose text in which Lorca recounts attending a funeral when he was aged seven: "El compadre Pastor," 443.

tive construction (e.g. "pechos de duro estaño").[18] However, when the entire phrase is considered in conjunction with the subject of the second half of the line, a subject—"el que llora"—to which the "feria de ceniza" is in turn attributed, it becomes clear that in fact *both* elements are figurative and that a descriptive genitive connects them. "Ceniza" strongly negates all the joyous connotations of "feria," and the resulting contradictory and quite unreal concept serves to characterize the experience of the subject, no doubt adult, who for unknown reasons is unfortunate and miserable enough still to be awake and weeping in the small hours of the morning. Underlying all this, and adding to it, is a palpable reminiscence of a technical ecclesiastic term: weekdays are known as "feria segunda" (Monday) through to "feria sexta" (Friday), and so the "feria cuarta de ceniza" refers to Ash Wednesday. Line 4 brings an explicit simile whose meaning is transparent yet whose elements of comparison are unexpected: "el corazón que tiembla arrinconado como un caballito de mar." The smallness and defenselessness of the seahorse are stressed and projected as emotions on to "corazón," just as the personifying verb and past participle, and their connotations, can easily be transferred on to the "caballito de mar." Lines 2-4 thus exemplify the variability and mixed nature of the writing here: line 2 is largely literal, line 3 offers a complex modern image approaching an objective correlative, and line 4 features a relatively conventional if unusual simile.

In stanza 2, the items named in lines 6-7, much as in line 2, can be taken quite literally, though at the same time they obviously have further, metonymic and symbolic significance. For one thing, their highly miscellaneous quality mimics the randomness with which small children notice some things and not others, and can be fascinated by them.[19] At the same time, they evoke aspects of life in a small rural farming community and the gradual discovery of the outside world: a pre-pubertal interest in sexuality and the "grapevine" among the local village boys regarding where the young girls were rumored to congregate, the impressive and possibly threatening snout of a bull, perhaps with a ring through its nostrils, and the colorful but dangerous toadstool that adults have warned against.

---

18   These terms form part of the categorization scheme established by Brooke-Rose; the examples are drawn from Lorca's "Romance de la luna, luna."

19   Marcilly writes: "Au fur et à mesure de leur déroulement théoriquement incontrôlé, les images se font peu à peu plus personnelles, se lient davantage à une expérience complexe [...]. C'est ici la vie sentimentale de l'enfant, éveil affectif tout à la fois pur et ambigu, qui assure l'unité interne des souvenirs apparemment disparates" (16).

In striking and immediate contrast, lines 8-9, which form a single, complex unit, present even greater challenges than line 3. The first phrase, "una luna incomprensible," follows on logically enough, both structurally and semantically, from the previously enumerated items: it is another of the child's observations, a presence in the night sky that for unspecified reasons he finds inscrutable. But then on arriving at the relative clause, which continues over the enjambment, the reader seeks to imagine a set of circumstances that will somehow integrate the diverse components. Lemon rounds are dried by cooks, but their location here "por los rincones" suggests, more probably, discarded slices of once-fresh lemon; the connection with bottles points to drinks, perhaps alcoholic; the simple synaesthetic metaphor of "negro duro" must describe the color and texture of the glass of the bottles, and contrasts with the color and organic nature of the shriveled lemon pieces, though why these features are foregrounded is impossible to say. As a whole, the clause perhaps evokes the leftover vestiges of an unruly party upon which, again, the child's inquisitive gaze happens to alight, but the tone implied by the scene is harder to determine. Are these remains of an innocent if raucous celebration, or of some more debauched episode? Are they just a token of the adult world that, as with the moon, the child finds unfathomable?

Structurally, stanza 3 echoes the pattern of stanza 2, with shorter, more transparent phrases in its first two lines, and longer phrases in the second two, one of which is quite opaque. The items identified in lines 10-11, "el cuello de la jaca," "el seno traspasado de Santa Rosa dormida," align with those mentioned in lines 6-7. Like the bull, the pony could be encountered in a barnyard or farm pen, and again one body part is focalized, one which a small child might cling to if set upon a horse's back for the first time. Line 11 clearly refers to a popular devotional print such as might be found hanging in many houses; the standard representations of Saint Rose of Lima depict her in an ecstatic, trance-like state ("dormida"), and so we should think of the "seno traspasado" in terms of the beam of divine light that similarly penetrates Mary in the iconography of the Annunciation (Marcilly, 17).

These are all objects that captivate the youthful viewer, and lines 12-13 are presented syntactically as continuing the list of sights that his eyes fell upon. Line 13 once more evokes a literal scene where the innocent observer was able to witness the Darwinian harshness of nature—his home's garden where the housecats hunted and ate frogs, attracted perhaps by a fountain or pond. Line 12—"en los tejados del amor con gemidos y frescas manos"— is more problematic. Is the child looking up at the roofs, or looking down on houses close to his own? How exactly are we to understand the genitive linking "tejados" with "amor"? Are these rooftops where some kind of love encounter takes place, do they shelter or hide that location, are they used to gain clandestine access to a lover's room, or is it something else again? When we read "amor," should we understand romance or sex? Is the reference to human beings, or animals (perhaps the same cats as in the next line)? The following phrase certainly suggests physical activity and humans ("manos"), though the dominant conceptual framework of sight ("Aquellos ojos míos") combines disconcertingly with two other sense perceptions, hearing ("gemidos") and touch ("frescas manos"), to create an imprecise and open-ended referent. What kind of connection between the two phrases does "con" imply? Are the "gemidos y frescas manos" related exclusively to the antecedent "amor," are they *on* the rooftops, or do they somehow accompany the viewing of the rooftops? Broadly speaking, in these four lines, 10-13, and via the four diverse concrete items/actions named and partially described, we pass rapidly through four more abstract notions: from familiar domestic animals to religion to sexuality to the "eat and be eaten" world of nature.

The fourth stanza dispenses with the familiar opening phrase, but it is still implied that what is listed here forms part of what was observed or, at the very least, part of the speaker's past. "Desván" immediately conjures another locale for specific experiences, alongside the farmyard, the street or alley, the countryside, the patio, the house's interior, and the garden. As a place for the storage of unused or outmoded possessions, the attic with its usual impedimenta of trunks and boxes obviously represents for a child a site of exploration, mystery, imagination, and possible adventure. Line 14 opens conventionally enough, with the most standard associations of attic with dust and age, but then, strangely, it is personified and given agency—"donde el polvo viejo congrega estatuas y musgos": instead of the fine powder just falling and gradually accumulating on the stored items, the text completely flips the idea, making the proposition on the literal level unreal, and turns the dust into an active force that gathers things there. Perhaps when a layer of dust coats everything it can be seen as a sort of leveler. Further surprises await at the end of the line, where the items mentioned—"estatuas" and "musgos"—are not what one stereotypically associates with attic storage. "Statue" has a wide range of possible references and here, given the domestic context, we might well think of fairly small, probably devotional, sculpted figures, or even, extending the term in a way that falls somewhere between the metaphorical and the metonymic, of mannequins or dress-forms. Similarly, one might reasonably expect to find mold rather than moss in the loft space ("moho" rather than "musgos"), though the two are undoubtedly related. Line 15 follows a similar pattern. "Cajas" are one of the most likely things to encounter in an attic, and of course are used for storage ("que guardan"). But then, partly one imagines under the influence of the idiom "guardar silencio" (to be/keep/ remain silent), they are described as containers of something as intangible as silence, rather than of old clothes, photographs, toys, etc., though silence can certainly be associated with the past as well as an attic space. "Silencio" is further modified in the descriptive genitive phrase that completes the line, and which as a whole creates a fairly extravagant image that only borders on the metaphoric. "Cangrejos devorados," not something one would ever expect to encounter stored in an attic, suggest the past (the tense of the participle) and, primarily, the empty carapace and other shell parts: crustaceans have been consumed, and only the hollow husks of the bodies and legs remain. The silence, then, is connected with the feast being long over, and with the enduring sense of emptiness and hollowness ("hueco" and "vacío" are two of the more insistent adjectives in *Poeta en Nueva York*, and both appear in stanza 5). If "cangrejos devorados" is viewed as the vehicle in a simple replacement metaphor, then the tenor is something more abstract than concrete, and serves in turn to characterize the aforementioned "silencio." At the same time, it is possible to respond to the emotional connotations of the phrase more immediately, without performing a fully metaphoric reading.

At all events, this blending of concrete with abstract, tangible with intangible, continues in line 16—"En el sitio donde el sueño tropezaba con su realidad." "Sitio" must refer to the attic and its boxes (there is no reason to think the scene has changed). Likewise, "tropezaba" denotes literally the collision of one concrete thing with another, but here "sueño" is almost personified in conjunction with the verb taking on its usual figurative meanings. At face value the proposition is quite general: in this place, dream stumbles over/bumps into its own reality, reality therefore acting as a hazard, an obstacle, and perhaps a block. Given the associations of the attic, certain more specific implications come to the forefront: the attic is where things that once held potential or promise ("sueño") but then lost their utility, efficacy, or appeal are now stored away, or if we still envisage a child, it is a place of fantasy/imagination/make-believe ("sueño") that trips up on itself. The reality of dream—"*su* realidad"—is probably to be understood in the sense of the realization of what a dream actually is, no more than an illusion, and hence liable to be punctured or implode (Marcilly, 18). This consciousness that a dream (like childhood itself) is not enduring prepares the way for the radical shift that occurs in the last stanza. This change in direction is signaled, too, by the last line of the stanza, "Allí mis pequeños ojos" (l. 17), which serves as a simple structural marker announcing that this section of the poem is at an end.

In stanza 5, the opening apostrophe—"No preguntarme nada"—directed to unspecified "others" (anticipating other similar moments, as in the *Llanto por Ignacio Sánchez Mejías*), anchors the discourse in the present, further reinforced by the use of the perfect tense in the next phrase. The speaker wants to be left alone, and/or has no answers to give. Likewise, the distancing ploy of referring to "Aquellos ojos míos" gives way to the implicit "yo" combined with the same verb as before—"He visto que las cosas"—but now it is much clearer that, as in English, the verb implies not just the act of seeing but also more generally perception and comprehension. In one sense these "things" could gesture to the various items identified in previous stanzas, but the statement here has more of the flavor of a generalization (as in, for example, "things aren't what they used to be"). These are then personified, or at least given agency, since they *seek* their course, rather than (more expectedly) *follow* it. In this clause and the next ("cuando buscan su curso encuentran su vacío"), which describe the action and the result, the two nouns function as simple replacement metaphors for more abstract tenors: "curso" for the way forward, the "path" of life, the natural evolution of events, fulfilment; "vacío" for the disappointing or nonexistent conclusion, an end-point that brings the realization that the "things" invested in (whatever they were) were in fact hollow or empty—vain, inoperative, unrealized, valueless, or meaningless. Additionally, both the grammatical structure of line 19 and the strong sense of disillusionment that it carries are strongly reminiscent of line 16 (noun–verb–possessive adjective–noun).

Other observations about the present moment—of adulthood—follow in lines 20-21, and although line 20 casts the assertion in generalized, impersonal fashion ("Hay"), it is clear that it corresponds very much to the speaker's individual perception of the state of affairs. The phrase "un dolor de huecos" presents yet another genitive construction, of which two syntactical readings are possible: one less likely, as a possessive genitive, where the physical pain and, by extension, the emotional sorrow actually correspond/belong to the (personified) hollow spaces; or a causal genitive, where the "huecos" are what occasion the "dolor." Neither term is truly abstract, but of course pain/sorrow is something attributed to sentient beings, whereas hollows are non-sentient and denote absence rather than presence. In addition, it is possible to read "huecos" as a simple replacement metaphor, standing for unspecified states or experiences characterized by hollowness. And, of course, it is precisely this *lack*, this feeling of widespread emptiness, which causes the distress. In a further, unreal, twist to the situation being evoked, the "dolor de huecos" is presented as floating in the air, carried on the wind, incorporeal, independent of anybody or anything. The modifier "sin gente" seems to qualify "aire," but it is also pertinent to the previous phrase. Thus the scene is completely abandoned, deserted, the speaker finds himself totally alone, and this solitariness may contribute to, or even cause, the "dolor de huecos."

The last line returns specifically to the speaker's eyes, but now in the present they are simply "mis ojos." What he sees aligns closely with the "vacío" and "huecos" of lines 19-20. The "criaturas vestidas" can be understood more or less literally, as referring to humankind ("creatures" who wear clothes). The two modifiers, "vestidas" and "¡sin desnudo!," both bear figurative—and emotional—connotations. Clothes here hide the person, enable them to present a "front" to the world; "vestidas" can be conceived of as an adjectival metaphor whose abstract tenor would be something like pretense, façade, inauthenticity. The fact that there is no naked body underneath turns these "criaturas vestidas" literally into the "trajes deshabitados" of Alberti and makes them analogous to Eliot's "hollow men." Rather like "vestidas," "desnudo" can be seen as a simple replacement metaphor for authenticity, a real self, an essence, etc. For the speaker, then, there is little to choose between the isolation of "sin gente" and the parallelistic lack of true presence of "¡sin desnudo!"

What figurative language does "1910 (Intermedio)" therefore contain? There is one very obvious simile (line 4), one simple metaphor (second half of line 9), and several examples of more or less overt personification (lines 4, 14, 15, 16, 18-19, 20). Various literal items (lines 2, 6, 7, 10, 11, 13) at the same time carry implied symbolic resonances, and might perhaps be grouped under the broadest category of "imagery." Finally, there are a number of complex phrases where various figurative operations are occurring simultaneously: sometimes these phrases incorporate less precise or nearly imperceptible metaphors (lines 3, 15, 19, 20, 21), sometimes they contain elements that appear more metonymic or synecdochical (lines 9, 12, 14), and sometimes neither (lines 8, 16).

One overriding feature, then, of the poetic discourse here is a feeling of hesitancy on the part of the reader with respect to exactly what kind of trope they are dealing with: we are uncertain as to the particular form of the metaphor (e.g. tenor + vehicle, vehicle alone [tenor elided], vehicle + vehicle, etc.), or even whether it is really a metaphor at all and not some other sort of less precise "imagery." Given the multiple semantic possibilities of the genitive construction "X de Y" (possessive, descriptive, material, attributive, causal, partitive, etc.), it is no surprise that this particular construction is found very frequently indeed in this poem (and throughout Lorca's work): "la feria de ceniza," "el negro duro de las botellas," "silencio de cangrejos devorados," "un dolor de huecos," and even just conceivably "los tejados del amor." But there are also other potential metaphors, such as "las cosas | cuando buscan su curso encuentran su vacío" and "criaturas vestidas ¡sin desnudo!" Overall, the effect produced, of multiple possible meanings and of ultimate undecidability, is distinctly unsettling, which was doubtless the intent.

Another important and related feature is language that functions as literal and symbolic expression simultaneously. Brooke-Rose demonstrates that in simple replacement metaphor "the noun not only can 'replace' more than one unstated idea, but [...] it can also be taken quite literally" (29). As a result, "there is this pleasant ambiguity, that the replacing word also makes literal sense in the sentence" (40), and she points out that "this kind of double meaning is a modern development, particularly noticeable after the advent of Symbolism" (29). In such circumstances, "the poet imagines a scene and describes it literally" (29); importantly, the imagined scene can just as well be fantastic as real or realistic (41). As one example among many:

> Eliot describes a Waste Land, with the dead tree, the cricket, the red rock and its shadow, all symbols which we have learnt to recognise, but the words are simply put down as if he were describing a real landscape. This is usually called "imagery" in criticism, and the technique has been described as that of the "objective correlative." It is the logical development of the Simple Replacement metaphor, stretched as far as it will go. (29-30)

Subsequently, Brooke-Rose refers to this specific technique as the "literal symbol" (31, 34) and then as the "image" (67), which operates thus:

> the poet simply mentions something and various connotations arise in our minds, as they might if we ourselves saw the same thing in fact; or he makes them arise in our minds by mentioning it in a context of other objects. Hence the importance of juxtaposition in modern poetry. (35)

> The mere putting down of one literal statement after another, even without rhetorical repetition, constitutes "imagery"; juxtaposition is enough to imply a connection, however remote, between one "image" and another. (91-92)

At this point let us remind ourselves, too, of Eliot's own characterization of the "objective correlative": "a set of objects, a situation, a chain of events which shall be the formula of that *particular* emotion" ("Hamlet and his Problems," 941).

It should be clear that a good deal of the "imagery" to be found in "1910 (Intermedio)" is described in the preceding paragraph. Items which I referred to earlier as being "literal" while at the same time carrying implied symbolic resonances square exactly with the post-Symbolist techniques that Brooke-Rose examines. The only addition that I would venture is that between the single "image" on the one hand and the entire "scene" on the other, an intermediate unit of some complexity, typically extending to a long phrase, may incorporate a miniature "scene" or a combination of two of three "images" in juxtaposition. These complex units correspond to how the "objective correlative" often operates in modern lyric poetry. There are manifest examples of just such a technique in several lines here: "la feria de ceniza del que llora por la madrugada," "una luna incomprensible que iluminaba por los rincones | los pedazos de limón seco bajo el negro duro de las botellas," "Desván donde el polvo viejo congrega estatuas y musgos. | Cajas que guardan silencio de cangrejos devorados" and "Hay un dolor de huecos por el aire sin gente | y en mis ojos criaturas vestidas ¡sin desnudo!" Furthermore, I would contend that these are also examples of precisely what Lorca meant by the "hecho poético."

The findings provided by this analysis of "1910 (Intermedio)" are one more piece of evidence in the ongoing task of attempting to situate *Poeta en Nueva York* more broadly within the landscape of modern poetry. Consultation of manuals of Spanish literature or an internet search for the title of the collection will rapidly reveal that it is very frequently classified as Surrealist. However, this adjective is all too often used as an imprecise catch-all, and really for no better reason than the fact that, alongside a number of fairly accessible texts (e.g. "Vuelta de paseo," "La aurora"), there are also more cryptic ones (e.g. "Asesinato," "Vals en las ramas") and more challengingly opaque ones (e.g. "Fábula y rueda de los tres amigos," "Luna y panorama de los insectos"). And regardless of how one understands Surrealism, and there are many ways, poetic difficulty and opacity are not, in and of themselves, any guarantee of its presence.[20]

Interestingly, most critics who closely examine Lorca's imagistic practice in *Poeta en Nueva York* tend to arrive at the conclusion that there is in fact lit-

---

20   I find Michel Riffaterre's approach generally persuasive, in "Semantic Incompatibilities" and "The Extended Metaphor." For Surrealism and Spanish poetry of the 1920s and 30s, see Harris, *Metal Butterflies*, 11-82.

tle or no Surrealist writing, or that there are only a few similarities common to various styles of modern, avant-garde poetry. Flys discounts the idea completely (47). Predmore notes that "Lorca denied, no doubt correctly, that he was a surrealist, but it is obvious that his New York poems show more than a little resemblance to the poetry of surrealism" (7, note 6). García-Posada attributes any apparent hermeticism to the complexity of the figurative expression and rejects any Surrealist influences (*Lorca: Interpretación*, 89, 91, 330-36). In his later article, of 1989, his position if anything hardens further, and he concludes that "me parece posible afirmar que [Lorca] es el menos surrealista de los grandes poetas de su generación" (García-Posada, "Lorca y el surrealismo," 9). Harris's stance evolves over time up to the book chapter of 1998. Like Posada, he points to Lorca's notion of "poetic logic," and finds the collection characterized by "the distorted and intensified emotionalism of Expressionism, not the bringing together of widely separate realities in the Surrealist abolition of contradiction" (*Metal Butterflies*, 86, 87-91). However, he is reluctant to banish all Surrealist influence, and in reconstructing—problematically—how Lorca may have generated some of his more impenetrable images, he discovers traces of Surrealist practice (*Metal Butterflies*, 98-111).

Monegal expresses serious reservations about the very notion of "Spanish Surrealist poetry," and finds that while the poetry of Lorca, Alberti, Cernuda, and Aleixandre displays typically avant-garde features, these are not attributable to the core ideals or practices of Surrealism (56-58, 61-63, 67, 69). Instead, invoking Riffaterre, he contends that the style of writing encountered here is "el resultado, no ya de la escritura automática de origen inconsciente, sino de operaciones metafóricas llevadas hasta el límite de lo posible" (63). For my part, I have shown how Lorca follows Dalí only so far, after which they part company ("García Lorca's *Poemas en prosa*," 169). Hence, beyond a good deal of more or less conventional metaphor and symbol, these New York poems also contain many "hechos poéticos," some of the "emotive image" type (objective correlative) and others more resolutely opaque ("García Lorca's *Poemas en prosa*," 177-81). But for me, as for Monegal, "el lenguaje oscuro de [...] *Poeta en Nueva York* no es oscuro por surrealista, sino porque aquello de lo que habla [...] se resiste a ser dicho con claridad. Es decir, que el significado de dichos textos no puede construirse sino mediante recursos que llevan el lenguaje al límite de sus posibilidades" (62).

"1910 (Intermedio)" is but one poem among the thirty-five that comprise *Poeta en Nueva York*, but Lorca's imagistic practice in this text—and, more broadly, his theoretical concept of the "hecho poético"—are nonetheless telling, inasmuch as they are more reminiscent of Pound and Eliot, Reverdy and Epstein, than they are of Lautréamont or the Surrealists. The commonalities are several. In all instances, what is important is the evocation or stimulation, in a non-rational and non-discursive fashion, of a mood (Pound) or emotion (Eliot) or "the state he feels" (Hulme). The image (Pound, Reverdy, Epstein) or objective correlative (Eliot) is always central to this process, though it is constructed in a variety of related ways in which juxtaposition always has a key role to play, as is stressed by Hulme, Pound, and Reverdy (as well as critics like Wheelwright and Brooke-Rose). The image can be one word/element, set in juxtaposition with others. It can also be a small unit of two or three words/elements, now more reminiscent of the traditional metaphor but without the strong epiphoric connection between the components. These individual units can again be set in juxtaposition with each other. The act of juxtaposition is not, however, utterly random: it corresponds rather to an "enchaîn[em]ent par association" (Epstein) or the "logic of the imagination" (Eliot)—Lorca's "hechos poéticos encadenados" and "lógica poética," even though the connectedness may be oblique or elliptical, difficult to grasp and not readily susceptible to ratiocinative analysis ("any obscurity of the poem, on first readings, is due to the suppression of 'links in the chain,' of explanatory and connecting matter, and not to incoherence": Eliot). Whatever the case, what is important is that the image or ensemble of images—the "set of objects"—should serve as the "equation" for the "mood" (Pound) or "the formula of that *particular* emotion" (Eliot), a mood or emotion that is, by definition, complex and not readily evoked/stimulated in any other way. Hulme puts the emphasis on expression, saying that the images serve "to suggest and to evoke the state he [the poet] feels," while Brooke-Rose focuses more on reception: "the poet simply mentions something and various connotations arise in our minds [...]; or he makes them arise in our minds by mentioning it in a context of other objects." This is exactly what happens in "1910 (Intermedio)," a composition that is centrally inscribed in various overlapping currents of European modernist and avant-garde poetry.

Works Cited

Anderson, Andrew A. "Lorca at the Crossroads: 'Imaginación, inspiración, evasión' and the 'novísimas estéticas,'" *Anales de la Literatura Española Contemporánea*, XVI, nos. 1-2 (1991), 149-73.

————. "García Lorca's *Poemas en prosa* and *Poeta en Nueva York*: Dalí, Gasch, Surrealism and the Avant-Garde," in *A Companion to Spanish Surrealism*, ed. Robert Havard (London: Tamesis, 2004), pp. 163-82.

————. "Introducción," in *Poeta en Nueva York*, by Federico García Lorca (Barcelona: Galaxia Gutenberg, 2013), pp. 7-138.

————. "*Paysage d'âme* and Objective Correlative: Tradition and Innovation in Cernuda, Alberti, and García Lorca," *Modern Language Review*, CX, no. 1 (2015), 166-83.

Aristotle. *Rhetoric*, ed. J. H. Freese, <http://www.perseus.tufts.edu/hopper/text?doc=Aristot.%20Rh>.

Auerbach, Erich. "'Figura,'" in *Scenes from the Drama of European Literature: Six Essays* (Gloucester, MA: Peter Smith, 1973), pp. 11-76.

Breton, André. *Manifestes du surréalisme* (Paris: NRF/Gallimard, 1972).

Brooke-Rose, Christine. *A Grammar of Metaphor* (London: Secker & Warburg, 1958).

Cernuda, Luis. *Estudios sobre poesía española contemporánea* (Madrid: Guadarrama, 1975).

Correa, Gustavo. *La poesía mítica de Federico García Lorca* (Madrid: Gredos, 1970).

Crow, John A. *Federico García Lorca* (Los Angeles: The Author, 1945).

Ducasse, Isidore Lucien, le Comte de Lautréamont. *Les Chants de Maldoror* (Paris: A. Lacroix, 1869).

Eliot, T.S. "Hamlet and his Problems," *The Athenaeum*, no. 4665 (26 September 1919), 940-41.

————. "Tradition and the Individual Talent–II," *The Egoist*, VI, no. 5 (1919), 72-73.

————. "Preface," in *Anabasis: A Poem, by Saint-John Perse*, trans. by T.S. Eliot (London: Faber & Faber, 1930), pp. 7-11.

Epstein, Jean. *La Poésie d'aujourd'hui* (Paris: Éditions de la Sirène, 1921).

Flys, Jaroslaw M. *El lenguaje poético de Federico García Lorca* (Madrid: Gredos, 1955).

Frazer, Ray. "The Origin of the Term 'Image,'" *ELH*, XXVII, no. 2 (1960), 149-61.

Furbank, P.N. *Reflections on the Word "Image"* (London: Secker & Warburg, 1970).

García, Carlos. "García Lorca, Jean Epstein y un tercero en concordia," *El Maquinista de la Generación*, no. 15 (2008), 28-31.

García Lorca, Federico. "La imagen poética de don Luis de Góngora," in *Conferencias*, ed. Christopher Maurer, 2 vols. (Madrid: Alianza, 1984), I, pp. 85-125.

———. "Imaginación, inspiración, evasión," in *Conferencias*, ed. Christopher Maurer, 2 vols. (Madrid: Alianza, 1984), II, pp. 13-31.

———. *Manuscritos neoyorquinos: "Poeta en Nueva York" y otras hojas y poemas*, ed. Mario Hernández (Madrid: Tabapress/Fundación Federico García Lorca, 1990).

———. "El compadre Pastor," in Federico García Lorca, *Prosa inédita de juventud*, ed. Christopher Maurer (Madrid: Cátedra, 1994), pp. 440-45.

———. *Romancero gitano*, ed. Mario Hernández (Madrid: Alianza, 1998).

———. "Corazón bleu y cœur azul," in *Poemas en prosa*, ed. Andrew A. Anderson (Granada: Comares, 2000), pp. 91-92.

———. *Poeta en Nueva York*, ed. Andrew A. Anderson (Barcelona: Galaxia Gutenberg, 2013).

García Lorca, Isabel. *Recuerdos míos*, ed. Ana Gurruchaga (Barcelona: Tusquets, 2002).

García-Posada, Miguel. *Lorca: Interpretación de "Poeta en Nueva York"* (Madrid: Akal, 1981).

———. "Lorca y el surrealismo: una relación conflictiva," *Ínsula*, XLIV, no. 515 (1989), 7-9.

Gracián, Baltasar. *Agudeza y arte de ingenio*, ed. Evaristo Correa Calderón, 2 vols. (Madrid: Castalia, 1969).

Harris, Derek. "Introducción: *Poeta en Nueva York*," in *Romancero gitano. Poeta en Nueva York. El público*, by Federico García Lorca (Madrid: Taurus, 1993), pp. 23-33.

———. "La elaboración textual de *Poeta en Nueva York*: el salto mortal," *Revista Canadiense de Estudios Hispánicos*, XVIII, no. 2 (1994), 309-15.

———. *Metal Butterflies and Poisonous Lights: The Language of Surrealism in Lorca, Alberti, Cernuda and Aleixandre* (Anstruther: La Sirena, 1998).

Hernández, Mario. "García Lorca y Salvador Dalí: del ruiseñor lírico a los burros podridos (poética y epistolario)," in *L'"imposible/posible" di Federico García Lorca*, ed. Laura Dolfi (Naples: Edizioni Scientifiche Italiane, 1989), pp. 267-319.

Hulme, T.E. "Lecture on Modern Poetry," in *T.E. Hulme*, by Michael Roberts (London: Faber and Faber, 1938), pp. 258-70.

Lewis, C. Day. *The Poetic Image* (London: Jonathan Cape, 1947).

Marcilly, C. *Ronde et fable de la solitude à New York: Prélude à "Poeta en Nueva York" de F. G. Lorca* (Paris: Ediciones Hispanoamericanas, 1962).

Marinetti, F.T. "Technical Manifesto of Futurist Literature," in *Futurism: An Anthology*, ed. Lawrence Rainey, Christine Poggi and Laura Wittman (New Haven, CT: Yale UP, 2009), pp. 119-125.

Maurer, Christopher. "García Lorca, Dalí, and the Metaphor, 1926-1929," *Avant-Garde Studies*, no. 2 (2016), 1-22.

McGavin, John J. *Chaucer and Dissimilarity: Literary Comparisons in Chaucer and Other Late-Medieval Writing* (Cranbury, NJ: Associated University Presses, 2000).

McLuhan, Marshall. *The Interior Landscape: The Literary Criticism of Marshall McLuhan 1943-1962*, ed. Eugene McNamara (New York: McGraw-Hill, 1969).

Mitchell, W.J.T. *Iconology: Image, Text, Ideology* (Chicago: The U of Chicago P, 1986).

Monegal, Antonio. "La 'poesía nueva' de 1929: entre el álgebra de las metáforas y la revolución surrealista," *Anales de la Literatura Española Contemporánea*, XVI, nos. 1-2 (1991), 55-72.

Pound, Ezra. "A Few Don'ts by an Imagiste," *Poetry: A Magazine of Verse*, I, no. 6 (1913), 200-06.

———. "Vorticism," *The Fortnightly Review*, XCVI (n.s.), no. 573 (1 September 1914), 461-71.

Predmore, Richard L. *Lorca's New York Poetry: Social Injustice, Dark Love, Lost Faith* (Durham, NC: Duke UP, 1980).

Reverdy, Pierre. "L'Image," *Nord-Sud*, II, no. 13 (1918), n.p.

Riffaterre, Michel. "Semantic Incompatibilities in Automatic Writing," in *About French Poetry from Dada to "Tel Quel": Text and Theory*, ed. Mary Ann Caws (Detroit, MI: Wayne State UP, 1974), pp. 223-41.

———. "The Extended Metaphor in Surrealist Poetry," in *Text Production*, trans. by Terese Lyons (New York: Columbia UP, 1983), pp. 202-20.

Ullmann, Stephen. *Language and Style* (New York: Barnes & Noble, 1964).

Urrutia, Jorge. "Federico García Lorca, Luis Buñuel y Jean Epstein, desde la poesía al cine," *El Extramundi y Los Papeles de Iria Flavia*, VIII, no. 31 (2002), 139-64.

Wheelwright, Philip. *Metaphor and Reality* (Bloomington: Indiana UP, 1962).

Ziolkowski, Theodore. *Disenchanted Images: A Literary Iconology* (Princeton: Princeton UP, 1977).

7

Lorca's "Tu infancia en Menton": A Reading

CCORDING TO LORCA'S OWN annotation, "Tu infancia en Menton" was composed on 3 January 1930 in New York.[1] It is written in
blank hendecasyllabics, taking its cue from the epigraph of Guillén,
which is repeated as the first, last, and nearly the middle line of the poem.[2]
Although the text is presented as continuous, in the original manuscript
there are very slightly larger breaks after four, eight, twelve lines, etc., and
there is a full stop at the end of lines 4, 8, 12, 16, etc., suggesting a possible
underlying organization in quatrains. This pattern is only broken around ll.
29-33, the emotional climax of the poem. If these lines are counted as an ex-
ceptional five-line stanza, the rest of the poem can similarly be divided into
three remaining quatrains.[3]

The text presents a poetic subject addressing another person with whom
he appears to have had a love affair. In the course of the poem, the subject
reviews the character and vicissitudes of the relationship, and it seems as if a
recriminatory note emerges, implying that the subject was more invested and
that the other person was emotionally distant, guarded, or unappreciative.
A series of references (to be discussed below) further suggests that this was
a homosexual relationship, but also that the other person may have had, or
gone on to have, relationships with women.

---

1   The autograph manuscript, with its original title "Ribera de 1910," is reproduced in facsimile in Anderson & Dennis, "The Manuscript of Lorca's 'Tu infancia
en Menton,'" 202-204; the date appears on 204.

2   The quotation is the last line of a poem entitled "Los jardines," from section 3 (first edition) of Jorge Guillén's *Cántico* (1928).

3   In this and the paragraphs that follow, line references correspond to the
"clean" text of "Tu infancia en Menton" offered at the end of this essay.

Difficulties in interpretation abound, due largely to the oblique language and cryptic imagery.[4] The definitive title seems to refer to the town of Menton on the French Côte d'Azur, and this in turn leads us to read "Ribera," in the original title, as a modified form of "Riviera." If the "present" of the poem is its date of composition, the original title would refer to a moment in time exactly twenty years earlier (1910). Thus the two titles appear as transformations or corollaries of one another, "Ribera" giving "Menton" and "1910" giving "Tu infancia."[5]

The opening lines (1-4) may offer, in highly abbreviated form, an outline of the other's life story. His childhood is situated at a good distance, having passed already into an "unreal" or fabled past, and the closure between childhood and adulthood may be represented by travel ("El tren") and an all-consuming interest in/curiosity about woman ("la mujer que llena el cielo"). Travel and assignations may be connoted by the mention of "los hoteles," but the main point seems to be that the negative qualities that the other demonstrated in the (later) relationship with the poetic subject already manifested themselves in the past: "tu soledad esquiva," "tu máscara pura." The other's distance, elusiveness, and aloofness lead to a feeling of solitude even when accompanied by another person, and the other puts on a mask, a façade, which impedes real knowing or communication. How one interprets "de otro signo" is more open to question: it could refer to either a heterosexual or a homosexual orientation, or else to the other's elusiveness in that he always appears "other" to the situation in which he currently finds himself. An alternative, but equally plausible, reading for ll. 2-4 would situate this imagined episode *after* the breakdown of the relationship with the subject, but with the rest of the details mostly the same: rupture, departure, a trip, hotels, a heterosexual affair that now commands the other's attention, but the other's continued elusiveness, sexual indeterminacy, and so on.

The dynamic of their relationship is presented perhaps most explicitly in ll. 9-12. Elsewhere, notably in "Oda a Walt Whitman," Lorca associates Apollo with homosexuality, and this is borne out at other junctures in Lorca's work (with several references to the Apollo and Daphne myth) and in classical tradition, where Apollo was depicted as bisexual (rejection by Daphne, love for Hyacinthus, other female loves). Apollo also embodies "youthful but

---

4   On the issue of the poem's extreme hermeticism, see, for example, Harris, *García Lorca*, 28.

5   This also avoids any confusion with one of the other poems in section 1, "1910 (Intermedio)."

mature male beauty."[6] The speaking subject asserts that he gave or demon-strated towards the other a "norma de amor," and this is glossed in the follow-ing line as "llanto con ruiseñor enajenado": the nightingale associated with night and romantic love, the bird a possible phallic form, the weeping a man-ifestation of his unhappiness or disappointment, the adjective "enajenado" referring to the extremity of his feelings (the vocabulary is very similar to that which reappears in the *Sonetos del amor oscuro*, 1935–36). By implication, the other seems to have been unwilling or incapable of appreciating the loftiness or intensity of this "norma," this model, exemplary mode of loving. Instead, the subject now describes this "hombre de Apolo" as "pasto de ruina." There may be a sense of a statue crumbling with the passage of time, but the pri-mary weight of this phrase suggests not transcendence but rather mortality or at the very least, absolute failure: the other, his nature or inherent char-acter, is "ruin fodder." It may function also as a variant on or a muffled echo of the "classical" morality phrase "pasto de gusanos."[7] Meanwhile, the verb *afilarse* ("te afilabas") strongly suggests a knife that cuts or wounds, and may well have phallic overtones, while the act of sharpening suggests preparation. What the other is readying himself for now or in the future, with the subject or possibly with a woman (ll. 2-4), is no more than "los breves sueños indeci-sos": there will be no romantic heights achieved, just short-lived, ill-defined dreams that offer no transcendence but rather hurtfulness.

The subject also appears to allude to their—unsatisfactory—relation-ship and lovemaking in ll. 5-8 and 13-16, though in each of the two "qua-trains" the latter two lines make the reference rather more explicit. The first phrase, "Es la niñez del mar," may gloss the title, along the lines of "it's your childhood beside the sea," though the ambiguous syntax also invites us to connect "niñez" with "mar" in a disconcerting combination: if the sea is age-old or eternal, how can it be youthful? The "soledad esquiva" and "máscara" (ll. 3-4) attributed to the other are picked up here in "tu silencio," a silence that—like a high-pitched and pure tone or note—shatters glass. The adjec-tive "yerta" may refer to the other's unresponsiveness (rigidity is also associ-ated with death), though also possibly to an erection. In whichever case, the other seems to be either truly ignorant, or else, more likely, inexperienced/ unschooled in matters of relationships or unknowing/unappreciative of the subject's passion, evoked in l. 8. "Ignorancia" also contrasts with the adjective "sabios" applied to the glass that breaks on his silence. Lines 7-8 suggest their

---

6   See Howatson, ed., *The Oxford Companion to Classical Literature*, 43.

7   Thanks are due to Professor James Whiston for suggesting this particular reading.

lovemaking, "fuego" with its usual connotations of physical heat and passion. The mention of "limitado," in a sense answering "yerta," may perhaps indicate that the subject felt that he was not able to transmit his physical passion to the other, or else that it exercised, simultaneously, a restricting, limiting influence on himself.

Likewise, picking up on "ignorancia," the other's thought—"pensamiento"—is figured as diametrically opposed to the subject, and constituting not a beacon for the present or future, but rather a "luz de ayer" (l. 13); with this notion it seems as if the whole course of their relationship has not been positively guided or purposeful, but rather merely haphazard: "índices y señales del acaso" (l. 14). "Tu cintura" in l. 15 answers "mi torso" in l. 8, but again with negative connotations. "Arena" may evoke the color of the other's skin, but primarily it connotes dryness, sterility, and constant shifting, an association reinforced by the restlessness in the phrase "sin sosiego." Unresponsiveness to the subject is suggested in l. 16, where it is possible that there may be another insinuation of the other's sexual interest in women. This reproach would contrast the "high points" of notions such as "norma" and "luz," with the physical lowliness, earthbound quality, and vestigial nature of "rastros que no escalan," which do not or cannot achieve any true elevation or transcendence.

Besides recrimination we find also, further into the poem, a kind of psychological denial—the (desperate) assertion of the survival and future of a relationship that has in all likelihood already ended (and here we are not far from the emotional world of *Diván del Tamarit*). The pivot is signaled by the "Pero" that opens l. 17. The subject now outlines what he envisages as his future actions in ll. 17-33, with three uses of the construction "he de" and one simple future tense (one every "stanza"). But rather than applying literally to how he foresees a possible outcome, this should be read rather as a kind of unreal fantasy or wish-fulfilment, projecting a relationship into the future that, almost certainly, has already foundered. Lines 17-20 depict the other's soul as separate and distinct from the rest of his body or self, with the implication that he is "soulless" ("sin ti") and that in its authenticity it is incapable of fathoming the falsity or duplicity that he represents ("que no te entiende"). The subject intends to try to discover this soul—the only "true" part of the other, in this last-ditch (but fantasized) attempt to establish a loving connection, as, according to l. 20, he has already been able to break through the mask (*cf.* l. 4) that the other wears. Line 19 could be read in a number of different ways. Breaking the mask (if indeed he has really done so) has clearly been a difficult and painful process; "Apolo detenido" could refer to occasions when Apollo was rebuffed by his love interests, or possibly to Apollo arrested in his physical, sexual, or emotional development: in "Oda a Walt Whitman" Lorca writes of "tus muslos de Apolo virginal."

In this desperate (yet illusionary) attempt to salvage something from the relationship, there appears to be both an active, dynamic aspect and a passive, self-sacrificial one, bordering on the masochistic. The subject now addresses the other first—and almost apocalyptically—as "león" and "furia de cielo," and then, suggesting the physicality and intensity of his passion, as "caballo azul de mi locura." The horse and the color blue are both associated with masculinity.[8] In a hypothetical but nonetheless clearly fixed place and time— the insistent "allí" of these lines—the subject envisages a kind of surrender or abandon: "te dejaré pacer en mis mejillas," "caballo" picking up "pacer" in the previous line, and "locura" relating to "enajenado" (l. 10). Place and time also come together in l. 24, where the other is figured as an elemental living being, a pulse, which is at once cosmically large, undefined, and incommensurate ("nebulosa") and at the same time tiny, discreet, and limited ("minutero").

As the subject's exclamations build toward their climax, his assertions also seem to become more general and less focused specifically on the other: thus the transition from "tu alma tibia" to "las piedras de alacranes" and "los vestidos de tu madre niña" as the objects of his quest. The first phrase suggests suffering (a desert landscape, stoning), combined with the possibility of being stung by the venomous insect hiding precisely under the stones, something (like the betrayals of the other?) that the subject now apparently willingly accepts. The second phrase goes in a very different direction, pointing again to the other's childhood and to the one "acceptable" face of femininity, the other's mother, now rendered "niña" (either through age, or through asexual innocence).

The next two lines (ll. 27-28) seem to describe the feelings or experience of the subject: "llanto de media noche" picks up the earlier "llanto con ruiseñor enajenado" but with a bleaker tone—this weeping now seems to be closer to despair, occurring in the very middle of the night and either because the subject finds himself actually alone or feels alone although with the other. The funereal connotations of "llanto" are activated by the following phrase. Although it lends itself to various interpretations, the "paño roto" suggests a scene where the (figuratively?) dead person's face ("la sien del muerto") had

8   A blue horse may appear in some of the drawings that Lorca did during the New York period. See Hernández, *Libro de los dibujos*, especially no. 164, "[Escena de domador y animal fabuloso]," and also nos. 162 and 166 (where the horse-like animal is blue and red).

been covered with a cloth. But the cloth is characterized negatively—"paño roto" (the rending of garments, or an echo of the rupture between them?)— and furthermore it seems possible also to read negatively the removal of the (light of the) moon from the face: in the middle of the night, the last glimmer of light (of dreams?) is denied the temple (by metonymy, the mind) of the subject.

After a moment's pause and the reiteration of the epigraph line, the search for the other's soul is reasserted. The subject represents his own body as a "hueco de venas": hollow, unfulfilled, purely corporeal; the other's soul is doubly an "alma extraña," as the subject is still looking for it and it is also alien to the other (as in l. 18). The tonality of "por los rincones" and "tibia" is picked up by "pequeña" y "sin raíces." At the climactic point of the poem (ll. 32-33), the speaking subject seems to transcend the other and the concrete specifics of the relationship; his ultimate goal is love itself, and here he invokes it explicitly, love that transcends—that is outside—time, love that is a universal principle, and love that the subject has never attained.

Starting in l. 33 he rebuffs any attempts to impede his search for it or to silence him. The focus shifts from the shortcomings and obstacles inherent in the relationship and the attitude of the other, to the more broadly social dimension, indicated first in the plural "Dejadme." In his complaint and in his quest he will not be silenced, by two related groups (or one large group that engages in two related activities). Saturn is a seed god and "espigas" are a clear symbol of promise, fertility, growth, etc.; however, snow is in opposition to this (cold, winter, etc.) and a negative, hence those that seek "espigas de Saturno por la nieve" are at the least seriously misguided or confused and possibly perverse.[9] The second group is more manifestly anti-nature. The phrase "por un cielo" could be taken in different ways: as in the sky or as in exchange for a heaven (animal sacrifice), while l. 37 appears to be in apposition to "cielo." This sky/heaven turns out to be anything but transcendent or spiritual: it is both a civilized, cold, hard, dry, antiseptic clinic and a wild, murky, untamed jungle, where with scientific dispassion fertility and/

---

9   Marcilly further points out that in "Pequeño poema infinito," "nieve" and "mujer" seem to be equated: see *Ronde et fable*, 49. This remark offers a further symbolic reading. Andrés Soria Olmedo devotes a good deal of attention to "Tu infancia en Menton" in *Fábula de fuentes*. His reading of the poem departs significantly from that offered by Marcilly, preferring to view it as a soliloquy rather than a dialogue. This substantially different perspective, however, introduces as many difficulties in the interpretation of the text as it resolves, and ultimately proves less than fully convincing (see 38-56).

or sexuality is negated. Besides being a seed god, we might remember also that Cronus, with whom Saturn is identified, castrated his father Uranus (a personification of the heavens), an association which may have determined the course of the thought in l. 36. Further, we should note that in ll. 2 and 43 it is "la mujer" "que llena el cielo."

The last eight lines present a kind of recapitulation combined with some minor further development. The invocations of "amor" open l. 38, with the repetition of a phrase from l. 15. Likewise l. 39 repeats l. 18. More invocations of "amor" open l. 40, while l. 42 recombines these elements. Line 43 repeats l. 2, and l. 45 repeats ll. 1 and 29. Of course, the tenor of some of these phrases is modified in the light of what has elapsed in the course of the poem since their first enunciation. In contrast to l. 32, the phrase in ll. 40-41 that is descriptive of love seems to foreground lightness and ephemerality, the passing of the swift but timid roe deer being rendered as "vuelo," love passing through the subject's breast (by metonymy, heart), but the breast then turning into an endless snowy plain, which expresses the subject's emotional state before and after the all-too-brief passage of the deer/love. The return to the epigraph line at the very end reinforces the stress on the inevitability of the passage of time and the irrecuperability of past experiences. Line 44 underlines this forcefully. The very identity of the subject and the other trail off into nothingness, the nothingness of the air and the nothingness of the autumn leaves as they are swept off in the breeze (the two senses of "aire").

If one were intent on seeking a strictly biographical reading of the poem, the best candidate for the "other" would seem to be Emilio Aladrén. Their relationship had come to an end before Lorca went to New York, and according to Martínez Nadal, Aladrén had embarked, in the spring of 1929, on a relationship with the woman, Eleanor Dove, whom he would marry in late 1931.[10] Even if these facts are not precisely accurate, Gibson describes Aladrén as a "mujeriego empedernido" who, because of his dalliances, drove Lorca to distraction.[11] Aladrén was born in 1906, which would have made him just four years old in 1910. According to Martínez Nadal, Aladrén told him and Lorca about the suicide of an elder brother in Venice, which occurred around 1918 while he and his mother were vacationing in or near Menton; on receiving the news, they immediately took an express train to Italy.[12] It has not been possible to verify any of these details.

* * * * *

10   See Martínez Nadal, *Cuatro lecciones*, 31.

11   Gibson, *Federico García Lorca*, I, 594.

12   Martínez Nadal, *Mi penúltimo libro*, 83.

VARIANTS IN THE ORIGINAL MANUSCRIPT

"Tu infancia en Menton" is, without doubt, an elusive, tantalizingly encoded text and constitutes a prime example of how the dense, personal register that characterizes Lorca's writing in New York frames a problem of expression and communication that may never be fully resolved. The reading offered above is shot through with uncertainties and is necessarily incomplete, but it can be further developed, albeit in a more acutely tentative fashion, by reference to the variants that appear in the autograph manuscript and which have been noted in the transcription offered below.[13] These variants could be said, in principle, to perform the same kind of function as do those in other manuscripts of poems from *Poeta en Nueva York*, pointing to ways in which interpretations can be nuanced, enriched, or reconsidered.[14] This provides an opportunity to sketch out some of these additional suggestions while readily acknowledging that their ultimate value is open to question.

Let us consider, for example, line 2: "[?]l tren y la mujer que llegan al cielo" (2i) / "El tren y la mujer que llena el cielo" (2ii).[15] The process at work here seems to correspond to a common creative strategy in Lorca that Derek Harris has identified in his discussions of *Poeta en Nueva York*, namely that during the revision of the first iteration, acoustic similarity (*llegan/llena* in this case) had a role to play in the alternative wording of the second.[16] The first iteration suggests a more mundane reading, pointing to a (possibly romantic) journey by rail, though with a literal destination being replaced by a more metaphorical one. The syntactic changes made in the second iteration, i.e. the shift in verb form, separate the train from the woman, clearly privileging the latter; the train becomes almost incidental while (heterosexual) love is affirmed as the principal goal or distraction.

Having said this, however, we still have to tackle the issue of the relationship between the opening four lines of the poem which, by virtue of their punctuation in the final version, are presented as three separate units. It is impossible to determine how they are connected. The syntactic and poematic structure would, on the face of it, suggest apposition, but this does not

---

13   This manuscript only came to light in the early 2000s and was presented and studied by Nigel Dennis in the first section of the article from which this current essay is excerpted.

14   A case in point would be "Poema doble del lago Eden." See Anderson, "*Et in Arcadia ego.*"

15   Line references from this point onward are to the diplomatic transcription offered below.

16   See Harris, "La elaboración textual."

resolve the problem. Are the train and the woman meant to function as some kind of gloss on the "infancia" of the title or the "fábula" of the epigraph? Or is there a change of emphasis and direction after l. 1? The second and third units (ll. 2 and 3-4) are easier to connect since they have more thematic material in common.

The discarded "carrito sin ruedas" in l. 3i is intriguing but perplexing and could simply be yet another example of the kind of encoded image found throughout *Poeta en Nueva York*, in which an initially positive idea is characteristically negated.[17] If it is to be understood as a wheeled cart or vehicle of some kind, it would logically link up, at least by association, with the train mentioned immediately before. The use of the diminutive form suggests that this could be a child's toy wagon or even a baby carriage (most normally *cochecito* but *carrito de bebé* is also found), an item from the *niñez* evoked in the poem's epigraph. The key idea here would be that of constrained movement or immobilization (reinforced by the use of the verb *atar*)—a derailment, as it were, of the figurative journey sketched out in the poem's opening line. This would frame and clarify the notion of failure and frustration that the text subsequently explores. However, as this same line continues ("los niños que lo ataban"), it becomes even more enigmatic. The pronoun "lo" appears to refer back to the *carrito* but could possibly refer to its owner. If the two parts of the line are read separately, side by side, as distinct though complementary, we may actually perceive two images of immobilization, applied, on the one hand, to the wagon/cart itself and, on the other, to its child owner/driver/occupant, now tied up by other children in some cruel game or prank. The fact that in line 9i the wagon appears with only a singular *rueda* is probably of little significance since it likely corresponds to a *lapsus* typical of the poet. The *mendigos* who appear in this line certainly suggest poverty and human suffering but could also link up with childhood, harking back to the world of Fuente Vaqueros in which the child curiously observes the beggars in the street as he plays. The allusion is so fleeting, however, that it is impossible to assign any definite meaning to it.

The discarded lines C and D ("O los guantes pequeños dominados / por el negro bullir de las hormigas") may be read as a fairly typical Lorquian vision of death. The poet closely associates formal attire (dress suits, black patent shoes, and the like) with burial, so the gloves would be entirely congruent in this context. Such a reading is reinforced by the location of the ants: in the earth, attacking the interred body. Lorca's vision seems to be that the (protec-

17   Correa identified many examples of this kind.

tive) gloves are no match for the ants, thereby opening up a broader perspective on the idea that love transcends corporeal death. The speaker seems to suggest that he wants one, or, if not that, then the other.

There may be a link between this "negro bullir de las hormigas" and the invitation to "pacer en mis mejillas" (l. 22), or the even more sinister "pacer sobre mis sienes" (l. 22ii), since it appears to tie in with the "blanco rostro devorado" mentioned later (l. 44i); but this is debatable. The attitude being struck here seems once more to be typically Lorquian, though in this case it is Christological. Many characters in Lorca's works offer themselves up in some kind of self-sacrifice, though within the parameters of the relationship suggested in this poem, the offer can also appear less altruistic and more passive-aggressive. In l. 21 we seem to see the slippage or superimposition of the lion and horse, reminiscent of the drawings alluded to earlier. Here the *león* is mentioned explicitly but the verb *pacer* can be more logically attached to the horse (the *caballo* of l. 23). Metonymically, *sienes* usually stand for the mind in Lorca's writing, while cheeks are places for kisses and caresses (*mejillas* appear at least once in the late sonnets). These lines make more compelling sense if they are understood to evoke the subject offering himself up to the other, for the other to do what he will with him. It is notable that the *león* is retained in the final version of the poem (l. 21) but the ants disappear with the suppression of the entire grouping of A/B/C/D and the reworking of l. 41i.

There are clearly no firm conclusions to be drawn. The meanings that can be assigned to the variants and reworkings are as uncertain as those that can be read into the final version, if not more so. Other readers may legitimately devise other interpretations that pursue different emphases. Beyond its intrinsic interest, however, the autograph manuscript at least provides a unique insight into its process of composition and revision. The diplomatic transcription that follows is presented in such a way as to make that process as clear as possible, differentiating between the successive iterations (where they exist) of individual lines.[18]

—Ribera de 1910—

---

18   In the transcription the numeration "9i 9ii 9iii" indicates successive iterations of the same line (first redaction, second redaction, etc.); square brackets enclosing question marks [??????] indicate an illegible letter, letters, or word; square brackets indicate an unsure reading of a word; and a dashed line ---------- indicates the end of a manuscript page.

Si, tu niñez: ya fabula de fuentes
—Jorge Guillen—

1   Si, tu niñez: ya fabula de fuentes.

2i   [?]l tren y la mujer que llegan al cielo
2ii   El tren y la mujer que llena   el cielo

3i   El carrito sin ruedas los niños que lo ataban
3ii   Tu soledad esquiva en los alambres
3iii   Tu soledad esquiva en los [????????]
3iv   Tu soledad esquiva en los [portales]

4i   y tu mascara pura de otra [?]
4ii   y tu mascara pura de otro signo.

5   Es la niñez del mar y tu silencio

6   donde los sabios vidrios se quebraban.

7i   Es tu yerta ignorancia donde gime
7ii   Es tu yerta ignorancia donde estuvo

8   mi torso limitado por el fuego

9i   El carrito sin rueda y los mendigos
9ii   norma de amor te di, hombre de estatua
9iii   norma de amor te di, hombre de Apolo

10i   despertaron en ti los otros cielos
10ii   despertaron en ti las otros lunas
10iii   llanto [???] ruiseñor enagenado
10iv   llanto con ruiseñor enajenado

11i   pero, pasto de niebla, te afilabas
11ii   pero, pasto de hierba, te afilabas
11iii   pero, pasto de ruina, te afilabas

12i   para la
12ii   para los breves sueños indecisos

13   Pensamiento de enfrente, luz de ayer

14   indices y señales del acaso.

15   Tu cintura de arena sin sosiego

16i   atiende solo [???]t[??] sin sombra
16ii   atiende solo   rastros que no escalan

17   Pero yo he de buscar por los rincones

18   tu alma tibia sin ti que no te entiende

19   con el dolor de Apolo detenido

----

20   con que he roto la mascara que llevas

21   Alli !leon! !alli! furia de cielo

22i   te dejare paecer
22ii   te dejare pacer sobre mis sienes
22iii   te dejare pacer en mis mejillas

23i   y aquel señor tam
23ii   y aquel señor blan
23iii   Alli !grande en la cripta de los ciegos
23iv   Alli !grande en la cueva de los ciegos
23v   Alli !grande en lo oscuro de las playas
23vi   Alli caballo azul de mi locura

24i   vivire por tu
24ii   pulso de nebulosa y minutero

25   He de buscar las piedras de alacranes

26i   y los [?????]dos de tu madre niña
26ii   y los   vestidos de tu madre niña

27   llanto de media noche y paño roto

28   que quitó luna de la sien del muerto

29   Si, tu niñez: ya fabula de fuentes

30i   Alma extraña de la que soy un hueco
30ii   Alma extraña de mi hueco de venas

31i   pero
31ii   te he de buscar pequeña y sin raíces

32   Amor de siempre amor !amor de nunca!

33i   !Oh si por [?]
33ii   !Oh si por Dios Amor ! Amor ! Dejadme !
33iii !Oh si yo quiero Amor ! Amor ! Dejadme !

34   No me tapen la boca los que buscan

35i   espigas de Saturno por el [?????]
35ii   espigas de Saturno por la nieve

36i   o castran animales por un mundo
36ii   o castran animales por un cielo

37i   clinica y selva de la atm
37ii   clinica y selva de la anatomía

A   Ahora soy yo que canto amor y puedo

Bi   Ahora soy yo que busca idea [????]
Bii   Ahora soy yo que busca dura idea

C   O los guantes pequeños dominados

D   por el negro bullir de las hormigas

38i   Amor amor amor. Niñe[?] del mar.
38ii Amor amor amor. Niñez del mar.

39   tu alma tibia sin ti que no te entiende

40i   Amor amor tus guantes dominados
40ii Amor amor un vuelo de la garza

41i   por el negro bullir de las hormigas.
41ii por el pecho sin fin de la blancura.

42   Y tu niñez amor y tu niñez

43   El tren y la mujer que llena el cielo

44i   ¿Donde a que blanco rostro devorado?
44ii Ribera de tu rostro devorado
44iii Libre [yo/ya] de tu boca ! libre ! libre
44iv ni tu ni yo ni el aire ni las hojas

45   Si, tu niñez: ya fabula de fuentes.

----

3 de Enero. 1930.
– New-York –

•

TU INFANCIA EN MENTON

Sí, tu niñez: ya fábula de fuentes.
Jorge Guillén.

1   Sí, tu niñez: ya fábula de fuentes.
2   El tren y la mujer que llena el cielo.
3   Tu soledad esquiva en los hoteles
4   y tu máscara pura de otro signo.
5   Es la niñez del mar y tu silencio
6   donde los sabios vidrios se quebraban.
7   Es tu yerta ignorancia donde estuvo
8   mi torso limitado por el fuego.
9   Norma de amor te di, hombre de Apolo,
10 llanto con ruiseñor enajenado,
11 pero, pasto de ruina, te afilabas
12 para los breves sueños indecisos.
13 Pensamiento de enfrente, luz de ayer,
14 índices y señales del acaso.
15 Tu cintura de arena sin sosiego
16 atiende sólo rastros que no escalan.
17 Pero yo he de buscar por los rincones
18 tu alma tibia sin ti que no te entiende,
19 con el dolor de Apolo detenido
20 con que he roto la máscara que llevas.
21 Allí león, allí furia de cielo,
22 te dejaré pacer en mis mejillas,
23 allí caballo azul de mi locura,
24 pulso de nebulosa y minutero.
25 He de buscar las piedras de alacranes
26 y los vestidos de tu madre niña,
27 llanto de media noche y paño roto
28 que quitó luna de la sien del muerto.
29 Sí, tu niñez: ya fábula de fuentes.
30 Alma extraña de mi hueco de venas,
31 te he de buscar pequeña y sin raíces.
32 ¡Amor de siempre, amor, amor de nunca!
33 ¡Oh, sí! Yo quiero. ¡Amor, amor! Dejadme.
34 No me tapen la boca los que buscan
35 espigas de Saturno por la nieve
36 o castran animales por un cielo,

37 clínica y selva de la anatomía.
38 Amor, amor, amor. Niñez del mar.
39 Tu alma tibia sin ti que no te entiende.
40 Amor, amor, un vuelo de la corza
41 por el pecho sin fin de la blancura.
42 Y tu niñez, amor, y tu niñez.
43 El tren y la mujer que llena el cielo.
44 Ni tú, ni yo, ni el aire, ni las hojas.
45 Sí, tu niñez: ya fábula de fuentes.

Works Cited

Anderson, Andrew A. "*Et in Arcadia ego*: Thematic Divergence and Convergence in Lorca's 'Poema doble del Lago Edén,'" *Bulletin of Hispanic Studies* (Glasgow), LXXIV, no. 4 (1997), 409-29.

———, with Nigel Dennis. "The Manuscript of Lorca's 'Tu infancia en Menton,'" *Bulletin of Spanish Studies*, LXXXII, no. 2 (2005), 181-204.

Correa, Gustavo. *La poesía mítica de Federico García Lorca* (Madrid: Gredos, 1970).

Gibson, Ian. *Federico García Lorca*, vol. I: *De Fuente Vaqueros a Nueva York (1898-1929)* (Barcelona: Grijalbo, 1985).

Harris, Derek. *García Lorca: "Poeta en Nueva York"* (London: Grant & Cutler/Tamesis Books, 1978).

Harris, Derek. "La elaboración textual de *Poeta en Nueva York*: el salto mortal," *Revista Canadiense de Estudios Hispánicos*, XVIII, no. 2 (1994), 309-15.

Hernández, Mario. *Libro de los dibujos* (Madrid: Tabapress/Fundación Federico García Lorca, 1990).

Howatson, M.C., ed. *The Oxford Companion to Classical Literature*, 2nd ed. (Oxford: Oxford UP, 1993).

Marcilly, C. *Ronde et fable de la solitude à New York. Prélude à "Poeta en Nueva York" de F. G. Lorca* (Paris: Ediciones Hispano-Americanas, 1962).

Martínez Nadal, Rafael. *Cuatro lecciones sobre Federico García Lorca* (Madrid: Fundación Juan March/Cátedra, 1980).

———. *Federico García Lorca. Mi penúltimo libro sobre el hombre y el poeta* (Madrid: Casariego, 1992).

Soria Olmedo, Andrés. *Fábula de fuentes. Tradición y vida literaria en Federico García Lorca* (Madrid: Residencia de Estudiantes, 2004).

8

Et in Arcadia Ego: Thematic Divergence and Convergence in Lorca's "Poema doble del lago Edén"

IN THE EARLY 1930S, when Lorca returned to Madrid literary life after his stay in the United States and Cuba, friends would ask him what he had done in New York, to which he was wont to reply: "He hecho lo más difícil: he sido poeta en Nueva York" (Entrambasaguas, 4). But Lorca did not spend all of his time in the city; during the last third of August and the first two-thirds of September 1929 he vacationed first in Eden Mills, Vermont, and then in two other rural locations in New York State. Being a "poeta en Nueva Inglaterra" was still arduous, but in a different way, for as he wrote to Ángel del Río from Vermont: "los bosques y el lago me sumen en un estado de desesperación poética muy difícil de sostener. Escribo todo el día y a la noche me siento agotado" (García Lorca, *Epistolario*, II, 130-31). Indeed, these weeks were a fertile period as far as his poetic output is concerned, and although the original autograph of the "Poema doble del lago Edén" has not survived, it must surely date from the ten or so days that Lorca spent with his young American friend Philip Cummings at his family's holiday rental cabin located deep in the Vermont countryside.[1]

---

1   See Schwartz, 50-53; Eisenberg, 237-38; Gibson, II, 34-46; and García Lorca, *Songs, passim*. Lorca was in Eden Mills from 17-19 August to 29-30 August (the precise dates have not been established). The poem "Cielo vivo" is dated on its manuscript 24 August 1929 and "Tierra y luna" 28 August 1929. Other possible candidates for composition during this brief Vermont stay are "Vaca" (Schwartz, 53) and "Ruina" (García Lorca, *Songs*, 123). In terms of its imagery, there are a host of links between the "Poema doble" and "Infancia y muerte," dated in New York, 7 October 1929.

The poem strikes a particularly autobiographical, confessional note, even for this collection where it is often difficult to keep separate the textual speaking subject and the historical García Lorca—a division which the poet himself tended to erase in his "conferencia-recital" of *Poeta en Nueva York*:

> Yo bajaba al lago y el silencio del agua, el cuco, etc., etc., hacía que no pudiera estar sentado de ninguna manera, porque en todas las posturas me sentía litografía romántica con el siguiente pie: ¡Federico dejaba vagar su pensamiento![2] Pero, al fin, un espléndido verso de Garcilaso me arrebató esta testarudez plástica. Un verso de Garcilaso:
>
> *Nuestro ganado pace. El viento espira.*
>
> y nació este poema doble del Lago de Eden Mills.[3]

The "Poema doble" is littered with highly characteristic details of the vicinity—the lake itself, mist, ferns, woods, spruces, pastures, and cows. Lorca's letters home and Cummings's vacation diary, entitled "August in Eden. An Hour of Youth,"[4] flesh out the references and provide occasional clues as to the genesis of some of the more difficult imagery.[5] Two of Cummings's descriptions are worth quoting at some length:

---

2   On the "romantic" atmosphere of the locale, see the letter to his family (García Lorca, "Cartas inéditas de García Lorca [II]," ix) and to Ángel del Río (García Lorca, *Epistolario*, II, 131).

3   García Lorca, "Conferencia-recital de *Poeta en Nueva York*," 262. In stanza 9 of the poem, the second line originally ran "Federico García Lorca, a la orilla de este lago"; the self-referential proper name was replaced with the phrase "rosa, niño y abeto" in all subsequent versions. On the issue of biographical readings, see Burshatin, 235-36; Dennis, 54, note 2; Geist, 549; Gibson, II, 42; and Ilie, 771.

4   In García Lorca, *Federico García Lorca escribe a su familia*, and García Lorca, *Songs*, 125-66, respectively.

5   From this point of view, the two most important letters are the one that Lorca sent to Ángel del Río from Eden Mills (*Epistolario*, II, 130-31) and the one dated 22 August 1929 written to his family (first edited by García-Posada, "Cartas inéditas de García Lorca [II]"), both already cited. There are several mentions of the lake, the woods, and the ferns, and Lorca observes at one point that "Hace frío y el agua parece de plomo oscuro. No se sabe dónde está el reflejo y dónde la cosa reflejada, y por la noche nos vemos y hablamos bajo la luz del petróleo" (García-Posada, "Cartas inéditas de García Lorca [II]," ix).

The lake has been lulled to a pure mirror-like placidity and the long files of hills and trees have been doubled inversely in the multiplication of the dusky hours. The solitary ghost-shadow of a low skimming bat moves over the clear reflection on the lake of the evening sky—a thing of patched clouds and sociable stars. (128)

The moon is only an hour high over the dark points of the steepled spruces. There is a soft thin mist that rises from the cooling lake... As the water laps the smooth stones of the shore the movement makes six small reflected moons do a symphonic dance. (149)

Furthermore, Cummings makes some acute and revealing comments on his new friend's approach to poetic composition and the relationship between lived experience and the literary text:

I went walking through the woodland this morning with the Spanish poet who has just come. He found many delightful thoughts in the woods ... One decaying stump was for him the ruin of a citadel of Babylon, another became a castle ... He watched me push over a few rotted trees and he said I was a Cyclops intent on destroying the weak and unfit. In other words what had always been a lovely woodland to me had become for him something symbolic. (159)

This same notion is fleshed out in another memoir by Cummings, "The Mind of Genius," also included in *Songs*:

Walking in Madrid on a clammy late autumn day of rain, Federico expanded in deep thoughts and one statement remains sharply with me: "*Oiga*, Felipe, this rain comes chattering out of the mountains, shivering with the cold. It came from the Escorial where all the cold dead rains are born" ... That whole walk he was in a mood of "translation" of the visible into the intangible. A similar walk in the forests of Mount Norris in Vermont was in just this key. When Federico was in his mood of tenseness he fastened heroic symbols onto the least of things. (179-80)

As for Cummings, he refers, among other things, to the pastoral mode (127, 159), a talc mine (131, 132, 136, 138, 142, 152), delicate sweet-scented ferns (134, 137, 146, 147, 154, 157, 158, 164), spruces (144, 147, 148, 149, 153, 158) and pastures and meadows (134, 157, 158); all references are from "August in Eden. An Hour of Youth."

Despite the suggestiveness of these observations, in what follows I shall try mainly to resist the biographical temptation and, rather, address certain basic literary-critical questions: how do various themes and preoccupations arise?, how are they focused?, where do they lead?, how widely do they range?, and, perhaps most importantly, how do they coexist and coalesce in the single text?

The poem opens with the speaker presumably beside the "Lago Edén" of the title (though this is not made explicit until stanza 9 and then stanza B),[6] and he finds himself in quiet, restful surroundings, as suggested by the epigraph; it is indeed an appropriate moment for solitary meditation. It may be that the reflection *on* self that constitutes much of the text is prompted by the reflection *of* self in the surface of the water, which would then constitute the most obvious and immediate instance of doubling in the text ("Poema *doble*"), but if that is the case it is not directly established or represented—no faces peer back at the speaker from the watery depths. The Narcissus myth and reflecting surfaces of all kinds appear frequently in Lorca's poetry, but here the motif is entirely implicit.[7] Rather the speaker is visited by "mi voz antigua," where his voice stands simultaneously for self and self-expression and for poetry and poetic expression. This voice is figured perhaps as a faithful, affectionate dog or else as the lake itself, lapping at his feet on the water's edge.[8] We should note the use of "ser" with "ignorante": his self and his poetry of the past were untutored in "los densos jugos amargos" of present-day, adult life. This last strongly negative phrase contrasts directly with "los frágiles helechos mojados" (with its identical syntactic structure: definite article-adjective-noun-adjective), ferns that concretely form part of the lakeside scene, a setting which in turn seems to have somehow enabled the re-establishing of contact. I am particularly put in mind of "San Rafael (Córdoba)" (from *Romancero gitano*), where likewise two Córdobas, past and present,

---

6   See my edition of the poem, given in the appendix. In the course of this article I shall refer to the variant stanzas quite frequently, and for the purposes of elucidation they will be used to supplement the reading of the final version of the text. A consideration of all the aesthetic consequences of their inclusion or exclusion is beyond the scope of the present study.

7   "Espejos" are mentioned in the first variant stanza, labelled A, which was later deleted. See Burshatin, 231-33; Delong-Tonelli, 252; and Ilie, 770, 772, 774, 777.

8   In his journal Cummings refers both to a dog that accompanied them on their walks (160) and to the water lapping the stones of the shore (149). See Ilie, 774, 777; and Predmore, 81.

real and illusory, Moorish and Roman, are suggested by the reflections in the Guadalquivir.

Various thematic lines lead off from this first stanza, and the first one that I want to pursue has to do with the writing of poetry. The acknowledgement of Garcilaso, which acts as a kind of opening framing device, makes it clear that Lorca is very conscious—self-conscious—of what he is doing, and at the same time he inscribes himself within Spanish poetic tradition.[9] In stanza 2, the line "cuando todas las rosas manaban de mi lengua" may be read as an evocation of the speaker's, possibly idealized, literary past: beauty, love, and nature were once the topics of his poetry, which flowed with effortless ease.[10] In stanza 7 he hopes that somehow this "voz antigua" can assert itself over and perhaps eradicate another voice, "esta voz de hojalata y de talco," his present style of poetry, metallic and powdery, artificial, sterile, inhuman, the product of—or perhaps the response to—an alienating, industrial society.[11] Stanza C adumbrates two of the principal stylistic options open to poets at the end of the 1920s, but the speaker appears to criticize and reject both.[12] Rather, as he writes in stanza 9, his ultimate goal would be achieved "matando en mí la burla y la sugestión del vocablo": language is tricky, slippery, and deceitful, and these qualities need to be controlled or eliminated in order to express authentically a simple but profound truth.[13]

Evidently, then, the composition is a metapoem, a poem about poetry past, present, and future, about poetic styles, and about the difficulty of writing poetry. But the text has one final surprise in store for us, at the beginning of the last stanza. The phrase "Así hablaba yo" acts as a retroactive framing device, putting the preceding stanzas into a different perspective: the "yo" of stanza 11 looks on knowingly, observing the "yo" of stanzas

---

9   See Burshatin, 230-31; Delong-Tonelli, 252; and Ilie, 774.

10   See Burshatin, 236; Geist, 554; Ilie, 776; and Pratt, 249. A very similar phrase, "veremos [...] manar rosas de nuestra lengua," is to be found in "Ciudad sin sueño" (*Poeta en Nueva York*). Notice that at the very beginning of Garcilaso's "Égloga segunda," the "claras ondas" of the spring bring to Albanio's mind "la memoria d'aquel día" (ll. 4-5): *Poesías castellanas*, 135.

11   See Burshatin, 236; Ilie, 772; and Pratt, 249.

12   See Cano Ballesta, *passim*.

13   See Ilie, 777-78. Compare this passage in the first of Lorca's *Alocuciones argentinas* (May/June 1935): "Cada día que pasa huyo con más angustia de lo artificioso, para entregarme a una sencillez que ansío en todos mis actos y en toda mi obra, y que me hace buscar la expresión vital con toda la mayor frescura que puedo captarla en el vuelo misterioso de la poesía y la naturaleza. Esta ansia, este deseo me lleva a huir de toda retórica fácil, de todo juego de palabras" (13).

1-10; the present of the verbs throughout the poem—"adivino," "Estás aquí," "no quiero," etc.—is suddenly transformed into a recollected and narrated past; and from this superior vantage point the speaker now seems privy to important information previously unavailable to him.[14] Besides creating a further doubling—the bulk of the poem is this final speaker's transcript of the prior scene—these different layers bring into focus various fundamental problems of self-reflection, autobiographical writing, and lyric poetry. How can the subject become, simultaneously, the object? Similarly, how can the poet-present accurately evoke the poet-past if his style has changed in the interim?; how can the poet write a poem about the inadequacy and shifting nature of language, if he has to use that very language to write the poem?; and how can he aspire to a direct, immediate, sincere, and truthful self-expression if again language is his only available mode of expression?

These perhaps unanswerable questions lead us to a final, more empirical one: what kind of poetic language does Lorca actually use? But here again the response is not entirely straight-forward. Occasionally the writing (if not the sense behind it) is fairly transparent: "Quiero llorar porque me da la gana / como lloran los niños del último banco" (stanza 8), a reference to misbehaving or poorly achieving schoolchildren being banished to the back of the classroom.[15] Sometimes the imagery is at first sight surprising but turns out to be quite easy to interpret, as, for instance, with "los densos jugos amargos" (stanza 1) or "Cuando todas las rosas manaban de mi lengua" (stanza 2). More commonly, however, the language is of a more advanced, "encoded" variety, which the reader has to struggle to decipher, although it does appear that there is usually a "meaning" there, behind the disconcerting linguistic surface, waiting to be perceived and extracted. A good deal of the text falls into this category, and is well represented by the second two lines of stanza 10, commented on in detail below. Finally, there are a few passages and images that virtually resist interpretation, such as "Eva come hormigas / y Adán fecunda peces deslumbrados." Here it is difficult if not impossible to know if the writing is genuinely hermetic (be that hermeticism willed or accidental), or if the ingenuity of readers and critics has not yet been sufficiently exercised to crack the imagistic code. Be this as it may, the conclusions are clear: the poem itself is spoken predominantly with that "voz de hojalata y de talco," and there is a profusion of "la burla y la sugestión del vocablo." In this sense the aims expressed in stanzas 7, 8, and 9 are still very much in the future; the

---

14   See Burshatin, 237; Craige, 15, 18; Ilie, 775-76; and Pratt, 251.

15   Unlike the Anglo-Saxon practice of bringing them to the front; see Gibson, I, 95; and Havard, 227.

speaker may consciously repudiate a certain mode of expression, but he finds it considerably harder to eliminate its traits from his current poetic speech.

Alongside these metapoetic explorations and to an extent in parallel to them, the theme of past and present and of past and present selves is also developed. In stanza 2 the "voz antigua" is apostrophized as the utterance of the love and the truth he once possessed, and as a medium through which it was once possible for him to express them. The anaphora leads us on down to "abierto costado," at which point the speaker is cast both as Adam and Christ, and it is hard not to recall the many Christological references in Lorca's earlier writings. Adam's task of naming things is that of every poet,[16] and the poet's lyrical voice ("la voz que es mi hijo" in stanza D) is part of him but separate from him in much the same relationship as Eve bears to Adam. The iconography of Christ's wound in his side directly recalls Adam's rib, while the gash left by the lance also figuratively has lips, and thus becomes a metaphorical mouth from which this voice issues, expressing suffering but also self-sacrifice, divine truth, and a love for mankind.[17] This raises the possibility of a further reading for "rosas"—remember the "trescientas rosas morenas" representing the blood stain in Lorca's "Romance sonámbulo"—and it also points forward to stanza 3.

Here the first impression is one of logical contradiction: the voice that emerged from the wound is now directly addressed, and its agency has apparently completely switched; equipped with lips, mouth, and tongue, it is "bebiendo mi sangre." The shift is most probably to be explained in terms of the change of time-frame. The opening lines of stanza 1 say what the voice was, and stanza 2 elaborates on what the voice once was to him. But in stanza 3 the past voice is in the here and now—"Estás aquí"—with the speaker in the present,[18] and these lines elaborate on the relationship between them, now that the voice has—at least temporarily—come back to him. Following the Christological lead, the first line could suggest that the bond between voice and speaker is analogous to that between communicants and Christ, with

---

16   See Craige, 16-17; Harris, 29; and Predmore, 81.

17   In this regard, see the reading offered by Havard: "The former prepubescent voice is, in its innocence, the voice of the poet's 'amor' and 'verdad,' but also the voice of his 'abierto costado' since his innocence has been crucified in the process of growing up" (225). On the symbolic significance of the wound in Christ's side, as treated by Lorca, see Anderson, "García Lorca como poeta petrarquista," 503.

18   See Havard, 225. Ilie (776) is one of the few critics to recognize the apparent incompatibility between the content of this stanza and what comes before and after.

the relevant related associations of transubstantiation and the Real Presence. On the other hand, if the speaker is metaphorically hemorrhaging, then this could represent the fact that he is rapidly losing what little remains to him of his childhood and childlike qualities. The "voz antigua," coming out of the past, feeds on that; indeed the voice, in order to survive in the hostile present, must nourish itself thus. The second line acts mainly as a gloss, the variant reading "amor" connecting back with stanza 2, while "humor" can be read as denoting either mood or else humor as liquid (cf. John 19:34). Overall, then, the tenor of stanza 3 is mixed: this visitation is not an entirely positive experience, and it is hard to avoid the perception of the "voz antigua" as some kind of bloodsucking creature that may be weakening him—being reminded of the past is certainly not an unalloyed good (Craige, 17).

On the other hand, the depiction of the speaker's present circumstances is entirely and unequivocally negative, taking its cue from those cloying bitter juices that he cannot avoid tasting and perhaps swallowing. The adjective "ignorante" in stanza 1 stands in direct counterposition to the emphatic "Yo sé" opening stanza 5. Here he asserts that he is now well instructed in the ways of the world, and in particular about violence, pain, and death: the first couplet refers, perhaps, to an age-old abortion practice,[19] and the second, through the explicit allusion to St. Lucy, to torture, dismemberment, and martyrdom. The gouged eyes are a horrendous sight, and by dint of being displaced and alone but still open and looking—"despiertos," they themselves experience horror.[20] Likewise, his recent experience in the city is captured in the second couplet of stanza 3, also, significantly enough, concerned with sight: his own eyes, with which he normally perceives himself, shatter in the harsh wind, which must be very different to the bucolic breeze of the epigraph; they appear to be dazzled and hurt by the bright reflections from the burnished aluminum of "high-tech" modern artefacts—buildings, cars, buses, trains, planes—while at the same time the wind carries to him the cries of the alienated urban masses who seek temporary solace in often highly toxic bootleg liquor.[21]

---

19   See the poem "Asesinato," also from *Poeta en Nueva York*, two of whose lines read: "Un alfiler que bucea / hasta encontrar las raicillas del grito."

20   In the "Égloga segunda" Albanio reveals his love to Camila by having her look in a spring pool; later, revisiting the scene, the chaste Camila reflects: "¿Sabes que me quitaste, fuente clara, / los ojos de la cara?, que no quiero / menos un compañero que yo amaba, / mas no como él pensaba" (ll. 746-49): *Poesías castellanas*, 157.

21   The importance of eyes in Lorca's imagery is a central point of Dennis's article (41-42); the notion of fragmentation/disintegration—suggested here by the

A third line of interpretation also leads off from the title of the poem and the epigraph. The quoted verse is l. 1146 from the latter half of the Second Eclogue. Nemoroso has started to tell the story about Severo and the Duques de Alba, and Salicio encourages him to continue, as the circumstances are ideal:

> 1146   Nuestro ganado pace, el viento espira,
>   Filomena sospira en dulce canto
>   y en amoroso llanto s'amancilla;
>   gime la tortolilla sobre'l olmo,
> 1150   preséntanos a colmo el prado flores
>   y esmalta en mil colores su verdura;
>   la fuente clara y pura, murmurando,
>   nos está convidando a dulce trato. (170)

Garcilaso's "Églogas" invoke Theocritus, Virgil, and the whole pastoral tradition, while here, clearly, the epigraph is the opening line of the description of a *locus amoenus*—a topos whose origin can be traced back to early pastoral poetry.[22] As Curtius reminds us, "To write poetry under trees, on the grass, by a spring—in the Hellenistic period, this came to rank as a poetical motif in itself" (Curtius, 187). But there were real forests, meadow-pastures, and cows grazing around Eden Mills, Vermont, which, in its literary transposition, becomes simultaneously a New England Arcadia and, by dint of its name, the biblical Garden.[23] This kind of slippage is nothing new—think of Virgil's so-called "Messianic Eclogue," the assimilation of features of the Elysian Fields into Christian poets' descriptions of Paradise, the Hellenized representation of Christ as an Arcadian shepherd, or the horns and cloven hooves of the Greek Satyrs that were transferred to Satan.[24]

---

verb "se quiebran"—is treated on 44-45.

22   Curtius, 185-200; Delong-Tonelli, 252; and Geist, 555. The "Égloga segunda" contains other similar descriptions: see ll. 431-51 (148) and ll. 733-45 (157). Burshatin (240, note 22) points out another instance of doubling: for Fernando de Herrera, the "Égloga segunda" "Es de doblado título y se introducen en ella dos pastores."

23   On Arcadia one may consult Hall, 30-31; Howatson, ed., 48-49; and Radice, 63-64.

24   Curtius, 200; Hall, 273, 280; Howatson, ed., 202; and Radice, 164.

Now, the village of Eden Mills, Lake Eden, and its immediate surroundings are and are not paradise.[25] Following quite closely the notion of *menos-
precio de corte y alabanza de aldea*, New York City is anathematized elsewhere
in *Poeta en Nueva York* as a kind of living hell, and opposed to the simple, bucolic virtues of the countryside.[26] Furthermore, as against the trend-setting,
go-head, ultra-modern, fast-paced rhythm of Manhattan—sky-scrapers,
suspension bridges, illuminated advertisements, the subway, cars, zeppelins,
airplanes, Broadway, and all the rest—rustic Eden is comfortably set back
in time: the daily pace is relaxed, the agricultural lifestyle is essentially the
same as always, the village is distant from the city and barely touched by the
hurly-burly of the modern urban environment (Pratt, 251; Predmore, 81). Indeed, Eden Mills is almost timeless, almost seemingly outside of time, and it
is precisely this setting that puts the speaker in mind of, and makes him long
for, the real Eden.

Another doubling occurs, then, in the conjunction of the Christian Garden of Eden with pagan Arcadia, which in turn is closely related to the allied
notion of the Golden Age. Pan—the "hombrecillo de los cuernos" of stanza 4[27]—presides over this decidedly heterodox Eden *cum* "locus amoenus"
cum Arcady *cum* Golden Age, and we should note that Saturn, mentioned
in stanza 11, was the ancient Roman god of agriculture who reigned during
the Golden Age.[28] While the Garden of Eden is, by definition, associated
with a pre-sexual state, and the Fall occasioned by the initiation into sexual
consciousness, there are mixed messages in the "Poema doble" about its version of an Edenic Arcadia. The last line of stanza 2 evokes a pre-pubescent
world before the appearance of the horse, but in stanza 4 the site gives the
impression rather of a place of robust physicality, playfulness, and indeed of
guiltless sexuality.[29] Pan himself had a powerful libido, as did his companions

---

25   As Lorca wrote to his parents: "Al cabo de estar un rato bogando, ya te en-
cuentras endulzado y como dormido en esta luz paradisíaca" (García Lorca, *Lettere
americane*, 118).

26   See García-Posada, 181. On Antonio de Guevara and his work *Menospre-
cio...*, see Jones, 38-48.

27   Hall, 232-33; Howatson, ed., 406; Radice, 183; and see Burshatin, 229, and
Semprún Donahue, 82. It is interesting to note that Lorca started on the composition of another poem entitled "Baco en New England"; the fact that it is dedicated
to the Misses Tyler, who lived in Eden Mills, allows us to date this brief, unfinished
manuscript to the Vermont period (García Lorca, *Manuscritos neoyorquinos*, 204).

28   Hall, 272-73; Howatson, ed., 509; and Radice, 213.

29   The image of "el jardín de los saltos" occurs in the postscript of a letter
to Jorge Guillén of 2 September 1926 (García Lorca, *Epistolario*, I, 160). There are

the satyrs and nymphs, the former often depicted with the tail and ears of a horse.[30] The briefly described actions attributed to Adam and Eve are frankly rather cryptic: does Eve demonstrate a childlike, carefree lack of discrimination in eating ants, or might ants symbolize death (as they do elsewhere in Lorca's poetry), vanquished and even used for sustenance? Likewise, Adam's powers of virility extend to different areas of creation, to fish who are dazzled—the faculty of sight yet again.[31]

It is this place that the speaker wants to enter, or perhaps, it is to this place that he wants to return. Both the story of the expulsion from the Garden and the classical fourfold division of the Ages of the World—Golden, Silver, Bronze, Iron—found in Hesiod, Virgil, and Ovid, enshrine the idea of decline, of things worsening rather than improving, and in addition the impossibility of return, the irrecuperable nature of the past, of the idyllic starting-point.[32] Furthermore, the idea of childhood as a lost paradise is a commonplace in modern literature, and in this the "Poema doble" is no different, though here the range of reference is perhaps richer and more complex than in many cases. It is to this place and time that the "voz antigua" corresponds, but the voice emerging from the past cannot necessarily enable the speaker's

---

also some rather arresting affinities with a passage in Ortega's *La deshumanización del arte* (1925): "el arte pierde seriedad y las cosas comienzan a brincar livianamente, libres de toda formalidad. Ese piruteo universal es para él el signo auténtico de que las musas existen. Si cabe decir que el arte salva al hombre, es sólo porque le salva de la seriedad de la vida y suscita en él inesperada puericia. Vuelve a ser símbolo del arte la flauta mágica de Pan, que hace danzar los chivos en la linde del bosque" (89).

30   Hall, 273; Howatson, ed., 510; Radice, 213; and see Burshatin, 229-30; Craige, 17; Geist, 554; Harris, 29-30; Havard, 225-26; Pratt, 249, 251; and Predmore, 82.

31   Various critics have struggled with these lines. The interpretation proposed by García-Posada (181-82) is not at all convincing, that suggested by Predmore (82) is debatable, while Burshatin (230-31) refers to "solitary erotic exertions" and "bewildering acts of onanistic sensuality"; my own reading is closer to those put forward by Delong-Tonelli (253) and Harris (29).

32   Hall, 9-10; Howatson, ed., 252; and Radice, 121. Dennis writes: "The subjects of Lorca's poems seem to be hounded by a sense of estrangement from their own representations, by their realization that from the moment at which that original edenic wholeness was ruptured, they have become somehow distinct and separate, disfigured, emptied, or sinisterly absent" (48).

return there. Similarly Eden Mills is again like Eden but is not Eden because it reminds him of his childhood but it is not his childhood.[33]

To recapitulate: the poem's Arcadian Eden is attractive for a number of predictable reasons: bitterness, disillusion, confusion, pain, and suffering are not known there, innocence and plenitude are its primary characteristics, things are what they appear to be, straightforward and easy, physicality, play, and sexuality are not frowned upon, all basic needs are presumably automatically satisfied. But there is one further feature, already alluded to, that is arguably the most telling of all: this place, just like childhood, is outside time.

Dotted through the text are painful reminders of temporality: stanza A, cut possibly because it was too explicit, contains one statement to this effect, the adjective "oxidado" (in stanza 5) reminds us that corrosion is a common process that takes place over time, while "el reloj encenizado" of stanza 10 drives the point home (Ilie, 776). Time ticks away, and the clock is covered with ash or else actually turned to ash because ash is what all sublunary material eventually becomes and is hence a conventional *memento mori*. These references acquire greater force when we remember that the ancient Italian god Saturn was subsequently identified with the Cronus of Greek mythology.[34] In Eden Mills Cronus temporarily suspends the trains and their rigorously regimented schedules and timetables. The nostalgic longing for childhood is thus also a flight from self-consciousness and from the adult's consciousness of time, and the desire to escape temporality is evidently also a desire to elude death.

Javier Herrero has elucidated the companion image in stanza 10 of the "luna de castigo," involving the classic Lorcan symbol of the horned moon combined with a reference to the *picador*'s role in a bullfight. The speaker is figured first as naked—defenseless but at the same time "authentic," and he finds himself inside a "laberinto de biombos" (148; see also Pratt, 250). On its own, the labyrinth suggests disorientation and an inability to chart

---

33   To his family Lorca wrote: "Ahora empiezan a encender las luces. Hay un ambiente que me recuerda mi niñez en Daimuz" (García Lorca, "Cartas inéditas de García Lorca [II]," ix), but to Ángel del Río he expressed himself less guardedly: "Han encendido las luces de petróleo y toda mi infancia viene a mi memoria envuelta en una gloria de amapolas y cereales ... Esto es acogedor para mí, pero me ahogo en esta niebla y esta tranquilidad que hacen surgir mis recuerdos de una manera que me queman" (García Lorca, *Epistolario*, II, 131).

34   Hall, 119-20; Howatson, ed., 161; and Radice, 148-49. My reading of the reference to Saturn is very different to those offered by García-Posada (183) and Havard (228).

one's own course; however, this maze is made of folding screens, which do not form very substantial walls but which rather serve for people to hide behind or to change their clothes behind. He is thus a lone, vulnerable, but truthful individual wandering in a confusing world of appearances, deceit, and mutability. To this basic reading is grafted the notion of the speaker as Theseus, confronting the Minotaur in Daedalus's labyrinth, and inasmuch as the hornèd crescent moon is a time-honored taurine image, it follows—in one sense at least—that this should be the site where "mi desnudo" "recibe la luna de castigo." However, this last phrase is calqued on the term "vara de castigo," which refers to the lance wielded by *picadores* in a bullfight. Consequently, a third metaphorical level emerges in which the speaker becomes the bull (rather than the fighter of the bull/minotaur),[35] confined in the arena of the bullring (whose perimeter is constituted by *barreras* and *burladeros*), and wounded by the "vara/luna de castigo," that is, by all that the moon most commonly connotes in Lorca's poetry. If the speaker is imagined in one of these figurative transformations as a sacrificial victim stabbed by the *picador*'s lance, then this in turn will remind us again of the Christological overtones, with a strong and very specific echo of the Roman soldier's spear.[36] The speaker has no option but to endure these various intimations of mortality, and he comes to what is perhaps the most important conclusion in the whole poem, that even in Eden Mills Death is always on the prowl—"la Muerte me estaba[...] buscando": *Et in Arcadia ego*.[37]

In the light of this consideration, the speaker feels the need to engage with the here and now and to seek a measure of self-fulfillment in the striving towards short-term goals. These reactions and priorities, charted principally in stanzas 6, 8, and 9, lead us to one further thematic nexus, which in turn looks back to the concerns about past, present, and future selves and voices: the issue of sexual identity and its expression, focused in the exclamation "¡Mi amor humano!" (stanza 6). The irremediable loss of childhood is tied to the onset of puberty—temporality and sexuality manifestly go hand in hand.

---

35   Herrero (149-50) addresses this apparent contradiction, which is also to be found in *Llanto por Ignacio Sánchez Mejías*.

36   In the very first stanza of Lorca's "Oda al Santísimo Sacramento del Altar" Christ is described as "desnudo" and "perseguido por siete novillos capitales," and in the second as "Punzado por tu Padre con aguja de lumbre."

37   Hall, 116-17; Howatson, ed., 49; and Radice, 63-64. In the chronology of the "conferencia-recital" (which does not correspond to the biographical information at our disposal) it should be noted that Lorca located the composition of this poem shortly after the (fictional) death of "la niña Mary" (261-62).

Thus it is easy to interpret the whole Genesis story as the aetiological myth of sexual awakening: Adam and Eve are initially innocent, pre-pubescent children, the Fall is the passage from the atemporal, unselfconscious world of the young child into the acutely self-aware and potentially sexually active world of the adolescent, and hence the Expulsion from the Garden is the insertion into the real, temporal—and finite—world of human reproduction and mortality.

No wonder, then, as has already been seen, that the Eden of stanza 4 is decidedly heterodox, and that it is conflated with Arcadia. This is so for at least two reasons: the guiltless, robust sexuality of the pagan ethos, already noted, and the unquestioning acceptance by pagan myths and culture of the homosexual paradigm within the general scope of sexuality. As noted above, the implicit allusions from the title onwards to reflections on the surface of water immediately invoke the Narcissus myth, and the allied identification of different voices likewise brings to mind the related myth of Echo. This is all the more coherent because Pan, the ruler of Arcadia, was involved with Echo, who bore him a daughter Iynx, though in general he was "amorous towards both sexes," and in Arcadia homosexual love between shepherds was far from uncommon—Corydon and Alexis are perhaps the best known example.[38] Furthermore, as Curtius writes:

> the shepherd's world is linked to nature and to love. One can say that for two millenniums it draws to itself the majority of erotic motifs. (187)

> As we have seen, the *locus amoenus* also formed part of the scenery of pastoral poetry and thus of erotic poetry. (199-200)[39]

As the "Poema doble" develops, a change of direction having been signaled by the conjunction "Pero" at the beginning of stanza 6, it becomes clear that the speaker wants the freedom to "be himself" and also the freedom—

---

38   On Narcissus and Echo, see Hall, 219, and Radice, 108, 169, but the clearest account of the two related stories (Hera's punishment of Echo; Aphrodite's punishment of Narcissus) is to be found in Howatson, ed., 201, 380. On Pan, Echo, and Iynx see Radice, 183, and additionally Graves, I, 101, 190 (sections 26d and 56a). On Corydon in Virgil's second *Eclogue*, see Howatson, ed., 201, and Radice, 94. See also Burshatin, 230-34, 236; Craige, 17; and Delong-Tonelli, 252.

39   On Garcilaso, nature, and love, see also Jones, 74-75. I cannot agree with Ilie's assertion: "The fact is that neither the subject of love nor of Nature concerns Lorca's narrating poet" (775).

together, perhaps, with the *ability*—to say what he is. Indeed, here philosophical, sexual, and linguistic concerns seem to coincide: he struggles simultaneously towards an authenticity of being, of identity, and of expression, and it appears impossible to have one of these without the others. Furthermore, this place of quiet meditation matches his mood and provides a suitable, even conducive site for what he presents as essentially modest aspirations (modest regardless of how difficult they may actually be to achieve). In stanza 6 the speaker rejects "mundo [y] sueño," which can be glossed respectively as society, fame, travel, or earthly pleasures (one of "los tres enemigos del alma"), and as ideals, otherworldliness, daydreams, or fantasies; rather he is willing to settle for his stated goals "en el rincón más oscuro de la brisa que nadie quiera," a description that could easily evoke Eden Mills (Havard, 226). The discarded stanza B runs in close parallel: here it is clearer that he concentrates not on his future and his end ("el vuelo que tendré"), whether it be a future of fame and glory and/or a death of transcendence and paradise ("luz") or an earthbound future/death of pain, erosion, and interment ("cal viva"). Rather he is alert to the potentialities of the present, and the last line may contain a rather opaque reference to the phenomenon of *aurora borealis* ("la bola del aire alucinado") (Schwartz, 52).

However, even such modest desires as these are beset with risks and dangers. What the speaker has to avoid is set out in stanza 7: he needs to assert and to live his homosexuality without falling prey to base and promiscuous manifestations such as are to be found both in the port of New York—"esos perros marinos se persiguen" (sailors as "sea dogs")—and in the countryside of Vermont, where the libidinous wind is always on the lookout—"el viento acecha troncos descuidados" (the pun is on tree trunks and human torsos).[40]

The voice corresponding to these perils is of course "esta voz de hojalata y de talco"—sterile and effeminate, and so the speaker hopes to put the stimulus from the past to good use: the revitalization of the "voz antigua," of his childhood, of sadness, but also of sincerity (stanza 8), and his consequent reconnection with those primary qualities, will contribute to the creation of a hypothetical third mode of expression, based on that "voz antigua" and not on the "voz de hojalata y de talco." In the future, then, he wants to be able to express himself with directness, simplicity, spontaneity, freshness,

---

40   See "Oda a Walt Whitman," with its extensive disquisition on "versions" of homosexuality, and for the wind, "Preciosa y el aire." See also Havard, 226; Predmore, 83; and Semprún Donahue, 83. In stanza A the phrase "el juego del tiro al blanco" may refer simply to a frivolous and fatuous leisure activity of "señoritos" in Madrid, but it could also have a much more sexual, carnal, symbolic significance.

and feeling, and he aims to reduce, if not eliminate, that distance between the referent and the linguistic sign and hence restore the immanence of the word (Pratt, 250). Note that in stanza 1 the "voz antigua" is "lamiendo mis pies," in stanza 6 it is addressed as "voz divina," while in stanza 10 it is "voz mía libertada, que me lames las manos," a voice that simultaneously retains the positive qualities of the past/childhood/Eden/Arcadia but yet has somehow broken free of the confines of that place and time.[41] Similarly, if the "voz antigua" of the past was "de mi amor" and "de mi verdad," nonetheless it was "ignorante de los densos jugos amargos"; the new voice would be the appropriate medium "para decir mi verdad de hombre de sangre"[42]—a truth pertaining, notably, to his present, adult self and adult sexuality, as well as to genuine emotion and personal identity (stanza 9).[43]

The most explicit stanza on this theme (D) is another of those subsequently discarded by Lorca. The description of "la voz que es mi hijo" may lead us back to Christological imagery, but equally I think it has to do with the fact that the speaker will have no other son, that is, he will not participate in the reproductive cycle, which makes his self-expression (and poetic legacy?) that much more important. He realizes that "turning the clock back" is impossible; the blushing awkwardness and embarrassment that accompanied the first sexual encounter and the new kind of pleasure that it occasioned cannot be relived or recaptured. Again the phrase "moneda de sangre" could put us in mind of blood money (Judas's thirty pieces of silver that are "the price of blood" [Matthew 27.3-8]), but I think it is probably more important here that coins very often carry the profiles of person's heads, and "perfil" in Lorca's metaphorical vocabulary is intimately bound up with life, identity, and individuality.[44] Thus "moneda de sangre" can be read in quite close parallel to "mi verdad de hombre de sangre," though here it is clearer that the speaker feels persecuted by society and perhaps not allowed

---

41   See Delong-Tonelli, 253; Dennis, 52-53; Geist, 554; and Pratt, 253.

42   When Leonardo confronts the Novia before her wedding (*Bodas de sangre*, Act II, Scene 1), they argue about what went wrong with their relationship and why they never married, to which Leonardo responds: "No quiero hablar, porque soy hombre de sangre, y no quiero que todos estos cerros oigan mis voces."

43   Note how the poet's own name is replaced by the phrase "rosa, niño y abeto" (with the further Argentinian variant "niña"). For a reading that suggests a homosexual interpretation for this string of three items, see Sahuquillo, 288-89; see also Havard, 227.

44   See Anderson, *Lorca's Late Poetry*, 192 and note 62, for a more extended discussion of the image.

to "be himself," that he is alone ("me quedo solo") and pitted against a name-less, likely conformist, mass of people ("todos").

The "Poema doble" closes with what may be the only allusion to the re-flection of the speaker in the waters of the lake (the earlier line "Aquí frente al agua en extremo desnuda" forms part of stanza B, which was discarded in its entirety). That he refers here in stanza 11 to "mi cuerpo" returns us to the disjunction of self that was mentioned earlier, and is curiously reminiscent of the "Égloga segunda": a "fuente clara" is a principal feature of the *locus amoenus* that is the locale for the poem's action, it is the means by which Albanio reveals his ill-fated love to Camila (ll. 470-78 [149]; *cf.* ll. 744- 49 [157]), and it is also the screen on to which the rejected Albanio's dementia is projected when he comes to believe that he has literally become disembod-ied (ll. 907-92 [162]) (Burshatin, 233-34, 238). Here the image suggests the reflection motionless on the still lake water, but we should remember that balance is achieved with *two* equal forces—or moments, in the language of physics—being exerted on opposite sides of a central point. The speaker is outside looking on, and what he witnesses, paradoxically, in these tranquil surroundings, where cows contentedly graze, chew the cud, and low, is a si-lent but tenacious struggle between opposing forces, within him and with-out. The doublings, then, that run through the poem, are multiple, and the themes numerous but all in some way interrelated. Tantalizingly, the "Poema doble" ends with the suggestion of a certain equipoise, but the existential predicament of the speaker[45] and the undercutting framing of stanza 11's ironic *reportage* mean that there can be no final resolution.[46]

45   Dennis offers an excellent summary of this philosophical condition (41). See also Ilie, 776.

46   I should like to thank Professor Monroe Z. Hafter, who was kind enough to comment on a draft of this article.

Appendix

POEMA DOBLE DEL LAGO EDÉN
Edem (M; P; T; B; Bv)

Nuestro ganado pace, el viento espira.
pace. El (M; P; T; Bv)

Garcilaso.

1   Era mi voz antigua
ignorante de los densos jugos amargos.
La adivino lamiendo mis pies
la que vino (M; P; T; Bv)
bajo   los frágiles helechos mojados.
sobre (M; P; T; Bv)

2   ¡Ay   voz antigua de mi amor,
    mi (P; T; Bv)
ay voz de mi verdad,
ay voz de mi abierto costado,
Ay   voz de mi verdad! Voz de mi abierto costado (M; P; T; Bv)
    mi (P; T; Bv)
cuando todas las rosas manaban de mi   lengua
        brotaban (M; P; T; Bv) *saliva* (M)
y el césped no conocía la impasible dentadura del caballo!
    [musgo] (M)

A   *Ay, voz antigua que todos tenemos*
pero que todos olvidamos
sobre el hombro de la hora, en las últimas expresiones
en los espejos de los otros o en el juego del tiro al blanco. (M; P; T; Bv)

3   Estás   aquí bebiendo mi sangre,
<u>Estáis</u> (Bv)
bebiendo mi humor de niño   pasado,
    amor (M; P; T; Bv) *<u>pesado</u>,* (B)
mientras mis ojos se quiebran en el viento
con el aluminio y las voces de los borrachos.
        soldados. (M; P; T; Bv)

4   Déjame   pasar la puerta
     Dejadme salir por la puerta cerrada (M; P; T; Bv)
     Déjame (P; T; Bv)
     Dejarme (H)
     donde Eva come hormigas
     y Adán fecunda peces deslumbrados.
                       peces ... (M)
     Déjame   pasar,   hombrecillo de los cuernos,
     Dejarme (H) *salir* (M; P; T; Bv) **hombrecillos** (H; B)
     al bosque de los desperezos
     y los alegrísimos saltos.
     al bosque de los desperezos y   los alegrísimos saltos. (M; P; T; Bv)
                              de (P; T; Bv)

5   Yo sé el uso más secreto
     que tiene un viejo alfiler oxidado
     y sé del horror de unos ojos despiertos
             el (P; T; Bv)   *[ ]* (M)
     sobre la superficie concreta del plato.

6   Pero no quiero mundo ni sueño, voz divina
                          sueno (H)
     quiero mi libertad, mi amor humano
     en el rincón más oscuro de la brisa que nadie quiera.
                          tierra (M)
     ¡Mi amor humano!
     [con mi nativo desprecio del arte y la correcta ley del canto.] (M)

7   Esos perros marinos se persiguen
     y el viento acecha troncos descuidados.
     ¡Oh   voz antigua, quema con tu lengua
     Ay, (M; P; T; Bv)
          mi (Bv)
     esta voz de hojalata y de talco!

8   Quiero llorar porque me da la gana
     como lloran los niños del último banco,

[por ti, por disciplina] (M)
porque yo no soy un hombre, ni un poeta,   ni una hoja,
                    poeta,   *hombre* (M; P; T; Bv)
pero sí un pulso herido que sonda las cosas del otro lado.
                    ronda (M; P; T; Bv)

9   Quiero llorar diciendo mi nombre,
     rosa, niño y abeto   a la orilla de este lago,
     Federico García Lorca, (M)
          niña (P; T)
     para decir mi verdad de hombre de sangre
     matando en mí la burla y la sugestión del vocablo.

B   *Aquí frente al agua en extremo desnuda*
     busco mi libertad, mi amor humano
     no el vuelo que tendré, luz o cal viva
     mi presente en acecho sobre la bola del aire alucinado. (M)

C   *Poesía pura. Poesía impura.*
     Vana piroteada [sic], periódico desgarrado.
     Torre de salitre donde se entrechocan las palabras
     y aurora lisa que flota con la angustia de lo exacto. (M)

10   No, no, yo no pregunto, yo deseo,
     voz mía libertada, que me lames las manos.
     En el laberinto de biombos es mi desnudo el que recibe
     la luna de castigo y el reloj encenizado.

D   *Aquí me quedo solo, hombrecillo de la cresta*
     con la voz que es mi hijo. Esperando
          [   ] (T; Bv)
     no la vuelta al rubor y al primer gusto de la alcoba
                    [   ] (P; T; Bv)
     pero sí mi moneda de sangre que entre todos me habéis quitado.
                    (M; P; T; Bv)

11   Así hablaba yo.
     [   ] (M; P; T; Bv)
     Así hablaba yo cuando Saturno detuvo los trenes

y la bruma y el Sueño y la Muerte me estaban buscando.
   broma (M: P; T; Bv)
Me estaban buscando
[   ] (M)
allí donde mugen las vacas que tienen   patitas de   paje
      mujen (H)   *rojas* (M; P; T; Bv) *paja* (H)
y allí donde flota mi cuerpo entre los equilibrios contrarios.
            sobre (M; P; T; Bv)

FEDERICO GARCÍA LORCA

(1) M: typescript, 2 pp., typed on the back of two sheets of out-of-date sta-
tionery from *Revista de Avance* (La Habana) headed with the characteristic typographical design of "1927. Revista de Avance." Presumably
typed from an autograph original; typed copy is corrected in Lorca's
own hand. Preserved and reproduced by Juan Marinello in *Contemporáneos. Noticia y memoria* ([Santa Clara]: Editora del Consejo Nacional de
Universidades/Univ. Central de las Villas, 1964), pp. 222-23.

(2) P: published in *Poesía* (Buenos Aires), I, no. 7 (November 1933), 26-28.

(3) T: published in Federico García Lorca, *Obras completas*, vol. 6: *Así que
pasen cinco años. Poemas póstumos*, ed. Guillermo de Torre, 1st ed. (Buenos Aires: Losada, 1938), pp. 162-64. ["Indicación de fuentes": from *Poesía*]

(4) H: published in Federico García Lorca, *The Poet in New York and Other
Poems*, trans. Rolfe Humphries (New York: W. W. Norton, 1940), pp.
70, 72.

(5) B: published in Federico García Lorca, *Poeta en Nueva York*, ed. José Bergamín (México D.F.: Séneca, 1940), pp. 79-81.

(6) Bv: published in Federico García Lorca, *Poeta en Nueva York*, ed. José
Bergamín (México D.F.: Séneca, 1940), "Variante a este poema de la
PARTE IV titulado POEMA DOBLE DEL LAGO EDEM," pp. 159-
61.

N.B. cases of variant punctuation (and resulting capitalization or non-capitalization) too numerous to note.

Works Cited

Anderson, Andrew A. "García Lorca como poeta petrarquista," *Cuadernos Hispanoamericanos*, nos. 435-436 (September-October 1986), 495-518.

———. *Lorca's Late Poetry. A Critical Study* (Leeds: Francis Cairns, 1990).

Burshatin, Israel. "'Poema doble del lago Eden': In the Aura of Garcilaso and Narcissus," in *Selected Proceedings of the "Singularidad y Trascendencia" Conference*, ed. Nora de Marval-McNair (Boulder: Society of Spanish and Spanish-American Studies, 1990), pp. 229-41.

Cano Ballesta, Juan. *La poesía española entre pureza y revolución (1930-1936)* (Madrid: Gredos, 1972).

Craige, Betty Jean. *Lorca's "Poet in New York." The Fall into Consciousness* (Lexington: UP of Kentucky, 1977).

Cummings, Philip H. "August in Eden. An Hour of Youth," in *Songs*, by Federico García Lorca, trans. by Philip Cummings, ed. Daniel Eisenberg (Pittsburgh: Duquesne UP, 1976), pp. 125-66.

———. "The Mind of Genius," in *Songs*, by Federico García Lorca, trans. by Philip Cummings, ed. Daniel Eisenberg (Pittsburgh: Duquesne UP, 1976), pp. 175-81.

Curtius, Ernst Robert. *European Literature and the Latin Middle Ages*, trans. by Willard R. Trask (Princeton: Princeton UP, 1967).

Delong-Tonelli, Beverly J. "In the Beginning was the End: Lorca's New York Poetry," *Anales de la Literatura Española Contemporánea*, XII, no. 3 (1987), 243-57.

Dennis, Nigel. "Lorca in the Looking-Glass: On Mirrors and Self-Contemplation," in *"Cuando yo me muera ...." Essays in Memory of Federico García Lorca*, ed. C. Brian Morris (Lanham: UP of America, 1988), pp. 41-55.

Eisenberg, Daniel. "A Chronology of Lorca's Visit to New York and Cuba," *Kentucky Romance Quarterly*, XXIV, no. 3 (1977), 233-50.

Entrambasaguas, Joaquín de. "Nota preliminar," in *Poeta en Nueva York. (Selección)*, by Federico García Lorca, Antología de la Literatura Contemporánea 1, Suplemento Primero de "Cuadernos de Literatura Contemporánea" (Madrid: Consejo Superior de Investigaciones Científicas, 1945), pp. 3-7.

García Lorca, Federico. *Songs*, trans. by Philip Cummings, ed. Daniel Eisenberg (Pittsburgh: Duquesne UP, 1976).

——. *Epistolario*, ed. Christopher Maurer, 2 vols. (Madrid: Alianza, 1983).

——. *Federico García Lorca escribe a su familia desde Nueva York y La Habana (1929-1930)*, ed. Christopher Maurer, special double number of *Poesía*, nos. 23-24 (1985).

——. *Alocuciones argentinas*, ed. Mario Hernández (Madrid: Fundación Federico García Lorca/El Crotalón, 1985).

——. "Cartas inéditas de García Lorca [II]," ed. Miguel García-Posada, *ABC Literario* (17 February 1990), vii-xi.

——. *Manuscritos neoyorquinos. "Poeta en Nueva York" y otras hojas y poemas*, ed. Mario Hernández (Madrid: Tabapress/Fundación Federico García Lorca, 1990).

——. "Conferencia-recital de *Poeta en Nueva York*," in *Manuscritos neoyorquinos. "Poeta en Nueva York" y otras hojas y poemas*, ed. Mario Hernández (Madrid: Tabapress/Fundación Federico García Lorca, 1990), pp. 245-66.

——. *Lettere americane*, ed. Gabriele Morelli (Venice: Marsilio, 1994).

García-Posada, Miguel. *Lorca: interpretación de "Poeta en Nueva York"* (Madrid: Akal, 1981).

Geist, Anthony L. "Las mariposas en la barba: una lectura de *Poeta en Nueva York*," *Cuadernos Hispanoamericanos*, nos. 435-436 (September-October 1986), 547-65.

Gibson, Ian. *Federico García Lorca*, vol. I: *De Fuente Vaqueros a Nueva York (1898-1929)* (Barcelona: Grijalbo, 1985).

——. *Federico García Lorca*, vol. II: *De Nueva York a Fuente Grande (1929-1936)* (Barcelona: Grijalbo, 1987).

Graves, Robert. *The Greek Myths*, rev. ed., 2 vols. (Harmondsworth: Penguin, 1990).

Hall, James. *Dictionary of Subjects and Symbols in Art*, rev. ed. (London: John Murray, 1979).

Harris, Derek. *García Lorca. "Poeta en Nueva York"* (London: Grant & Cutler/Tamesis Books, 1978).

Havard, Robert. "Dream and Nightmare in Lorca's *Poeta en Nueva York*," in *Catholic Tastes and Times. Essays in Honour of Michael E. Williams*, ed. Margaret A. Rees (Leeds: Trinity and All Saints College, 1987), pp. 199-232.

Herrero, Javier. "The Horned Moon, Queen of the Waters, Images of Death in Lorca," in *"Cuando yo me muera ...." Essays in Memory of Federico García Lorca, ed. C. Brian Morris (Lanham: UP of America, 1988), pp. 147-57.

M.C. Howatson, ed. *The Oxford Companion to Classical Literature*, 2nd ed. (Oxford: Oxford UP, 1989).

Ilie, Paul. "The Vanguard Infrastructure of 'Poema doble del lago Eden,'" *Hispania*, LXIX, no. 4 (1986), 770-78.

Jones, R.O. *Historia de la literatura española*, vol. 2: *Siglo de Oro: prosa y poesía (siglos XVI y XVII)* (Barcelona: Ariel, 1974).

Ortega y Gasset, José. *La deshumanización del arte y otros ensayos de estética*, ed. Valeriano Bozal (Madrid: Espasa-Calpe, 1987).

Pratt, Heather. "Place and Displacement in Lorca's *Poeta en Nueva York*," *Forum for Modern Language Studies*, XXII, no. 3 (1986), 248-62.

Predmore, Richard L. *Lorca's New York Poetry. Social Injustice, Dark Love, Lost Faith* (Durham: Duke UP, 1980).

Radice, Betty. *Who's Who in the Ancient World* (Harmondsworth: Penguin, 1973).

Sahuquillo, Ángel. *Federico García Lorca y la cultura de la homosexualidad masculina. Lorca, Dalí, Cernuda, Gil-Albert, Prados y la voz silenciada del amor homosexual*, 2nd ed. (Alicante: Instituto de Cultura "Juan Gil-Albert"/ Diputación de Alicante, 1991).

Schwartz, Kessel. "García Lorca and Vermont," *Hispania*, XLII, no. 1 (1959), 50-55.

Semprún Donahue, Moraima de. "Una franca interpretación de 'Poemas del Lago Edem Mills' de García Lorca," *García Lorca Review*, III, no. 2 (1975), 79-90.

Vega, Garcilaso de la. *Poesías castellanas completas*, ed. Elias L. Rivers (Madrid: Castalia, 1979).

9
Lorca's "Cielo vivo": the Other Lake Eden Poem

COMPARED WITH A GOOD number of other poems in *Poeta en Nueva York*, "Poema doble del Lago Edén" has attracted more than an average amount of attention from critics over the years. The same cannot be said of its companion piece, "Cielo vivo"; indeed, quite the reverse. Together, the two compositions constitute the entirety of one of the shorter sections in the collection, IV, "Poemas del Lago Eden Mills." All of the poems in *Poeta en Nueva York* are, to varying degrees, difficult, and my purpose here is to provide a close reading of "Cielo vivo" in an attempt to elucidate a somewhat neglected text from the collection and also to gauge to what extent it shares similar or complementary themes with "Poema doble."

Lorca arrived in Eden Mills, Vermont, from New York on August 22, 1929.[1] He had been invited by Philip Cummings to come and stay with him and his family in their summer rental cabin overlooking Lake Eden and the Green Mountains. He stayed for approximately a week and likely left on August 29 to go and spend some time with Ángel del Río and his wife Amelia Agostini in their vacation rental cottage in Bushnellsville, Shandaken, in the Catskill Mountains of New York State. The autograph manuscript of "Cielo vivo" is inscribed at the end "cabaña de Dew-Kum-Inn | Edem [*sic*] Mills Vermont | 24 de Agosto – 1929"; the name, invented by Lorca's friend, is a pun on the phrase "do come in" and on the Cummings's surname. "Tierra y luna," a contemporaneous poem not included in *Poeta en Nueva York*, is dated

---

1   Or possibly August 21, 1929: see Maurer and Anderson, 43, note 1. He traveled by train and then was picked up by car from a nearby station, seemingly either Montpelier Junction or Waterbury. On his departure, he was again dropped off by car at Burlington Station.

"28 de August [*sic*] 1929 | cabaña de Duw Kun Inn. [*sic*]|Edem [*sic*] Mills |
Vermont" (García Lorca, *Manuscritos neoyorquinos*, 122-25, 212-17). No first-
draft autograph for "Poema doble del Lago Edén" survives, but it is clear that
its inspiration derives from this stay even if the composition took place later.
"Vaca" (again with no original manuscript) may also reflect an incident that
occurred there (Schwartz, 52-53).[2] Several photographs show Lorca on the
banks of the lake, in front of the cottage, and in other locations nearby.[3] Cummings's memoir "August in Eden. An Hour of Youth" provides an evocative, if
flowery, narrative of the stay and some of their activities together, though the
strict accuracy of every detail in the account may be open to question; in later
decades, he provided Lorca's biographers (Mildred Adams, Daniel Eisenberg,
Ian Gibson, etc.) with supplementary material. The historical starting point
for the poem that concerns us has been documented by Kessel Schwartz, who
collected information directly from Cummings: "'Cielo vivo' was inspired by a
night of brilliant aurora borealis activity as the lake reflected the lights against
a pitch black Mount Norris" (52).[4] In addition, the ferns mentioned in the
poem are a characteristic feature of the Vermont landscape; rather more "generic"—though still typical of the region—are the rotted trees, the swimmer,
the cows, or the beached boats.

Much more important, of course, is what Lorca did with these raw ma-
terials. The title "Cielo vivo" puns on what the words mean literally and how
the phrase can be interpreted: the constantly swirling light show of aurora
borealis makes it look as if the sky has "come alive," while Catholic theology
holds out the promise (for some) of eternal life in heaven. The poem, then,
turns out to be a meditation on nature, mutability, and human mortality: the
lyric voice contemplates the beauty but yet also the transience of the natural
world and explores different conceptions of what lies beyond, while contrasting what might "realistically" be expected with a more appealing alternative

---

2   Cummings stated that "Ruina" was "written at Eden Lake" (123), but Ángel del Río remembered it being composed during the Catskills days (xvii); again,
this poem is one of the relatively few poems for which we have no autograph original
(which are often dated). Most or all of the texts included in section VI of *Poeta en
Nueva York*, "Introducción a la muerte (Poemas de la soledad en Vermont)," were
actually written later than the brief time spent in Vermont.

3   Maurer and Anderson, 46-47, 51-52, 231-32; García Lorca, *Songs*, plates
between 20 and 21.

4   Curiously, Cummings did not describe witnessing the Northern Lights in
"August in Eden," though he did provide a notably purple description of a spectacu-
lar thunderstorm (142-43).

that looks back to the prebirth experience in order to capture imaginatively a momentary glimpse of some kind of transcendence *post mortem*.

In his opening words, the speaker envisages a future ("Yo no podré," l. 1) from which he will survey his past ("si no encontré," l. 2), a set of temporal shifts that ends up locating the point of utterance in the present ("lo que busco," l. 9), even though a search, a quest, is by definition future-oriented.[5] Stanza 1 posits a future in which the speaker has not been successful in attaining his goal (which is as yet undefined; l. 2), but he nonetheless responds to this situation with stoic acceptance (l. 1). The reason for this relative lack of concern seems to be that the coming experience of death that he envisages for himself will be nonconscious and nonsentient. He will be reduced to the same status as "las piedras sin jugo y los insectos vacíos" (l. 3), two typical images of Lorca's style in the New York period. The first image stresses the inertness, the dry lifelessness of stone, without any vital juices,[6] while the second evokes the husks of insects, the exoskeleton, devoid of any matter within; both emphasize absence beyond the obvious connotation of death. In this state of atemporal nonbeing, he will not see—that is, he will not be able to see—the ongoing struggle for existence, which is expressed figuratively in the daily "duel" between the sun and living creatures, a fight both "in the raw" and with creatures (animals and human beings) that do contain "living flesh," unlike the dead insects ("el duelo del sol con las criaturas en carne viva," l. 4).

Stanza 2, by contrast ("Pero," l. 5), seeks to express what it is that he would ideally like to achieve and what he needs to do to conceive of it and understand it fully. Although we encounter another verb in the future tense, here it refers to a "strategy" that the speaker plans to put into effect in the present. The travel to which he refers ("me iré," l. 5) is of course entirely imaginative, and it involves a trip not forward but rather back in time to the womb/childhood and to the Garden of Eden (Anderson, 417-23; Román Román, 438-41). The two destinations share a good deal in common: they are both "places" of primordial union, security, innocence, and atemporality before the expulsion into the adult world of separation, solitude, self-consciousness, work, temporality, and mortality. The image of the "primer paisaje / de choques, líquidos y rumores" (ll. 5-6) combines a reference to the Garden of Eden (which, biblically speaking, is indeed the *first* landscape) with one evoking the intrauterine experience, a reading confirmed by the fact that the "paisaje" gives off the

---

5   All references to "Cielo vivo" are by line number in García Lorca, *Poeta en Nueva York*, 217-18 (henceforth abbreviated as *PNY*).

6   Cf. "la piedra inerte / ni conoce la sombra, ni la evita" ("El poeta pide a su amor que le escriba," *Sonetos*, 17).

characteristic smell of a newborn baby (l. 7; Nandorfy 93). In the prenatal oneness of the womb, as in the prelapsarian Garden, there are no boundaries and hence no surfaces, and in addition, there is an original authenticity and hence no false appearances, a concept that Lorca frequently renders with the term "superficie" (l. 8). The imaginative immersion in these primal states of plenitude enables the speaker to grasp that his future objective shares more than a few traits in common with them: his quest ("lo que busco") will culminate ("tendrá su blanco de alegría," l. 9) when (and if) he flies "mezclado con el amor y las arenas" (l. 10). He seeks the transcendence of flight, rather than the earthbound company of rocks and dry insects, and a fusion reminiscent of the "lost paradise" of the past, wherein he will be simultaneously combined with the abstract, absolute principle of love and with "las arenas," a more negative symbol connoting dryness, barrenness, changeability, fugacity, temporality, etc., and a recognition perhaps that this "ideal" future does not conform to any conventionally theological view of "la vida de ultratumba."[7] A rather different reading would propose that the speaker asserts that he needs to (re)visit the womb, synonymous with procreation, to focus his own particular goal as involving a love that also incorporates an element of sterility ("las arenas").[8]

Stanza 3 elaborates on that "primer paisaje." This place or state (the deictic "Allí" in ll. 11, 13, 19) is cut off from all manifestations of mutability, decay, and mortality. Thus, it is isolated from "la escarcha de los ojos apagados" (l. 11), the flicker or flame of life extinguished and replaced by the deathly cold whiteness and rigidity of frost, or tears of sadness turned to ice. Nor can be heard there "el mugido del árbol asesinado por la oruga" (l. 12), the tree, imagined as a stricken animal, devastated and felled by an infestation of caterpillars. Rather, insulated from the natural processes of the world, of change and inevitable decline, here forms endure, they come together ("entrelazadas" [l. 13] develops on "mezclado" [l. 10]), and they are not stopped in their tracks (frozen, snuffed out, felled), but rather are able to maintain "una sola expresión frenética de avance" (l. 14).

Stanza 4 returns to the here-and-now and develops on the idea already present in lines 11 and 12 that, both literally and figuratively, the worm is in the

---

7   Compare this sentiment with that expressed in poem VIII from Bécquer's *Rimas*, where the speaker yearns to defeat gravity and, freed from his human form, "flotar con la niebla dorada / en átomos leves / cual ella deshecho" (110).

8   In the first version of this line, Lorca wrote, instead of "arenas," "frutas secas" (*Manuscritos neoyorquinos*, 122). This option does not seem quite as negative as "arenas," nor does it serve to bolster this alternative reading.

bud. Lines 15 to 16 provide a good example of Lorca's imagery in action. Taking "los enjambres de corolas" first as a straightforward metaphor, with "enjambres" as the vehicle standing for an unspoken tenor, it can be interpreted as betokening a profusion of blooms such as one might encounter in a luxuriant garden or meadow.[9] But the subsequent mention of "azúcar" indicates that "enjambres" is to read literally as well as figuratively, generating a long associative chain: *swarms*–bees–flowers–*corollas*–petals–stamens/anthers–pollen–nectar–honey–*sugar*, although only three of the elements (italicized) are actually named in the text.[10] The thrust of the two lines becomes clear; in this sublunary natural world, it is impossible to experience beauty without also experiencing its concomitant downside, desolation and destruction, or at the very least without being reminded of it: hence, walking through a garden or meadow filled with flowers and buzzing with bees is irreparably linked with tooth decay.[11] Lines 17 and 18 sketch an even more stark contrast. The delicacy and fragility of a single fern leaf is explicitly described as "fugaz" (l. 17; in "Poema doble del Lago Eden," they are "los frágiles helechos," *PNY* 215), while the verb chosen, "acariciar," rather than other possible candidates ("tocar," "rozar," etc.), emphasizes the affectionate bond with and appreciation for nature. In line 18, "marfil," unlike the "helecho," is hard and unyielding and associated with a closely related substance, bone; likewise, "fugaz" and "definitivo" are polar opposites. A proposition running in parallel to lines 15 and 16 emerges: even in the momentary act of enjoying and celebrating the beauty and grace of the fern, it is impossible not to be reminded, shockingly ("asombro," l. 18), of evanescence and death. Essentially the same thought pattern and structure will be repeated in "Gacela de la huida" (*Diván del Tamarit*):

> No hay nadie que, al dar un beso,
> no sienta la sonrisa de las gentes sin rostro,
> ni hay nadie que, al tocar un recién nacido,
> olvide las inmóviles calaveras de caballo. (218)

---

9   Cummings recounted the discovery of a "Garden of Eden" in the village and referred to "these semi-cultivated flowers which [...] have become such hardy perennial blossomers" (163-64).

10   Compare the line from "Vuelta de paseo": "el árbol de muñones que no canta" (*PNY*, 165), which similarly deploys a technique of radical ellipsis: The *tree* that has been pollarded has only the *stumps* of its branches left, so there is nowhere for birds to perch and then be able to *sing*.

11   The phrase "dientes de azúcar" could be read as a simple metaphor, of whiteness, but if present at all, it is a very secondary meaning.

Stanza 5 returns to that "edenic" place or state already described in stanza 3. Here all tensions, all contradictions, are resolved, are held in balance and harmony, and misconceptions ("cosas equivocadas," l. 20) are perceived to hold a truth all their own. In a slightly different reading, "verdad" could also be understood in the sense of "cause" or "reason for." The only locations where this extraordinary phenomenon can occur are necessarily extreme: "Allí bajo las raíces y en la médula del aire" (l. 19), in the very depths of the earth and in the very core of the air (or sky), both of which would correspond to different versions of death/the afterlife. Syntactically, lines 21 to 22 appear to be offered as two specific examples of those "cosas equivocadas," though how they are "mistaken," "wrong," or "in error" is not immediately clear. Line 21 seems to involve a human being in the water during the day and line 22 seems to involve animals on dry land at night, so these instances could be taken as encompassing a wide range of possibilities. The light glinting off the water on the swimmer's back produces the silvery effect ("El nadador de níquel que acecha la onda más fina," l. 21), and perhaps the conundrum is that this seemingly metallic swimmer is somehow able to float and make headway. Likewise, the bulky girth of the cow's body is supported on four feet that look remarkably delicate for the weight that they are carrying: "el rebaño de vacas nocturnas con rojas patitas de mujer" (l. 22).[12]

A very different, more metaphorical interpretation is also possible, stemming from Lorca's predilection for *trompe l'œil* images. The "nadador de níquel" might not be real and could simply be the reflection of the moon on the water's surface, hunting, or hunted by, "la onda más fina."[13] Following from this, the "rebaño de vacas nocturnas" may represent not animals but a group of clouds, either in the night sky or again reflected on the lake, though the precise reasoning behind the "rojas patitas de mujer" remains elusive. In "Danza de la muerte," Lorca writes: "En mis ojos bebían las dulces vacas de los cielos" (*PNY*, 195), where the same image is more explicit.[14] Domínguez Gil developed this

---

12   Evidently, this detail caught Lorca's attention: in "Poema doble del Lago Edén," he refers to "las vacas que tienen patitas de paje" (*PNY*, 216).

13   Lorca often uses silvery metals as descriptors for the moon. See Domínguez Gil, 334; as he pointed out, it is impossible to determine which is subject and which object. Cf. Cummings: "The moon is only an hour high over the dark points of the steepled spruces. [...] As the water laps the smooth stones of the shore this movement makes six small reflected moons do a symphonic dance" (149).

14   Compare, too, "Norma y paraíso de los negros" with another vision of the night sky: "azul donde el desnudo del viento va quebrando / los camellos sonámbulos de las nubes vacías" (*PNY*, 177), and "Oda a Walt Whitman": "y el cielo desem-

reading further, pointing out that in the autograph manuscript, Lorca had written in "egipcias" as an alternative adjective to "nocturnas."[15] For him, this opens the door to seeing a reference to the Egyptian cow-goddess Hathor and a connection between the cow's horns and the moon (Domínguez Gil, 335). Lines 21 to 22, then, come to exemplify how "cosas equivocadas"—that is, things perceived metaphorically as other things (the moon as a swimmer, clouds as cows)—can have a (figurative, poetic) truth of their own, even while they are literally wrong or mistaken.

Stanza 6 ushers in the closing section of the poem, with a recapitulation that combines parts of stanzas 1 and 2: the exact repetition of lines 1 and 2, a variation on lines 5 and 6, and the repetition of lines 9 and 10. Line 25, "pero me iré al primer paisaje de humedades y latidos," only serves to confirm the reading of line 6 as referring to the preborn's experience of the womb—amniotic fluid and heartbeats. Stanza 7 then develops on this recapitulation, picking up the verb "vuele" with the noun "Vuelo" as the first word in its first line (l. 28). As the speaker elaborates on this notion, it increasingly seems almost within reach. The fact that it is outside of time is repeatedly stressed: "Vuelo fresco de siempre" (l. 28), "la dura eternidad fija" (l. 30), "amor al fin sin alba" (l. 31). Flight again brings with it the idea of transcendence over the mundane. "Lechos vacíos" (l. 28) can suggest beds where love-making has taken place or, equally, death beds; either way, they are now empty, vacated, indicating that the event occurred in the chronological past. Line 29 is strongly redolent of Lake Eden. Cummings referred to the placid surface of the lake that sometimes became choppy when the wind would pick up, and while he was there, Lorca supposedly wrote while resting his paper on the hull of an overturned boat on the shore.[16] Again these are almost random events that occur over time: a breeze picks up and then subsides, a boat is rowed across the lake and then beached.[17] The closing lines become much more abstract. The speaker

---

bocaba por los puentes y los tejados / manadas de bisontes empujadas por el viento" (*PNY*, 266).

15   Neither is crossed out: García Lorca, *Manuscritos neoyorquinos*, 124.

16   "The lake has been lulled to a pure mirror-like placidity"; "The lake was rough-shod this afternoon and the gusts of wind swept in on us"; "I sit alone on the bow of my beached boat and look out over the great piece of glossy black satin" (Cummings, 128, 149). "Lorca spent a good part of the day at Eden scribbling away on an overturned boat" (Schwartz 50).

17   The specific values that García-Posada assigned to these three images could easily be challenged: for him, "lechos vacíos" betokened "una existencia sin amor," while "brisas" combined with "barcos" symbolized "una vida en que los hombres son

also imagines the experience as disconcerting, as if he were almost in a fog: "Tropiezo vacilante" (l. 30), even though eternity possesses these qualities of hardness and fixity.[18] There, as before ("mezclado con el amor," l. 10), he finds love, a kind of love that is timeless. Both modifiers are double-edged. Alone, the expression "al fin" (l. 31) brings with it the impression of a long and repeatedly frustrating search, now rewarded, and also conjures the sense of closure—but these are both temporal ideas. When "al fin" is connected with "sin alba" (l. 31), it suggests that the love is now, finally, outside, freed, beyond the cycle of day and night (cf. the significance of "sol" in l. 4), but dawn conventionally carries positive connotations of optimism, a fresh start, renewed hope, etc., so the phrase "*sin alba*" also carries a negative charge, and we are reminded that line 10 ends with the mention of "las arenas."[19] Still, stanza 7 ends on an exultant note: "Amor. ¡Amor visible!" as if the speaker had been vouchsafed an epiphanic glimpse of this "blanco de alegría."[20]

In his lecture on "Juego y teoría del duende," Lorca referred to Santa Teresa and how she stole from the *duende* "su último secreto, el puente sutil que une los cinco sentidos con ese centro en carne viva, en mar viva, del Amor libertado del Tiempo" (*Conferencias*, II, 105). This last notion, "Amor libertado del Tiempo," seems to be very close to what is identified here, where "amor al fin sin alba. Amor. ¡Amor visible!" is located "por la dura eternidad fija."[21] Perhaps too the "Amor" that is now visible is to be connected with the "Cielo vivo" of the title; although there may be no belief in an orthodox, theological, heavenly "vida de ultratumba," the sky/heavens are visibly alive with the almost otherworldly aurora borealis.

---

brisas fugaces y mueren sin pena ni gloria" (*Lorca: interpretación de "Poeta en Nueva York*," 269). Still, in "Oda a Walt Whitman," Lorca writes "mañana los amores serán rocas y el Tiempo / una brisa que viene dormida por las ramas" (*PNY*, 269), and *Llanto por Ignacio Sánchez Mejías* closes with "una brisa triste por los olivos" (308).

18   Nandorfy pointed out that in the phrase "por la dura eternidad fija," "por" can be read both spatially and temporally (96).

19   Cf. Predmore, 31, 42. As in line 10, here too he found that "'Love without dawn' is surely dark love" (70)—that is, homosexual and hence non-procreative love. Be that as it may, the kind of love suggested by "¡Amor visible!" would likely transcend such categories.

20   Craige went further and saw here a mystical, ecstatic moment actually experienced rather than vividly anticipated (19-20). Nandorfy was—rightly—much more cautious: "the final outcome cannot be interpreted as the successful termination of a linear process but as a utopian desire" (96).

21   Domínguez Gil pursued this connection further (334-35).

The idea of a nonspiritual life after death appears with some frequency in Lorca's poetry. Indeed, it would perhaps be more accurate to refer to a number of nonspiritual afterlives, because the notion is represented figuratively in several different spatial/material ways, and each seems to correspond to the conception of a slightly different fate. The hard, rocky, hostile place envisaged by "El emplazado" (*Romancero gitano*) is quite rare:

> mis ojos miran un norte
> de metales y peñascos
> donde mi cuerpo sin venas
> consulta naipes helados.
> [...]
> Aprende a cruzar las manos,
> y gusta los aires fríos
> de metales y peñascos. (84-85)

On the other hand, one of the "versions" most commonly imagined is an afterlife in the earthy grave; it is also conceived of as the most unpleasant and hence the one that the poetic subjects make the most strenuous efforts to avoid. Mentions and descriptions run throughout *Poeta en Nueva York*. For instance, in "Paisaje de la multitud que vomita," "Son los muertos que arañan con sus manos de tierra" (*PNY*, 197), in "Ciudad sin sueño," "Hay un muerto en el cementerio más lejano / que se queja tres años" and "Nos caemos por las escaleras para comer la tierra húmeda" (*PNY*, 204), in "Nocturno del hueco," "Los rostros bogan impasibles / bajo el diminuto griterío de las hierbas" (*PNY*, 234), and in "Grito hacia Roma," "ni quien cultive hierbas en la boca del muerto" (*PNY*, 263).[22]

In "Ciudad sin sueno," after the second line just quoted, the poem continues: "o subimos al filo de la nieve con el coro de las dalias muertas" (*PNY*, 204). Here we find evoked a third locus for the afterlife, imagined now as a cold, white, snowy expanse. The late occasional sonnet, "A Mercedes en su vuelo," develops on this notion:

> Una viola de luz yerta y helada
> eres ya por las rocas de la altura.
> [...]
> Tu pensamiento es nieve resbalada

---

22   For more on this topic, see García-Posada, "La vida de los muertos."

en la gloria sin fin de la blancura. (57)

Nevertheless, the "version" that seems to be generally preferred is the one characterized not by rocks and metals or earth or snow but rather by water. In "El emplazado" the protagonist is denied this more soothing possibility:

Ojos chicos de mi cuerpo
[...]
ni miran al otro lado
donde se aleja tranquilo
un sueño de trece barcos. (84)

It is in *Llanto por Ignacio Sánchez Mejías* that this alternative is perhaps most fully explored:

Yo quiero que me enseñen dónde está la salida
para este capitán atado por la muerte.

Yo quiero que me enseñen un llanto como un río
que tenga dulces nieblas y profundas orillas,
para llevar el cuerpo de Ignacio y que se pierda
[...]
que se pierda en la noche sin canto de los peces
y en la maleza blanca del humo congelado. (302-03)

Although certainly no paradisiacal afterlife, the river and the sea bring a restfulness and a release from suffering rarely associated with the other mediums.

When set against this broad context, "Cielo vivo" appears to have a rather less bleak outlook than some other poems in *Poeta en Nueva York*. Certainly, the speaker recognizes the difference between reality and his imagined ideal, and some of the negative processes of the natural world are explicitly enumerated in lines 4, 11, 12, and 15 through 18. But in the tranquility of the countryside and in the face of the extraordinary (natural) phenomenon of the aurora borealis, the speaker achieves this momentary vision of a transcendent principle that he describes—and apostrophizes—in the closing lines.

In comparison with "Poema doble del Lago Eden" then, "Cielo vivo" does not address as many themes: it does not have a metapoetic component, there is no mention (or barely any) of the topic of homosexuality, it does not deploy any Christological imagery, and there is a different focus on the

Garden of Eden and early childhood.[23] There is, though, in "Poema doble" a similar contrasting alternation between what is presented as desirable but not attained (and probably not attainable)—the repeated pleas of "Déjame pasar" in stanza 4 versus the harsh realities of the world that the speaker knows to be all too true—"Yo sé el uso [...] y sé del horror" in stanza 5 (*PNY*, 215). "Poema doble" is very much concerned with temporality, from the "voz antigua que todos tenemos / pero que todos olvidamos / sobre el hombro de la hora"[24] through to "mi desnudo [...] que recibe / la luna de castigo y el reloj encenizado" (*PNY*, 216). But although temporality always implies mortality, the text does not make explicit mention of the latter until the very last stanza, where "la Muerte me estaba[...] buscando" (*PNY*, 216).

In general terms, in "Poema doble," the speaker is very dissatisfied with the state in which he finds himself in the present and looks back nostalgically to the past in an attempt to define and express what it is that he wants to be and wants to do in the present. It ends with him seemingly stuck, caught between two poles, unable to resolve his existential dilemma: "allí donde flota mi cuerpo entre los equilibrios contrarios" (*PNY*, 216). In a sense, "Cielo vivo" picks up where "Poema doble" leaves off: the speaker now looks to the future, takes cognizance of his own mortality, and at the same time looks back in an effort to capture or conjure the essence of an alternative future to which he aspires (but knows, really, that he will never attain). A variant stanza from "Poema doble del Lago Edén" (the second of four stanzas that were originally part of the text) clearly reveals the differences between the two poems:

> Aquí frente al agua en extremo desnuda
> busco mi libertad, mi amor humano
> no el vuelo que tendré, luz o cal viva
> mi presente en acecho sobre la bola del aire alucinado.
>   (Marinello, 223)

The phrase "busco mi libertad" is picked up in the second poem by the similar "lo que busco," but in "Poema doble," the scene is very much rooted in the present: "Aquí frente al agua," whereas in "Cielo vivo," the perspective is clearly oriented to the future: "lo que busco *tendrá* su blanco de alegría" (my italics). The discarded stanza goes on to sideline explicitly what will become the central concern of "Cielo vivo": "*no* el vuelo que tendré" (my italics) versus "su

---

23   On "Poema doble," see Anderson, 412-25.
24   Lines from a stanza later discarded by Lorca; see Marinello, 222.

blanco de alegría / cuando yo vuele" and "Vuelo fresco de siempre." And finally, it makes the time-frame a point of emphatic insistence: rather than "el
vuelo que tendré," what interests him for the moment is "mi libertad, mi amor
humano / [...] / mi *presente* en acecho" (my italics).

In this same stanza from "Poema doble," "el vuelo que tendré" is glossed
as "luz o cal viva," two contrasting images of the speaker's anticipated future,
death, and indeed "afterlife." These brief, almost telegrammatic mentions tap
into another important opposition that runs through Lorca's poetry, that of
the "muerte de luz" versus the "muerte oscura."[25] "Gacela de la huida" (*Diván
del Tamarit*) closes with these two lines: "Ignorante del agua, voy buscando
/ una muerte de luz que me consuma" (219), while another poem from the
same collection is entitled, "Gacela de la muerte oscura." Here two potential
alternatives are evoked, and the negative one of suffering in the grave—"[el]
tumulto de los cementerios" (211)—is developed in the second stanza:

> No quiero que me repitan que los muertos no pierden la sangre;
> que la boca podrida sigue pidiendo agua.
> No quiero enterarme de los martirios que da la hierba,
> ni de la luna con boca de serpiente
> que trabaja antes del amanecer. (212)

To this is opposed one of restfulness, in the fifth and last stanza:

> ...quiero dormir el sueño de las manzanas
> para aprender un llanto que me limpie de tierra;
> porque quiero vivir con aquel niño oscuro
> que quería cortarse el corazón en alta mar. (214)[26]

This basic dichotomy, then, is articulated around the notion of survival
after death through sacrifice, remembrance, or even fame[27] versus a death of
passivity, forgetfulness, and possible oblivion. The "muerte de luz/oscura" binary stands alongside, and sometimes combines with, the other set of "versions" of mortality already adumbrated. Thus, the "muerte oscura" is associ-

---

25   Throughout his book, this is one of the principal topics explored by
Domínguez Gil; see especially 107-10.

26   Notice here the twin references to Edenic apples and reconnection with
early childhood.

27   A notion that seems to pick up certain ideas from Unamuno's *Del sentimiento trágico de la vida*.

ated with earth—interment and the fear of "los martirios que da la hierba"—
and set against this we find an "alternative" that is connected with water—"un
llanto que me limpie de tierra" and "aquel niño oscuro / que quería cortarse el
corazón en alta mar." And so while in "Poema doble" the speaker asserts that
he is *not* seeking "el vuelo que tendré," whether that end up being either "luz o
cal viva," the light of renown or the quicklime in the earthy grave, we can see
that in "Cielo vivo" the development of these ideas is somewhat different: the
state of nonexistence described in its lines 3 and 4, although far from ideal,
is not nearly as ominous as the notion of a "muerte oscura," and the "vuelo,"
rather than involving survival in memory ("muerte de luz"), becomes one of
the possibility of plentitude and the experience of a truly transcendent, all-
encompassing love.

Works Cited

Anderson, Andrew A. "*Et in Arcadia Ego*: Thematic Divergence and Con-
    vergence in Lorca's 'Poema doble del lago Edén.'" *Bulletin of Hispanic
    Studies*, vol. 74, no. 4 (1997), pp. 409-29.
Bécquer, Gustavo Adolfo. *Rimas*. Edited by José Carlos de Torres, Castalia,
    1977.
Craige, Betty Jean. *Lorca's "Poet in New York": The Fall into Consciousness*.
    UP of Kentucky, 1977.
Cummings, Philip. "August in Eden. An Hour of Youth." *Songs*, by Federico
    García Lorca, Duquesne UP, 1976, pp. 125-66.
Domínguez Gil, José. *La voz de la piedra: Lorca y la "muerte oscura" del verbo*.
    Universidad de Extremadura, 2008.
García Lorca, Federico. *Conferencias*. Edited by Christopher Maurer, Alian-
    za, 1984. 2 vols.
———. *Diván del Tamarit. Llanto por Ignacio Sánchez Mejías. Seis poemas
    galegos. Poemas sueltos*. Edited by Andrew A. Anderson, Espasa-Calpe/
    Clásicos Castellanos, 1988.
———. *Manuscritos neoyorquinos. "Poeta en Nueva York" y otras hojas y po-
    emas*. Edited by Mario Hernández, Tabapress/Fundación Federico Gar-
    cía Lorca, 1990.
———. *Poeta en Nueva York*. Edited by Andrew A. Anderson, Galaxia
    Gutenberg, 2013.
———. *Romancero gitano*. Edited by Mario Hernández, Alianza, 1998.
———. *Sonetos*. Fundación Federico García Lorca/Comares, 1996.

―――. *Songs*. Edited by Daniel Eisenberg, translated by Philip Cummings, Duquesne UP, 1976.

García-Posada, Miguel. "La vida de los muertos: un tema común a Baudelaire y Lorca." *1616. Sociedad Española de Literatura General y Comparada. Anuario*, vol. 1 (1978), pp. 109-18.

―――. *Lorca: interpretación de "Poeta en Nueva York."* Akal, 1981.

Marinello, Juan. *Contemporáneos. Noticia y memoria*. Editora del Consejo Nacional de Universidades, Universidad Central de Las Villas, 1964.

Maurer, Christopher, and Andrew A. Anderson. *Federico García Lorca en Nueva York y La Habana. Cartas y recuerdos*. Galaxia Gutenberg, 2013.

Nandorfy, Martha J. *The Poetics of Apocalypse. Federico García Lorca's "Poeta en Nueva York."* Bucknell UP, 2003.

Predmore, Richard L. *Lorca's New York Poetry: Social Injustice, Dark Love, Lost Faith*. Duke UP, 1980.

Río, Ángel del. "Introduction. *Poet in New York*: Twenty-Five Years After." *Poet in New York*, by Federico García Lorca, translated by Ben Belitt, Grove P, 1955, pp. ix-xxxix.

Román Román, Isabel. "Espacios y escenas en la poesía surrealista del 27. La deixis de la fantasía." *Anuario de Estudios Filológicos*, vol. 25 (2002), pp. 433-44.

Schwartz, Kessel. "García Lorca and Vermont." *Hispania*, vol. 42, no. 1 (March 1959), pp. 50-55.

10
Un puente entre dos poetas: García Lorca y Hart Crane

E L LIBRO EN CUESTIÓN no es tanto una colección de poemas como un largo poema articulado en varias partes, cada una de éstas con su propio subtítulo; no obstante, varios de los poemas se publicaron primero individualmente en conocidas revistas literarias. Su tema principal es los Estados Unidos al final del decenio de los años 20, con muchas descripciones fragmentarias de la vida urbana y sus supuestos "adelantos" modernos. Este libro fue escrito por un poeta nacido justo antes del principio del siglo XX, un escritor que luchó con la expresión de su homosexualidad, y cuya corta vida tuvo un fin trágico y sin sentido. Tras un largo proceso de composición y pulimiento, el poemario se publicó el mismo año en dos países distintos y en dos ediciones distintas, con ligeras diferencias textuales entre sí.

Me refiero, no a *Poeta en Nueva York,* de Federico García Lorca, como podría parecer el caso, sino a *The Bridge (El puente)* del poeta estadounidense Hart Crane. Crane nació en el pueblo de Garrettsville, cerca de Cleveland, Ohio, el 21 de julio de 1899, poco más de un año después de Lorca, y se suicidó lanzándose al mar de un buque que hacía la travesía de Cuba a Nueva York, en el mediodía del 27 de abril de 1932, algo más de cuatro años antes del asesinato del poeta granadino. Crane dejó un legado poético relativamente escueto: dos colecciones poéticas—*White Buildings (Edificios blancos)* (1926), y *The Bridge* (1930)—, bastantes poemas sueltos y pequeños ciclos poéticos. En este trabajo, me propongo fijar los paralelos biográficos y literarios entre los dos escritores, y también las discrepancias, para intentar entender mejor la significación y la novedad de *Poeta en Nueva York.*[1]

---

1   Sobre la relación Crane–Lorca existen ya dos artículos, de Higginbotham y Bartra. Higginbotham señala algunos de los puntos de contacto más sustanciales,

Para empezar, las conexiones entre las circunstancias familiares, la infancia y juventud, y la educación de los dos poetas son, curiosamente, escasas o más bien nulas. El padre de Crane era hombre de negocios, dueño de fábricas de azúcar y de chocolate, así como de varias tiendas y restaurantes. Hart era hijo único, y su familia se mudó de casa varias veces durante su infancia, llegando a la gran ciudad de Cleveland en 1908. Pero la relación entre sus padres fue difícil y estuvo llena de conflictos y peleas, hasta que por fin en 1916 se divorciaron. Poco después, sin haber terminado sus cursos para el diploma de educación secundaria, Crane abandonó la casa familiar y se estableció en Nueva York. No tuvo estudios universitarios, y se entregó más bien a una vida algo bohemia en que ya empezaba a aflorar el joven poeta con una voz distintiva.[2] Todo esto contrasta notablemente con lo que sabemos de Lorca: el trasfondo agrícola, la familia grande, la vida en Fuente Vaqueros y Asquerosa, la infancia aparentemente feliz, incluso mimada, la relación estable entre sus padres, y el paso, aunque si algo penoso, por el instituto a la Universidad de Granada y de allí a la Residencia de Estudiantes. La única coincidencia quizás digna de señalar es el cambio de la provincia al centro: para Crane, del pueblo a Cleveland, y de allí finalmente a Nueva York; para Lorca, del pueblo a Granada, y de allí a Madrid.

Donde sí encontramos cierto parecido es en su vida íntima y en su sexualidad. Según su más reciente biógrafo, Crane tuvo su primera experiencia homosexual entre los doce y los dieciséis años de edad, después de la cual empezó a explorar esa faceta de su personalidad, pero desarrollando al mismo tiempo una cuidadosa reserva, casi una fachada (Unterecker, 26). Aunque los Estados Unidos de 1915 no eran exactamente la España de la misma época, no obstante, en una "buena familia," en una ciudad de provincias, este rasgo de su personalidad no era algo que se pudiera expresar ni mostrar. A partir de este momento tiene frecuentes encuentros sexuales y relaciones sentimentales más o menos cortas, y ya adulto sus paseos nocturnos por los astilleros en busca de marineros adquirieron cierta notoriedad entre su pequeño círculo literario de Nueva York (Giles, 163).

De otra señal, y quizás de más trascendencia, fue el encuentro con Emil Opffer, marinero de la marina mercante, con quien llegó a tener una relación casi ideal, mezcla de amistad, entendimiento mutuo, cariño y devoción. En abril de 1924 Crane se trasladó a vivir a una habitación en la misma casa don-

---

pero discrepo de unos de sus planteamientos básicos, sobre todo con referencia a la influencia del surrealismo; el artículo de Bartra parece aportar muy poco a la discusión.

2   Para la vida de Crane, se puede consultar la biografía de Unterecker.

de vivía Opffer, 110 Columbia Heights, en el barrio neoyorquino de Brooklyn (Yingling, 87-88; Unterecker, 355-365). La gran coincidencia fue que se trataba de la misma casa que había ocupado cincuenta años antes John Augustus Roebling, el ingeniero principal del Puente de Brooklyn, quien, después de un accidente que le dejó lisiado, había tenido que supervisar el resto del trabajo "a distancia," desde una ventana que daba al puerto y al puente. Cuando, algo después, Crane cambió de habitación en la misma casa, ocupó el mismo cuarto desde el cual había observado y dirigido Roebling (Clark, 114-115).

Aquí las experiencias de Crane nos recuerdan las de Lorca hasta cierto punto, aunque Crane, según parece, era más proclive a los excesos, tanto de alcohol (y esto, durante la Ley Seca) como de promiscuidad sexual, aunque parece que podría existir cierto paralelismo entre las experiencias de Crane en los muelles neoyorquinos y el período de gran libertad—incluso, posiblemente, de libertinaje—en el puerto de La Habana de que gozó Lorca durante su estancia en Cuba (Gibson, II, 102-106).

Estas observaciones nos conducen a uno de los puntos más sorprendentes de esta pesquisa doble: el hecho de que Hart Crane y Federico García Lorca se conocieran en Nueva York en el otoño de 1929. Gracias a las investigaciones de Bussell Thomson y Jack Walsh, sabemos bastante de lo que ocurrió. Crane volvió a los Estados Unidos a finales de julio de 1929, después de pasar unos seis meses en Francia. De vuelta a Nueva York, se estableció otra vez en Brooklyn, esta vez en el 130 Columbia Heights, a unos pocos metros de la casa de Opffer y Roebling (Unterecker, 599-601). No sabemos exactamente cuándo tuvo lugar el encuentro, pero es posible que se verificara durante la primera quincena de agosto, antes de las vacaciones estivales de Lorca en Nueva Inglaterra, o bien hacia finales de septiembre, cuando ya estaba de vuelta a Manhattan y Columbia University.[3]

La fuente principal de Thomson y Walsh fue Ángel Flores, un portorriqueño radicado en Nueva York en aquel entonces, director de la revista *Alhambra,* que era el órgano de la Alianza Hispana y Americana, un grupo de bohemios e intelectuales españoles y latinoamericanos. Gabriel García Maroto, el viejo amigo de Lorca, y uno de sus primeros impresores, era director artístico de la revista. Una vez en Nueva York, es perfectamente comprensible que la Alianza fuera uno de los círculos en que se moviera Lorca, y que fuera uno en el que se sintiera más relajado, entre literatos y artistas hispanohablantes. Según parece, Lorca solía asistir a la tertulia del grupo, constituido,

---

3   Thomson & Walsh; también se refiere al encuentro, aunque con menos pormenores, Adams, 120-122.

entre otros, por Flores, Maroto y León Felipe, que se reunía para almorzar en uno de los restaurantes del barrio chino de Manhattan. Flores se interesaba en la poesía española y norteamericana, y trabajaba en aquel momento en una traducción de *Tierra baldía* (*The Waste Land*) de T.S. Eliot. Un día, después del almuerzo, se le ocurrió llevar a Lorca a conocer a Crane, y le llevó por Chinatown a través del mismísimo Puente de Brooklyn al piso del poeta estadounidense. Pero, para seguir con la narración, vayamos al artículo de Thomson y Walsh:

> [Cuando llegaron] Crane estaba bastante ebrio y tenía reunidos en su piso a media docena de marineros ya borrachos con el alcohol ilegal que Crane les había proporcionado. Flores hizo las presentaciones, sirviendo de intérprete. (Crane, aunque muy aficionado a lo hispánico, no hablaba español; [...].) [...] [Flores] se dio cuenta de pronto de que Lorca y Crane tenían mucho en común, que a Lorca "le interesaban también los marineros" y que la situación despertó en Lorca la curiosidad. En efecto, Crane invitó a Lorca a quedarse en la compañía de los marineros; Flores se despidió, y Lorca permaneció con el grupo. El último recuerdo de Flores fue un vistazo de Crane bromeando con un grupo de marineros, y de Lorca ya con otro grupo en su alrededor. (12)

De modo que se queda en la oscuridad el desenlace de la anécdota; además, parece muy poco probable que se vieran o se tratasen otra vez durante la estancia neoyorquina de Lorca. Como veremos a continuación, es muy difícil averiguar si este encuentro tuvo algún impacto en la obra lorquiana: por ejemplo, el manuscrito original del poema "Ciudad sin sueño (Nocturno de Brooklyn Bridge)" es del 9 de octubre de 1929, fecha, según parece, poco posterior al día en cuestión,[4] pero si miramos otros títulos de *Poeta en Nueva York* aparecen otros nombres de lugares de la ciudad—Harlem, Coney Island, Battery Place, Riverside Drive, el río Hudson, Wall Street, etc.—, así que es imposible establecer un impacto o una influencia directa.

Donde sí se presenta una serie de paralelismos y coincidencias llamativas, es en el poemario de Crane, *El puente,* libro que, por sus fechas de publicación y distribución (a finales de marzo de 1930, unas pocas semanas después de la salida de Lorca con rumbo a Cuba), el poeta granadino casi seguramente no llegaría a conocer directamente (Unterecker, 615). *El puente* está articulado en ocho secciones, cada una con su propio título—"Ave Maria," "Powhatan's

---

4　García Lorca, *"Poeta en Nueva York" y otras hojas y poemas,* 106-111.

Daughter," "Cutty Sark," "Cape Hatteras," "Three Songs," "Quaker Hill," "The Tunnel," "Atlantis"—, más una composición "Proem: To Brooklyn Bridge" introductoria.[5] La sección II consta de cinco poemas y la sección V de tres. Todas las otras secciones sólo contienen un poema, cuyo título es siempre igual al de la sección correspondiente. *El puente,* pues, cuenta con un total de quince poemas, todos bastante largos, algunos muy extensos. Para señalar las estadísticas correspondientes, *Poeta en Nueva York* está articulado en diez secciones, cada una con su propio título. Cada sección contiene varios poemas (menos la última): cuatro, tres, nueve, dos, tres, seis, tres, dos, dos y uno, respectivamente, para un total de treinta y cinco.[6] Casi todos los poemas lorquianos son más cortos que los de Crane.

Aún más interesantes son las peripecias de composición de *El puente.* Crane concibió el proyecto para el libro y empezó a redactar la primera versión del primer poema en febrero de 1923; no puso los últimos toques a la última versión del manuscrito hasta diciembre de 1929, un lapso de casi siete años, en los que hubo períodos de intensa composición y revisión, y largos y frecuentes períodos de inactividad, faltos por completo de inspiración cuando sufría un bloqueo creativo total (Butterfield, 122-151).

Además, y aquí debemos prestar bastante atención, el diseño y la estructura del poemario sufrió una serie de cambios a lo largo de estos siete años. Por ejemplo, según una carta a un amigo de marzo de 1926, en ese momento integraban el poemario seis secciones: "Columbus," "Pocahontas," "Whitman," "John Brown," "Subway" y "The Bridge" (Butterfield, 125). Aquí la primera sección, "Columbus," corresponde a la primera definitiva, "Ave Maria," con un cambio de título; la segunda, "Pocahontas," es efectivamente "la hija de Powhatan," el nuevo nombre de la segunda sección; la tercera, "Whitman," será en la organización final la cuarta sección, ahora titulada "Cape Hatteras"; la cuarta sección, "John Brown," esencialmente desaparecerá; la quinta, "Subway," se renombra "The Tunnel" y aparece como la séptima sección; de manera similar, la sexta, "The Bridge," se rebautiza "Atlantis," y constituirá la octava y última sección.

En otra carta a otro amigo de principios de 1927, la organización ya se había modificado considerablemente (Brunner, 187-188). Ahora había diez secciones, más un poema designado como una dedicatoria al Puente de Brooklyn. La forma final se ve ahora con bastante claridad, con la mayoría de las secciones y de los títulos definitivos. Sin embargo, surgen varias discrepancias: el orden de las secciones tercera y cuarta, "Cutty Sark" y "Cape Hat-

---

5   Crane, *The Poems of Hart Crane.*
6   García Lorca, *Poeta en Nueva York.*

teras," está invertido; aparece una nueva sección quinta, "The Mango Tree,"
que luego sería suprimida; aparece también una sección séptima, "The Cal-
gary Express," nuevo nombre para la sección "John Brown," que también sería
suprimida; y la sección octava, "1920 Whistles," sería reemplazada por una
completamente nueva, "Quaker Hill," que se compondría después.

A lo constatado hasta aquí podemos añadir un proceso largo y compli-
cado de revisión—y, a veces, de reelaboración—a que fueron sometidos los
poemas individuales. Todo esto puede compararse provechosamente con lo
que sabemos del proceso de plasmación del libro que sería finalmente *Poeta
en Nueva York,* con una excepción notable: Crane concibió el proyecto de
The Bridge antes de componer sus poemas integrantes; *Poeta en Nueva York*
es el resultado esencialmente de la creación de un libro *a posteriori,* después de
escritos los textos individuales. En efecto, ya durante su estancia neoyorquina
Lorca pensaba en dos colecciones poéticas, que denominaba a veces *Nueva
York* y *Tierra y luna.* También es posible que hubiera vislumbrado la posibilidad de una tercera obra, probablemente en prosa, que se titularía, curiosamente, *La ciudad.* De *Nueva York* nació *Poeta en Nueva York,* mientras que
en el verano de 1931, surgió otro poemario proyectado, *Poemas para los muertos,* relacionado con *Tierra y luna.* En 1933 hubo otro cambio de título—de
Poeta en Nueva York a *Introducción a la muerte,* una sugerencia nerudiana—,
y con este cambio, el desmembramiento de *Tierra y luna* y la distribución de
sus poemas integrantes entre, sobre todo, *Introducción a la muerte* y *Diván
del Tamarit.* Para 1935 ya se había impuesto otra vez el título preferido—*Poeta en Nueva York*—, y quizás con algún otro cambio de composición menor
el poemario se preparó para la imprenta durante los meses anteriores al es-
tallido de la guerra civil (Anderson, "The Evolution"). Como parte de esta
compleja evolución, encontramos casos de creación o supresión de secciones,
cambios de título de secciones, adición o eliminación de poemas individuales, cambios en el orden de los poemas y cambios en las secciones a las cuales
corresponden, además de bastante revisión textual. En fin, la elaboración de
un gran proyecto poemático articulado en varias partes o movimientos, con
las modificaciones de todo tipo que inevitablemente conlleva la creación literaria concebida a esta escala tan ambiciosa.

Cuando estuvo en París durante la primera mitad de 1929, Crane entró
en contacto con una pareja estadounidense fabulosamente rica, Harry y Caresse Crosby. Harry tenía una pequeña editorial de lujo, financiada, evidentemente, con su propio bolsillo, que se llamaba Black Sun Press. Cuando Crane
le conoció, la editorial/imprenta estaba a punto de publicar secciones de *Fin-
negans Wake,* de James Joyce. Durante estos seis meses franceses se propuso

y se ratificó el plan de sacar la primera edición de *The Bridge* en Black Sun Press; Crane pudo discutir hasta los últimos pormenores tipográficos con sus editores, mientras trabajaba en lo que esperaba fuesen las últimas revisiones. Pero cuando se marchó de Francia en julio, todavía no había puesto el punto final, así que los manuscritos definitivos se enviaron desde los Estados Unidos a Europa, dejando a veces, incluso, al criterio de Caresse la selección entre dos versiones variantes de una frase o un verso.[7]

Como esta edición del Black Sun Press iba a ser de una tirada muy limitada—250 ejemplares—, Crane también se entendió con la editorial estadounidense que había publicado su primera colección poética, Horace Liveright de Nueva York.[8] La publicación escalonada en dos ediciones también proporcionaba a Crane la posibilidad de introducir unas últimas revisiones en la edición americana después de cerrada la francesa, y así lo hizo efectivamente. Aunque, en un principio Crane había esperado que la lujosa edición de Black Sun Press—impresa a gran formato y en rojo y negro—saliera para el Día Acción de Gracias o las Navidades de 1929, no se publicó hasta febrero de 1930 (su colofón fecha la impresión del libro en enero). La edición más corriente de Liveright la siguió a finales de marzo. Esto explica el que haya, en cierto sentido, dos "primeras" ediciones de *The Bridge,* publicadas con unas seis semanas de diferencia una de la otra en distintos continentes y con unas discrepancias textuales.

Otra vez, las similitudes con la historia editorial de *Poeta en Nueva York* son bien curiosas. En este caso, por el inicio de la Guerra Civil y la muerte de Lorca, el manuscrito del libro, a veces no completamente ultimado, fue sometido en distintos momentos a varios esfuerzos de transcripción, desciframiento, revisión y corrección, lo que explica las diferencias en las dos "primeras" ediciones del poemario, una, bilingüe, aparecida en Nueva York en mayo de 1940, y la otra, española, publicada en la Ciudad de Mexico en junio del mismo año (Anderson, "Las peripecias").

Pero, volvamos a las coincidencias entre ambas obras, porque hasta en la manera en que sus autores respectivos querían ilustrar los volúmenes, surgen paralelos llamativos. En el caso de Hart Crane, en un principio había querido utilizar como frontispicio a la edición de Black Sun Press la reproducción a todo color de un cuadro de Joseph Stella, precisamente uno de los llamados "cuadros del Puente de Brooklyn" que había pintado este artista americano. En la práctica este deseo no pudo realizarse, pero en lugar de este frontispicio

7   Giles, 120; Unterecker, 577-602; Lewis, 232.
8   Clark, v, 38; Giles, 120; Lewis, 221; Unterecker, 601-602, 615; Paul, 181, nota 46.

la edición parisiense se ilustró con tres fotografías del puerto de Brooklyn y del puente sacadas por su amigo Walker Evans. Una de estas fotografías se utilizó para la sobrecubierta y el frontispicio de la edición de Liveright (Unterecker, 556, 562, 579, 595, 609, 611). En cuanto a *Poeta en Nueva York*, Lorca también barajó una serie de posibilidades para su ilustración, y nunca abandonó el deseo de que aparecieran imágenes al lado de sus poemas. Lorca volvió de Nueva York con una extensa colección de tarjetas postales, y es posible que estas figuraran en tempranos proyectos de ilustración del libro. Con el manuscrito de *Poeta en Nueva York* se conserva una lista de ilustraciones fotográficas, aunque es difícil establecer con certidumbre a cuál de las fases de elaboración del libro corresponde. La mayoría de las ilustraciones pedidas son fotografías más o menos documentales, pero también figuran algunos fotomontajes. De todas maneras, parece que Lorca no se había decidido definitivamente, porque, aunque hay testimonios del verano de 1936 que apoyan el uso de fotografías sacadas de libros de viaje, también hay otros que sugieren el uso de una mezcla de reproducciones de postales y dibujos originales de Lorca, o exclusivamente dibujos (Anderson, "The Evolution," 231-233). Es elocuente esta preferencia por parte de ambos poetas por las fotografías, que quieren combinar con el texto, intercalándolas, lo que quizás nos dice algo de la estética vanguardista de ese momento.

En cuanto a la relación entre su estructura y su temática, *The Bridge* es una especie de nueva épica, condición a la que no aspira exactamente *Poeta en Nueva York*. Si la obra del poeta granadino es, en cierto sentido, un *voyage aux enfers,* con la salida y la "huida" al final, hacia el paraíso terrenal de Cuba, *The Bridge* también implica un viaje al interior, al lejano pasado americano, e incluso a las profundidades infernales modernas—la sección del "Túnel"—, en un rito de paso, para luego salir y lanzarse a una apoteosis—la sección final de "Atlantis"—(Butterfield, 122, 131, 138, 201-210). Crane se expresó varias veces sobre sus propósitos al componer este poema: quería crear "una nueva síntesis cultural de valores en términos de nuestra América"; observó que "el afianzamiento firme de la maquinaria en nuestra vida ya ha producido una serie de nuevas responsabilidades que constituyen un reto para el poeta"; y afirmó que "a menos que la poesía pueda absorber la máquina, es decir, aclimatarla tan natural y tranquilamente como los árboles, el ganado, los galeones, los castillos y todas las otras asociaciones humanas del pasado, entonces la poesía habrá fracasado en su plena función contemporánea."[9]

---

9   Butterfield, v; Giles, 105-106; Dembo, 8.

Para Crane los Estados Unidos de los años veinte se habían equivocado de camino, o más bien ya no tenían camino; la conexión crucial, vivificadora, espiritual con el pasado, con el país antes y después del "Encuentro," se había perdido, y el capital, la industria, la tecnología y la máquina dominaban la escena contemporánea. Pero para él, esto no era motivo de desesperación: su concepto del poeta era fuertemente romántico, y su percepción de su papel como tal no era sólo el de llamar la atención sobre este estado lamentable, sino también el de señalar la necesidad de un ajuste de conciencia nacional e incluso presentar la materia necesaria para una re-conexión espiritual (Butterfield, 138, 143, 182, 214; Lewis, 243).

En la poesía estadounidense, para finales del decenio de los veinte, el tema—a secas—de la máquina era un motivo bastante trillado. Varios críticos de Crane citan poemas como "La turbina" de Harriet Monroe (1910) o el libro poético *Machinery,* de MacKnight Black (1929), donde trasluce una admiración casi ilimitada por la nueva tecnología, mientras un poeta como e.e. cummings gustaba enormemente del parque de atracciones de Coney Island (Giles, 30, 105, 107). Por contrario, Allen Tate compuso en 1928 un soneto donde se expresaba lo repugnante y lo horrífico del tren metropolitano— "the subway"—, y de igual manera, en libros de ensayo como *Our America* (*Nuestra América*) de Waldo Frank, o en novelas como *Manhattan Transfer,* de John Dos Passos, se presentaba una perspectiva fundamentalmente desengañada y crítica (Brunner, 173; Giles, 29-30). Pero lo que nos interesa subrayar aquí es que la actitud de Crane no era ni incondicionalmente positiva ni negativa. No le gustaban muchos aspectos de la vida moderna, pero se daba cuenta de que no podía sencillamente rechazarlos; era cuestión, más bien, de aprovecharlos, de—como decíamos arriba—absorberlos, de aclimatarlos, de identificar y reconocer su realidad y su utilidad potencial. De ahí parte de la significación simbólica del Puente de Brooklyn, que da nombre al poema y lo domina: es una maravilla de la tecnología aplicada, de la ingeniería, es una cosa en sí bella, con el diseño complejo que hacen sus miles de hilos, y es un símbolo de un puente al pasado y, sobre todo, al futuro.

En la literatura—y especialmente la poesía—europea, la situación es igual o aún más compleja. Por un lado, hay el entusiasmo por la máquina y el progresismo desbocado de la literatura vanguardista de tinte futurista, que había florecido durante los quince años antes de la composición de *Poeta en Nueva York.* Por otro lado, podemos identificar otros textos poéticos anteriores—"La gran cosmópolis (Meditaciones de la madrugada)," de Ruben Darío, "Les Pâques à New York," de Blaise Cendrars, *Diario de un poeta reciencasado,* de Juan Ramón Jiménez, o *Pruebas de Nueva York,* de Jose Moreno Villa—en los que ya empieza a aflorar una visión menos que positiva y elogiosa de la gran urbe. En la novela y el libro de viaje, encontramos una gama de actitudes, desde el optimismo de Joaquín Belda, *En el país del bluff. Veinte días en Nueva York,* hasta posiciones más matizadas, como las de Paul Morand en su *New York* o Georges Duhamel en *Scènes de la vie future,* llegando a las relativamente más negativas: *Anticípolis* de Luis de Oteyza; *...Pero ellos no tienen bananas. (El viaje a Nueva York),* de Jacinto Miguel Arena, *Singladuras. Viaje americano,* de Concha Espina, o *La ciudad automática,* de Julio Camba, sin decir nada de la película alemana de gran resonancia, *Metrópolis,* de Fritz Lang.

Dentro de este esquema, *Poeta en Nueva York* aparece como un hito importante: ofrece una crítica mucho más explícita y acerba que cualquier otro poemario—y casi nos atreveríamos a decir que cualquier otro libro—hasta la fecha, con su denuncia de la ciudad moderna industrializada, con una de las primeras descripciones en profundidad de la "jungla de asfalto," con su diagnóstico de una sociedad que no tiene raíces o que ha perdido contacto con ellas.[10] Esta delineación de sus calidades e innovaciones nos ayudará a juzgarlo y a situarlo al lado de *The Bridge.* La actitud de Crane me parece la más original, aunque probablemente la menos "realista" o viable; muchos críticos han señalado cómo, con el paso de los años y el creciente desengaño personal del poeta, el deseo de síntesis y de re-conexión en un futuro constructivo se convierte en una especie de acto de fe más que en una esperanza o en una meta factible. En cuanto a *Poeta en Nueva York,* el libro, estrictamente hablando, no inaugura pero sí define toda una modalidad en la literatura moderna que se fija en Nueva York identificándolo de algún modo como el síntoma más destacado de los males del siglo veinte.

Pasemos ahora de estas generalidades a puntos concretos o textos individuales, porque hay algunas observaciones útiles que podemos hacer acerca de *The Bridge* y *Poeta en Nueva York.* Llama la atención, por supuesto, el que Lorca compusiera un poema titulado "Ciudad sin sueño (Nocturno de Brooklyn Bridge)," fechado el 9 de octubre, y por ende posiblemente poco después de su encuentro con Crane. Pero el autógrafo original de la composición lorquiana demuestra que su título primitivo era "Vigilia," sustituida luego por "Ciudad sin sueño," y con la adición también posterior del subtítulo "(Nocturno de Brooklyn Bridge)." El énfasis recae, entonces, en la ciudad que no duerme, que no puede dormir, bajo un cielo nocturno donde tampoco el sueño es posible. El texto del poema no menciona ni describe el puente sobre

---

10   Sobre este aspecto de *Poeta en Nueva York,* véase Cano Ballesta, 209-231.

el East River, y tengo la impresión de que la mención del Puente de Brooklyn en el título es para identificarlo más bien como un mirador, un lugar adecuado desde donde apreciar el alcance de la ciudad con sus rascacielos y millones de luces encendidas.

Más sugestiva es la comparación del poema de Crane, "The Harbor Dawn" ("El amanecer en el puerto," o quizás mejor "El amanecer del puerto"), con "La aurora" de Lorca. Aunque no hay lo que podríamos llamar coincidencias textuales, cada poema utiliza las connotaciones convencionales del alba para invocarlas y al mismo tiempo negarlas o contrastarlas con lo que es la experiencia del amanecer en la gran ciudad: los primeros ruidos, la neblina, la gente que sale de sus casas para ir al trabajo, etc. Otra referencia pertinente proviene de "Cutty Sark" de Crane (el nombre del barco de vela, y también su marca preferida de whisky): después de una noche de excesos, el protagonista se separa de su compañero: "Outside a wharf truck nearly ran him down /—he lunged up Bowery way while the dawn / was putting the Statue of Liberty out—that / torch of hers you know—/ I started walking home across the Bridge": "mientras la aurora estaba apagando la Estatua de la Libertad—esa antorcha suya, ¿sabes?—" (*The Poems of Hart Crane*, 73). Aunque es posible leer los versos al pie de la letra—la luz del día que viene "apaga," en el sentido de hacer invisible, la llama de la antorcha de la estatua—, queda claro que el lector también debe dar al detalle una carga figurativa, una carga otra vez completamente en disonancia con las connotaciones convencionales del amanecer. Además, en "Cape Hatteras," encontramos los versos "The nasal whine of power whips a new universe... / Where spouting pillars spoor the evening sky, / Under the looming stacks of the gigantic power house," "donde chorreando, pilares ensucian el cielo del atardecer, / bajo las erguidas columnas de humo de la gigantesca central eléctrica" (78), imagen que nos remite a las "cuatro columnas de cieno" que tiene Nueva York en "La aurora."

Si buscamos huellas del puerto en los textos de Lorca, éstas aparecen no en "Ciudad sin sueño" sino en otros poemas de la misma sección, la tercera, "Calles y sueños." El subtítulo de "Paisaje de la multitud que orina (Nocturno de Battery Place)," por ejemplo, lo sitúa en la punta extrema del sur de Manhattan, al lado de unos muelles y con la vista directa al puerto de Brooklyn al otro lado del East River. Aquí se alude a "un mundo de la muerte con marineros definitivos / que se asomarán a los arcos y os helarán por detrás de los árboles," y a "¡Las sirenas de los transatlánticos!" (*Poeta en Nueva York*, 145-146), mientras los marineros metidos en una especie de lucha a muerte vuelven a aparecer en "Navidad en el Hudson." Más allá de estos rasgos de la ciudad, es de notar que Crane dedica uno de sus poemas más impresionantes, por la descripción lingüísticamente vertiginosa, al metro—"The Tunnel"—, pero quizás sorprendentemente este elemento de la vida urbana no aflora en el poemario lorquiano.

Crane presta mucha atención a la historia de los Estados Unidos antes de la llegada de los europeos, e invoca la presencia y el recuerdo de los americanos nativos. Por otro lado, aunque una sección de *The Bridge* iba a titularse "John Brown," en la cual, según Crane, el protagonista iba a ser un portero negro que trabaja en un coche cama Pullman, el poema en cuestión se suprimió y casi no percibimos la presencia de los negros en la versión definitiva del libro.[11] Podemos recurrir, no obstante, a su libro anterior, *White Buildings,* y a un poema corto en particular, "Black Tambourine" ("Pandereta negra") (*The Poems of Hart Crane,* 4), para atisbar la actitud de Crane, que resulta parecerse mucho a la expresada por Lorca en "Oda al rey de Harlem." El protagonista del poema de Crane, un portero de tienda, se queda en una especie de limbo entre un mundo y otro: está desconectado de sus raíces africanas, pero no ha logrado integrarse en el mundo estadounidense, dominado y definido por los blancos:

> The black man, forlorn in the cellar,
> Wanders in some mid-kingdom, dark, that lies,
> Between his tambourine, stuck on the wall,
> And, in Africa, a carcass quick with flies.

> El negro, triste y desamparado en el sótano,
> errante en algún reino intermedio, oscuro, que yace,
> entre su pandero, pegado al muro,
> y, en África, un cuerpo de animal muerto que hierve de moscas.

Sin poder salir de este "reino intermedio," el pasado inaccesible hecho un cadáver, se queda su creatividad, su expresión artística, "pegada al muro" (Butterfield, 32-33; Unterecker, 188).

En otro poema, titulado "Quaker Hill" ("Colina de los cuáqueros"), Crane evoca el paisaje de Nueva Inglaterra con una descripción bastante pastoril de la hierba, las vacas que pacen, y el cambio de las estaciones, de una manera que nos recuerda el "Poema doble del lago Edén" lorquiano, cuya acción se sitúa en el estado de Vermont. Pero a partir de aquí hay más bien diferencias: la colina de Crane ha sido invadida por gente de la ciudad, que

---

11   Butterfield, 125; Giles, 50; Higginbotham, 220.

viene a pasar allí nada más que el verano, y que traen consigo sus costumbres y valores superficiales, urbanos. Lorca, en cambio, evoca un paisaje, una aldea, un rincón del campo que conservan su belleza natural, para poder, siguiendo una larga tradición, ponerlo en contraste directo con la ciudad—la corte—.

No será motivo de sorpresa si el lugar donde Crane y Lorca probablemente se acercan más resulta ser en su admiración por Walt Whitman. La sección, y el largo poema correspondiente, "Cape Hatteras" ("El cabo Hatteras," un cabo en la costa del estado de North Carolina), fue descrita por Crane en una ocasión precisamente como una "oda a Whitman" (Clark, 67; Higginbotham, 221). Aquí Crane se dirige al gran poeta estadounidense, invocándole como antepasado intelectual y poético que también tenía una visión del destino nacional de su país, una visión, además, que se parecía mucho a la de Crane: la idea de una combinación redentora de los mundos material y espiritual. Una parte considerable del poema es, pues, un himno a Whitman, cuyo ejemplo servirá para regenerar América. Algo en particular que le atraía de Whitman era su capacidad para asimilar el mundo del dinero y de la máquina dentro de su poesía, un mundo que despreciaba pero que reconocía como parte de la realidad americana, exactamente tal y como Crane pretendía hacer.

De manera bastante parecida, Lorca abre su "Oda a Walt Whitman" con una descripción del trabajo manual y las necesidades de la industria:

> Por el East River y el Bronx
> los muchachos cantaban enseñando sus cinturas
> con la rueda, el aceite, el cuero y el martillo.
> Noventa mil mineros sacaban la plata de las rocas
> y los niños dibujaban escaleras y perspectivas.
> ....
> Por el East River y el Queensborough
> los muchachos luchaban con la industria,
> y los judíos vendían al fauno del río
> la rosa de la circuncisión,
> y el cielo desembocaba por los puentes y los tejados
> manadas de bisontes empujadas por el viento. (219)

Al lado de esta visión de una explotación laboral brutal, Lorca señala la resultante enajenación moderna: "Pero ninguno se dormía," "ninguno quería ser nube," "ninguno buscaba los helechos," etc., antes de lanzar la pregunta "¿qué voz perfecta dirá las verdades del trigo?" (219-220). La respuesta, evidentemente, es la de Walt Whitman, quien aparece en el primer momento como alguien no enajenado, en contacto directo con la naturaleza—"tu barba llena de mariposas"—, pero que rápidamente se convierte en un símbolo de una homosexualidad igualmente "sana," natural, no enajenada: "y amante de los cuerpos bajo la burda tela" (220). Como bien se sabe, casi todo el resto del poema es una diatriba contra los homosexuales perversos, enajenados, y una apología por los que se identifican, o que Lorca identifica, con Whitman. No obstante, justo al final del poema, en la última estrofa, hay una vuelta al principio, y Lorca trata otra vez el mundo industrial enajenante y la necesidad de un nuevo futuro definido por la reafirmación de valores primitivos y naturales:

> Una danza de muros agita las praderas
> y América se anega de máquinas y llanto.
> Quiero que [...]
> [...]
> [...] un niño negro anuncie a los blancos del oro
> la llegada del reino de la espiga. (224)

La importancia que tiene Whitman para Crane nos impele, pues, a fijarnos en estos pasajes de la oda lorquiana, que podrían pasar relativamente desapercibidos, y a ver que los "maricas de las ciudades," contra quienes clama tan estridente y violentamente Lorca, son "de carne tumefacta y pensamiento inmundo" precisamente porque son "de las ciudades" (223): todo el sistema capitalista y la evolución tecnológica tienen la culpa no sólo de enajenar al hombre moderno en su trabajo diario y su vida cotidiana, sino también de crear un mundo, un medio ambiente, que tiende a producir estos homosexuales tan radicalmente inauténticos.

Para terminar. En el título me he referido a "un puente entre dos poetas." Es un puente que tiende la mano, que relaciona al español con el estadounidense, y un puente que a la vez surge en medio, separando al uno del otro. El estudio comparativo de Lorca y Crane muestra similitudes y también diferencias. Leer *Poeta en Nueva York* a la luz de *The Bridge* nos ayuda a captar lo que en *Poeta en Nueva York* es novedoso, original, lo que sigue y desarrolla una tradición incipiente, lo que sería exclusivamente español y lo que es realmente cosmopolita, nos alerta sobre aspectos poco vistos, y nos obliga a aquilatar aún más cuidadosamente su posición cimera dentro de la poesía vanguardista del siglo veinte.

Obras Citadas

Adams, Mildred. *García Lorca: Playwright and Poet*, New York, George Braziller, 1977, pp. 120-122.

Anderson, Andrew A. "The Evolution of García Lorca's Poetic Projects 1929-1936 and the Textual Status of *Poeta en Nueva York*," *Bulletin of Hispanic Studies*, LX, no. 3 (1983), 221-246.

———. "Las peripecias de *Poeta en Nueva York*," *Boletín de la Fundación Federico García Lorca*, V, nos. 10-11 (1992), 97-123.

Bartra, Agustí. "Dos poetes a Nova York: Hart Crane i García Lorca," *Els Marges. Revista de Llengua i Literatura*, no. 38 (septiembre 1987), 11-20.

Brunner, Edward. *Splendid Failure. Hart Crane and the Making of "The Bridge*," Urbana, U of Illinois P, 1985.

Butterfield, R.W. *The Broken Arc: A Study of Hart Crane*, Edinburgh, Oliver & Boyd, 1969.

Cano Ballesta, Juan. *Literatura y tecnología. Las letras españolas ante la revolución industrial (1900-1933)*, Madrid, Orígenes, 1981.

Clark, David R., ed. *The Merrill Studies in "The Bridge*," Columbus, Charles E. Merrill Publishing Company, 1970.

Crane, Hart. *The Bridge. A Poem by Hart Crane*, Paris, The Black Sun Press, 1930; *The Bridge. A Poem by Hart Crane*, New York, Horace Liveright, 1930.

———. *The Poems of Hart Crane*, edición de Marc Simon, New York, Liveright, 1986.

Dembo, L.S. *Hart Crane's Sanskrit Charge: A Study of "The Bridge*," Ithaca, Cornell UP, 1960.

García Lorca, Federico. *Poeta en Nueva York*, edición de María Clementa Millán, Madrid, Cátedra, 1987.

———. *"Poeta en Nueva York" y otras hojas y poemas*, edición facsímil, edición, transcripción y notas de Mario Hernández, Madrid, Tabapress/ Fundación Federico García Lorca, 1990.

Gibson, Ian. *Federico García Lorca*, vol. II: *De Nueva York a Fuente Grande (1929-1936)*, Barcelona, Grijalbo, 1987.

Giles, Paul. *Hart Crane: The Contexts of "The Bridge*," Cambridge, Cambridge UP, 1986.

Higginbotham, Virginia. "García Lorca and Hart Crane: Two Views from the Bridge," *Neophilologus*, LXVI, no. 2 (1982), 219-226.

Lewis, R.W.B. *The Poetry of Hart Crane. A Critical Study*, Princeton, Princeton UP, 1967.

Paul, Sherman. *Hart's Bridge*, Urbana, U of Illinois P, 1972.

Thomson, B. Bussell, & J.K. Walsh. "Un encuentro de Lorca y Hart Crane en Nueva York," *Ínsula*, XLI, no. 479 (octubre 1986), 1, 12.

Unterecker, John. *Voyager. A Life of Hart Crane*, New York, Farrar, Straus & Giroux, 1969.

Yingling, Thomas E. *Hart Crane and the Homosexual Text. New Thresholds, New Anatomies*, Chicago, The U of Chicago P, 1990.

CPSIA information can be obtained
at www.ICGtesting.com
Printed in the USA
FSHW011352271221
87165FS